3 0600 00455 8079

# The Poetics of ARIOSTO

Marianne Shapiro

# The Poetics of ARIOSTO

Wayne State University Press

Detroit 1988

Library of Congress Cataloging-in-Publication Data

Shapiro, Marianne.
    The poetics of Ariosto.

    Bibliography: p.
    Includes index.
    1. Ariosto, Lodovico, 1474–1533. Orlando furioso.
2. Roland (Legendary character)—Romances—History
and criticism.   3. Ariosto, Lodovico, 1474–1533—
Technique.   4. Ariosto, Lodovico, 1474–1533—Influence.
5. European literature—Renaissance, 1450–1600—
History and criticism.   I. Title.
PQ4603.S5   1988      851'.3      87-25307
ISBN 0-8143—1894-0 (alk. paper)

For Pomme

# Contents

# Preface

This book is about the conditions that determined the writing of fiction in the Renaissance, particularly one of its great masterpieces, *Orlando Furioso*. It is not another introduction.

The scholar expecting documentation of Ariosto's multiple sources and an account of the ways in which he treats them, the general reader interested in grasping something of the transforming effect *Orlando Furioso* produces in Renaissance literature, the student wishing to know why his reading of the *Furioso* will illuminate his entire understanding of its culture—all have had little to resort to that was written after the sixteenth century.[1] I am not referring to a quantitative lack. The number of student manuals is legion, and introductory works proliferate, some accompanied by abbreviated versions of the poem or by "crib sheets" of citations. *Orlando Furioso* continues to suffer the fragmentation that Dante's *Comedy* is known to have undergone in many a classroom.

Teaching Ariosto has moved me to look outside Italian traditions for guidance in my readings as well as for helpful analogies to my own trends of thought. To some extent I have been encouraged by tendencies in current criticism to regard Ariosto as a master of subversion, particularly of the undermining of textual authority. This is indeed one of the traits that clearly distinguish him from forebears such as Pulci and Boiardo who used Carolingian and Breton material. But it is only one.

College courses on something called the *ciclo cavalleresco* persist in serving up poems from Pulci through Tasso, which have in common the features of similar subject matter and often daunting length. Neither the synchronic nor the diachronic study of Ariosto is satisfied by this approach. In crucial ways Castiglione and Machiavelli have more to tell us about Ariosto's worlds of discourse than any of the other *poeti cavallereschi* (chivalric poets), although they are not studied chiefly for their fictional writing. Where literary history is concerned, late medieval fictions such as those of Chrétien de Troyes, who knew how to measure the distance between his text and its mythological or fabulous precedents, have more to tell us about the subtleties of transmitting medieval content and filtering it through classical modes of thought.

There remains afterward too much in Ariosto that cannot be laid at the feet of precedent. With the intention of concentrating on Ariosto's own exemplification of Renaissance writing I have refrained from tracing the community of interests between Ariosto and Chrétien, or Machiavelli, or Cervantes. The best justification for this decision is that Ariosto himself stands most in need of clarification and close analysis. To this end, it is important that *Orlando Furioso,* which towers over the poems of other chivalric Italian poets, be freed from the comings and goings of comparison that would result in a leveling of his achievement. *Orlando Furioso* is the only long narrative poem in Italian that can even begin to mount a critique of Dante in serious terms. Our own time being one that distrusts the concept of masterpiece, the fact that Ariosto sums up for narrative poetry an age that began with Petrarch and has not yet ended may have more utility than the awed and tongue-tied appreciation his poem has garnered many times already. I do not pretend to deal here with every time-honored Ariosto topic (such as the link with Boiardo). In fact, the arguments of my first two chapters oppose a traditional reliance on purely genetic theories of influence.

A point that must be made by way of preamble to these chapters concerns a crucial difference between Ariosto and his predecessors. Although they have a common subject matter, it is dominated in Ariosto's case by a kind of abstract construction of formal language. This is not to say that Ariosto designed his poem on a blueprint or that it lacks relevance to human character and event. What it means is that Ariosto subjected his material and the vast cultural world that he summarizes to a scrutiny that elevates all of it to a level where pure relations are at issue. To allege, then, that Ariosto's work is only or even chiefly a demolition process engaging textuality in a self-conscious battle is to vulgarize and greatly reduce his achievement. At the level of relations between relations this poem simply cannot be dismissed as harmonious "noise" (in the sense employed by information theory).

The numerous incidental, courtly formalities in which Ariosto chose to embed much of his diction function in aid of an overarching formality. In elegant self-correcting language he produced a poem that stands "above it all" in true princely fashion, discriminating between sentiment and sentimentality so as to speak this language unhindered.

His departure from previous poets does not reside mainly in the fact that Ariosto could survey the mores of a cultural world as a detached observer of the past, whereas it was still alive in the works of his predecessors. It is delineated by Ariosto's own relationship to his work, or better, by the perspective from which he views it. The ability to see panoramically, to enfold in the sweep of an unbroken style cataclysmic events and trivial detail, and perhaps most of all, the ability to convey enormities through persistent restraint are particularly his own and not to be found in such measure in any other work of the same period.

Each chapter of this book examines a particular aspect of

Ariosto's art (with chapters 2 and 3 together forming an exception that deals with mythography). The chapters are connected, even interlaced, and each method comments on the next: satirical writing points to one of its implementations in Ariosto's original readings of entwined classical myths and of their medieval commentators. The sheer abundance of writing that Ariosto controls in his use of myth adumbrates the mad Orlando's complementary deficiency, his single-mindedness and lack of self-distancing. Patterning and aesthetic values in the "writing" Orlando sees on the trees and in the cave contain *in nuce* the exemplar of multiplicity and division that are revealed in the bifurcations of the poem. Any interpretation argues for the profound internal meanings of doubling as it relates to the conditions of princely patronage in Ariosto's Ferrara. In the interests of developing the aspect of historical necessity, the final chapter departs more than the others from the text of *Orlando Furioso* to discuss a wider set of issues to which the poem persistently calls us: the balance between idea and reality, Platonism and pragmatism, the need for reconciling oratory with visual depiction due to the fact that vision was still the main supplier of images to the mind, so as to require for the successful outcome of an encomiastic poem the enhancement of belief in its aesthetic qualities and those of the material it described. In sum, the five aspects of Renaissance writing dealt with here may be termed satire, mythography, picture-writing, amplification, and ecphrasis. They are clearly not only proper to the Renaissance but constitute particular features of poetic and critical practice in the *Furioso*. By *critical* I mean that the poet himself evidently engaged in various reading processes that he reversed in turn so as to allow the reader to take part in the full genesis of his poem as an aesthetic object and as a focus of meaning.

This study, then, takes its point of departure from some major aspect or textual locus in *Orlando Furioso*, but seeks to go far beyond this beginning to illuminate an epistemological characteristic of Renaissance writing. Chapter 1, "Ariosto's Eighth Satire," begins by showing how the satirical writings corroborate (or challenge) the stance of the narrator in the epic poem. The primary example of Ariosto's use of the Hercules myths and the topoi that became attached to them preface the next two chapters, which also deal with mythography. As a whole this chapter summarizes the quotient of allegoresis implicit in Ariosto's masterwork. I have included the vexed question of allegory within the purview of satire without devoting a separate chapter to it for two main reasons: first, that analysts from Thomas Greene to Patricia Parker have already put to rest the Ruggiero allegory as the red herring that it is; and second, that for Ariosto allegory is actually part of a larger critique of reality.

Chapter 2, "Atlante," presents this member of the dramatis personae as a nexus of literary signs and explores Ariosto's dialectical relationship with such precursors as Petrarch and *Ovides moralisés* to uncover new information about the significances of Atlante—both those confirmed by traditional patterns and those that disrupt them. I consider these data within the cultural context of Ariosto's age, which continued to read the moralized myths as well as the classical poets and drew on a variety of applicable heuristic means. The semiotic aspects of characters reveal themselves in this chapter as examples of Ariosto's approach to commentary, and of the fragmentation of the "book of the world" known to medieval minds.

The fruitfulness of a mythographic examination of *Orlando Furioso* emerges further in the following chapter. Perseus and Bellerophon are fraternal myths that run through the salient narrative assigned to Ruggiero and his kinsman Astolfo. These myths and their reworking in various readings occur at the heart of Ariosto's "journey to the Moon" and other journeys on the Hippogryph of imagination. Again, Ariosto's readings do not constitute mere analogies or imitations but new ways of seeing and of comparing. The saying "Comparaison, ce n'est pas raison," I trust, receives a serious challenge in this quarter.

Chapter 4, "Madness and the Writing on the Wall," offers a new interpretation of the central scene of the poem, refuting the notion that it is knowledge that drives Orlando mad. I suggest that two models for *Orlando Furioso* exist in small: Medoro's little "nonpastoral" inscription and the curvilinear Arabic writing that offers delight to the eye and despair to the beholding mind. The entwined names of Angelica and Medoro together with the seamlessly composed poem remind us of the labyrinthine plenitude of folly and anticipate the "Arabic" and translated context of *Don Quixote*.

"Ariosto's Multiple Vision" (Chapter 5) discusses the practice of doubling and multiplying characters and narratives both as amplification and as diminution in another sense, both within the context of Romance culture and in terms of psychologically based theories of mirroring and doubling.

Of these chapters the sixth and last, dealing with the topoi of oratorical praise and the allied practice of description as if through works of visual art, most obviously takes wing and flies beyond the immediate precincts of the chapter title. It constitutes an effort to assess the attraction of ecphrasis as a bridge between the still medieval, psychological conception of imagination that was the one known to Ariosto, and the aesthetic, creative conception that was to succeed it.

A study more narrowly based on sign systems would have had to present an arsenal of competing theories (and probably, of jargons). Here I can assert beyond doubt, however, that Ariosto did two things that are of clear semiotic value. First, he demonstrated that everything is to be seen and comprehended in its immediate context, case by case; and that rules, but for simple compositional ones (such as verses, stanzas, and cantos), emerge from examination as distant resonances. In other words, the very object pursued at any given moment is subject to ontological change: once nearly found, it either becomes transformed or disappears. As perhaps he read in Ovid, this change is a creative principle and inherent in interpretation. Second, Ariosto documented the change in the status of poetry in Italy after Dante from symbol to icon. This is not merely to state a literary-historical fact—whose proof would encompass material from Boccaccio's lyrics to Poliziano's *Stanze*—but to point out also that visual art and the growing body of art theory had themselves become sources of further poetic creativity, and even little more at times than an index of what was happening in the realms of the plastic arts. This development taken together with a flattening of poetic allegory and the removal of the active element of interpretability was inherited by Ariosto and becomes a source, in *Orlando Furioso,* of great amusement and fertile interpretation.

I trust that these points will emerge from the book itself, gradually and steadily, rather than as they might from a manifesto that takes wing from its own *parti pris* and is therefore grounded by it.

Versions of chapters 2 and 3 appeared as articles in *Comparative Literature* and *Modern Philology,* respectively. Translations not attributed are my own, except for *Orlando Furioso* itself: I have availed myself of the version by William Stewart Rose, ed. Stewart A. Baker and A. Bartlett Giamatti (Indianapolis: Bobbs-Merrill, 1968).

# Chapter 1

## Introductory: Ariosto's Eighth Satire

Anyone who has studied *Orlando Furioso* in some depth will surely attest to the challenges presented by its sheer profuseness. This trait is not to be equated with length. The first canto provides a kind of dress rehearsal for the rest of the poem. The opening line alerts the reader to the principle of amplification that informs the whole work. "Le donne, i cavallier, l'arme, gli amori, / Le cortesie, l'audaci imprese" (ladies, knights, arms, loves, courtly gestures, bold undertakings), crosscut by the doubled *furore* of Agramante the Saracen king and of Orlando and epitomized by the dynastic tale of Ruggiero and Bradamante, are the given subjects of their embellishment, which may seem as apparently aimless as Astolfo's and Ruggiero's rides on the Hippogryph; it may even seem pointless. Within the labyrinthine confines of a single, linear reading it is virtually impossible to grasp the *purely relational* meanings of the whole, for the *Furioso* is "a world poem."[1] The reader, like the characters (e.g., Ferraù and Sacripante from the first), is regularly put "in arbitrio di

Fortuna," (in the will of Fortune), and Fortune spares them all few tricks.

Human folly underlies all but the dynastically oriented principal events. The Olympian laughter of *Orlando Furioso* is heard amid the clash between "voler divino" (divine will, or fortune, or providence) and the willfulness of human desire. All the matter and every manner that treats of narrative poetry are reviewed in it. No wonder, then, that the reader may have to dive into this text and rise to the surface frequently, having made dissociated discoveries. This kind of discontinuity falls under the Narrator's scrutiny together with his other habits. As he bids farewell to Angelica with the invitation to some other poet to continue her story if he likes, that instance is merely singled out by explicit recognition from a number of other and similar possibilities of suspended animation. The main heroes are gathered in, to be sure, and returned from far-flung adventure, but to the neglect of a host of incidental appearances and exits. This structural nonchalance is a clear instance of the caprice of all "sublunary" vanity. Ariosto's laughter spares nothing and no one. Concomitantly the freedom of *errare* that Ariosto arrogates to himself and that so annoyed his detractors may be said to correspond in scope and daring to the overweening desires and ambitions that drive the characters in his poem. Ariosto's prolixity manifests his freedom above and beyond his subject matter. Amplification represents in literary terms the uncontainable and insatiable thirst of ambition and self-aggrandizement.

Ariosto's *Satire* provide us with documentation of attitudes on the most concrete aspects of ambition driven by unreason. From the first, these seven poems are all motivated by specific and seminal experiences in his life that are countered by an overarching desire for freedom. The following citation comes from a poem whose "occasion" is Ariosto's break with Cardinal Ippolito in 1517:

> Or, conchiudendo, dico, che, se'l sacro
> Cardinal comperato avermi stima

con li suoi doni, non mi è acerbo e acro
renderli, e tôr la libertà mia prima.

(I.262–65)[2]

(Now in conclusion I say that if the holy Cardinal thinks he
has bought me off with his gifts, it would not be bitter or
harsh for me to return them, and recover my lost freedom.)

The poet of the *Satire* does not once counterfeit narrative self-
abasement or display the servile stance of the courtier. Unlike
Horace's epistle to Maecenas, whom he had offended by over-
staying his leave in the country, this *Satira* justifies the con-
templative man by means of its many gross images of service
and patronage. Not surprisingly, it remained, with the other
*Satire,* unpublished during his lifetime.

The fourth satire records Ariosto's disgust with public
service as governor of the swampy Garfagnana and pivots on
the contrast between public repute and intrinsic worth. The
fifth *Satira* warns a friend about to take a wife against con-
tracting marriages such as are exemplified in the enclosed
catalogue of ill-married men. These two poems continue to
stress the value of privacy and liberty, as well as the simplicity
of the undesiring life. But the other *Satire* even more explicitly
link the problems of the humanist to the constancies of ser-
vice and patronage, and thereby to the vagaries of unbridled
ambition. Self-interest, greed, personal glory, and love in its
ineluctable character of desire constitute disruptive elements
that undermine world-order and are the agents of sudden,
otherwise inexplicable change:

E di poeta cavallar mi feo.

(VII.238)

(And from a poet I became a knight.)

But poets are not exempt from judgment as men. Ariosto's
search for a tutor for his son (VI) and his refusal of a post in
Rome (VII) serve as pretexts for a denunciation of humanistic

poets charged with heresy, pedantry, and sodomy (in a straightforward acceptance of Dante's category of sodomites in *Inferno*). Far from limiting himself to historical examples, Ariosto extends his diatribe to the contemporary ambitions of *signori*, sophists, poets, and courtiers—all prey to the encompassing embrace of unreason. Folly not only marks the blindness of human ambition and self-delusion but also, to a lesser degree, even includes what would seem to be its exact contrary. Ariosto's own visit to Rome, to safeguard a threatened benefice, occasions turns of thought that pause on the rejection of all illusion.

> Questa opinion mia so ben che folle
> Diranno molti, ch'a salir non tenti
> La via ch'uom spesso a grandi onori estolle.
>     Queste povere, sciocche, inutil genti,
>     Sordide, infami ha già levato tanto,
>     Che fatti gli ha adorar dai re potenti.
> Ma chi fu mai sì saggio o mai sì santo,
> Che di esser senza macchia di pazzia,
> O poco o molta, dar si possa vanto?
>     Ogniun tenga la sua, questa è la mia:
>     Se a perder s'ha la libertà, non stimo
>     Il più ricco cappel che in Roma sia.
>
> (II.142–53)

(I know that many will think my view mad, since I believe one should not attempt the road that so often raises man to high honor. It has elevated poor, foolish, useless, sordid, infamous persons so as to make them adored by kings. But who was ever so wise or holy that he could boast of being without a spot of madness, great or small? To each his own, this is mine: If you have to lose your freedom, the holiest hat in Rome is as nothing.)

The important metaphor of *salir* (climbing) is set against a pervasive background of the wars, conquests, fratricide, poverty, and unhappiness fostered by ambition, which remains the experience of greater blindness than its contrary. And as in the events of *Orlando Furioso,* unsatisfied desire accumulates and increases through gain:

> Ah, che'l desio d'alzarsi il tiene al fondo!
>
> (II.202)

(Ah, how the desire to rise keeps them grounded!)

*Orlando Furioso* is a poem that has much to do, if only implicitly or *per contrarium,* with climbing—on the ladder of the patron's favor; on the neo-Platonic ladder of love; on the Moon from which the sublunary world is viewed in small. But the *Satire* deal explicitly with another sort of climbing, epitomized in the possibilities of social mobility that dangled themselves before ambitious opportunists. For Ariosto, enlightened despotism, embodied in the measure of poetic license that the Estensi accorded to the ambiguities of the *Furioso,* and in the measure of *onore* accruing to him as a functionary of the Estense court, constitute an index of his actual possibilities of social mobility. Avarice expressed as social climbing in the third *Satira* (1518) serves as pretext for a little fable that joins with many a narrated ascent to the Moon, including that of Astolfo. The scramble for honor and riches is compared to the struggle of a primitive people who climbed a mountain to try to reach the Moon, carrying their sacks and baskets. A trick of perspective makes them appear successful, so that the contagion of desire motivates those below to follow them:

> Quei ch'alti li vedean dai poggi bassi,
> credendo che toccassero le luna,
> dietro venian con frettolosi passi.
>     Questo monte è la ruota di Fortuna.
>
> (III.226–29)

(Those who viewed them on high from low perches thought they had touched the moon and followed them with hurried steps. But that mountain is the Wheel of Fortune.)

Therefore no rest is to be found upon its summit, nor does access to the (temporary) summit of this wheel lead to any eventual transcendence. In the sixth *Satira,* movement upward on the Wheel of Fortune only implies the possibilities of inverse movement. On another level, social progress is a temptation to human regress:

> Quella ruota dipinta mi sgomenta,
> Ch'ogni mastro di carta a un modo finge:
> Tanta concordia non credo io che menta.
>     Quel che siede in cima, si dipinge
> Uno asinello: ognun lo enigma intende,
> Senza che chiami a interpretarlo Sfinge.
>     Vi si vede anco che ciascun che ascende,
> Comincia a inasinir le prime membre
> E resta umano quel che a dietro pende.
>
> (VI.46–54)

(That painted wheel confuses me which every papermaster describes in the same way: such agreement surely cannot lie! The being seated upon its summit is depicted as an ass; everyone understands this riddle so that no Sphinx need be called to interpret it. There you see that everyone upon ascending it begins to turn into a donkey, first frontwards so that what hangs in back remains human.)

As medicine for the desire to ascend Ariosto can recommend only that the poet put *bontà* (goodness) before *dottrina* (learning), though both are necessary to his calling:

> Dottrina abbia e bontà, ma principale
> Sia la bontà, che, non vi essendo questa,
> Né molto quella, alla mia estima, vale.
>
> (VII.16–18)

(Let him have learning and goodness, but let goodness come first, for if that isn't present then learning, in my view, means little.)

The meaning of ascent as social climbing is not absent from the poet's aspect of the "climbing" paradigm, for *poetare* and *arrivare* meet on the level of occasion, encomium, and the pragmatic translation of neo-Platonic fervor. To write may be viewed also as yet another sort of ambition. In respect of this consideration, *Orlando Furioso* is a poem about its own possibilities of existence.

Perhaps for this reason, the metaphor of ascent occurs as half of a dyad whose other half we experience more often in the direct sequence of narrative events of *Orlando Furioso:* the horizontal, geographically delineated "natural" world traversed by the Hippogryph after he has risen sufficiently for takeoff and for a view of the earth. The ascent that knows no such curb turns out to be that of an ass: it is the literal, prosaic, ambitious, and impatient desire to reach the summit of the Wheel of Fortune. But the *dottrina* of the idealized poet (not of those whom Plato forbids his Republic, V.67), subordinated to his *bontà*, brings about a process of fictionalization that embodies the way in which poetic imagination differs from social ambition and the greed for power. Poetry can be a vehicle of *bontà* if the poet is aware at all times that it is an illusion, a product of the imagination. And at the moment of enunciating this belief, a nostalgia for the authoritarian text moves Ariosto to characterize these poets with all seeming innocence as Cicero's Orator:

> Che col buon stile e più con l'opre buone
> Persuasero a gli uomini a doversi
> Ridurre insieme, e abbandonar le ghiande,
> Che per le selve li traen dispersi.
>
> (VII.72–75)

(He who with fine style and good works persuaded men to their duty, to come together, and leave off eating acorns, which custom had kept them dispersed through the woods.)

The failure implied, in contrast, by social climbing is either a failure of the goal of the enterprise itself or the failure to gain happiness from success. In the *Satire* Ariosto makes himself explicitly the poet of the lateral world and appears a happy armchair voyager apt to undermine the notion of ascent wherever possible. Whereas the *Satire* discuss the pitfalls of imagination in the social realm, the *Furioso* also deals expressly with the poetic. For example, the Narrator of *Orlando Furioso* speaks as one whose madness is of a lesser intensity than that of his characters:

> Chi salirà per me, madonna, in cielo
> a riportarne il mio perduto ingegno?
>
> . . . . . . . . . . .
>
> Per aver l'ingegno mio m'è aviso
>    che non bisogna che per l'aria io poggio
>    nel cerchio de la luna o in paradiso;
>    che'l mio non credo che tanto alto alloggi.
>
> (XXXV.1.1–2; II.1–4)

> (Madonna, who will scale the high ascent
> Of heaven, to me my judgment to restore,
> Which, since from your bright eyes the weapon went,
> That pierced my heart, is wasting evermore?
> Yet will not I such mighty loss lament,
> So that it drain no faster than before;
> To have anew that judgment, through the skies,
> I deem there is no need for me to fly.)

Imagination provides the illusion of mobility, that is, the poetic ascent to middle height. The progression in actuality consists of the fashioning and transformation of words on a page, the horizontal, low-flying voyage. Whereas an epic poem that Ariosto read closely, Dante's *Commedia*, presupposed the possibility of ascent by election and transcendence, Ariosto's human comedy presupposes the impossibility of that ascent in any realm but that of poetry, counterposed to the opportunities of concrete, pragmatic social mobility. The concomitant of mobility is freedom to the point of whim, that of rearranging narrative according to the dictates of the imagination. If the relations governing the poem are those among men, not between men and God, the threads that bind them must be horizontal and synchronic. Into this great web Ariosto wove the poetic *auctoritates* who furnished him with paradigms and occasionally with kindred thought. From this perspective there cannot be one *figura poetae* in *Orlando Furioso* but many, such as "Astolfo," "Atlante," and "Agramante." The poet returning to port in canto XLVI contains all of these *figurae* and transcends them, because in the long journey they have been proved necessary but transitory. None could embody the poet by itself.

In compositional far more than thematic terms, *Orlando Furioso* displays the workings of an imagination attempting to understand itself and to understand its world. It thereby approaches Hegel's definition of art, according to which man satisfies his general need to be at home in the world by "strip [ping] it of its inflexible foreignness"[3] and making it into his own product. Thus does Ariosto appropriate a poetic world. But for this purpose he has first to "defamiliarize" it, and the compositional strategies of this enhanced, deconceptualized seeing command an immensely varied repertoire that also serves to comment on its own rhythms: repetition and rhyme (including the two lines of deflating commentary at the end of a strophe), tautology and parallelism, and "stepped" *emboîtement des structures*, temporal suspension of time, or the multiplication and expansion of *peripeteia*. Defamiliarization, or more precisely, "making strange," can go so far as to render the world an artifact. It can accordingly point not only toward the making of ever finer discriminations case by case (as such Renaissance thinkers as Guicciardini advocated) but toward the creation of a world-view that tends toward aesthetic discovery and satisfaction.

If the process of perception in poetic art can function as an end in itself and therefore be heightened as a way of breaking down automatism, then impeded form, which delays and augments the difficulty of perception, may be understood as a cardinal aspect of Ariosto's compositional hermeneutic. His art exploits the unique property of language to capture artistically a moving—indeed, a perpetually moving—subject, a feat visual art could only muse on and dream of. The suddenness or fluidity of Ariosto's transitions belongs to his subject and in fact constitutes it. The amplitude and expansiveness of the poem belong to its means more than to its material.

Edgar Wind recounts in *Pagan Mysteries in the Renaissance* that the duke of Ferrara, Alfonso d'Este, like Federigo da Montefeltro before him, had used a bombshell as a heroic emblem, a symbol of concealed power to be released propitiously. In a painting by Titian, he places his hand on a cannon, which was his emblem of statecraft and of prudent *virtù*. On certain medals he is portrayed with a flaming bomb on his cuirass, with the following motto: *A lieu et temps,* roughly "all in good time" and in the right place. "It is essential to the stylishness of Titian's portrait that the duke, while touching the cannon as his emblem, is dressed in civilian attire, with a courtier's sword at his hip."[4] Apart from the localized sense of princely or chivalric virtue allied to the symbols of military strategy, apart from the more general acceptance of the two weapons as representing the combined personal attributes of force and prudence, the magic infused into the figure of Alfonso points to a wider understanding of how force is best reserved and unleashed—a combative deliberateness that chooses its moment to find the target. On such lines *Orlando Furioso*'s plot is drawn and extended. Its compositional breadths betoken a reserve as abundant and as controlled an aim.

Even the most immediate consequences of a given action may be felt many cantos later and reverberate well beyond the few cantos in which they are explicitly recounted. An action set afoot by a character—such as Ferraù's and Sacripante's pursuit of Angelica, or Mandricardo's contention for Doralice, or a struggle between two paladins for a horse or arms—functions as part of a relentless concealed logic. Like the characters themselves the reader is probably trapped in a linear progression, never sure till the end of an arc that it will take a certain shape and form. Fortuitous events intersect with one another in Ariosto's famed interlace patterns. Characters are flung out of France and around the Romance world with a long arm. Separately initiated and propelled into motion, enormous results grow from the slightest beginnings, apparently maintaining separate life and direction until they merge at certain nodes (such as the scene of Orlando's madness) to reveal a calligraphically graceful design. So fluid are the cursive transitions that changes are registered almost without surprise.

Although the momentary must not be confused with the spatial simply because time can be annotated only in space, nevertheless if a diagram of the poem (with directional arrows) were constructed, it would display the lineaments of a huge illuminated capital letter, traceable by the reader only after the fashion of its own unfolding. Such a letter would form an analogy to the literally concealed messages within the poem, the most obvious of these being the Arabic inscription on the cave that informs Orlando of his crucial "loss" of Angelica. These anagrams, ciphers, and codes, as cherished by the shaping imagination as the execution of Islamic calligraphy itself, could be borne by Orlando so long as they remained primarily decorative. When the script recovered its main function of annotating thoughts and communicating facts, the maddened knight found its message "senseless." When once again he appears blessedly cured of his madness and ready for battle, his arms are of the Tower of Babel, celebrating the Babelic condition of noncomprehension.

As important as the seductively decorative aspect of writing is its sheer proliferation. Not only does Ariosto expand and embellish by way of attracting and inveigling attention, but his procedure reproduces the quandary in which every wanderer in the poem finds himself. The very example that denotes Orlando's madness serves as a case in point. The title of the poem leads straight to its core.[5] Orlando's substituting for Hercules of Seneca's tragedy itself obscures *Ercole,* the name of the illustrious forebear of Ippolito d'Este.[6] Hercules had been read by mythographers since Fulgentius as an exemplar of heroic virtue, as the protector and savior of man against monsters and tyrants, conqueror of the giants against the gods,

Cacus and Antaeus.[7] An ambiguous Hercules returns beneath the surface of Ariosto's work at a time that had recently witnessed the reconquest of the classical Hercules as the embodiment of Fortitudo and Virtus.[8] Giambattista Pigna, to whom the attribution of Ariosto's title to the suggestion by Seneca is credited, observes that Orlando is like Hercules especially in that *stupende cose* (stupendous deeds) were attributed to each, in the latter case by the ancients and in the former by the moderns.[9] Orlando would then represent for Christian mythology what Hercules represented for ancient mythography. If the title seems to embody a perfect contradiction in terms, it should be kept in mind that like Hercules, the Roland of the oldest poem (the "Oxford" *chanson de geste*) already contains the germ of that *furor*.

In accordance with the fundamental compositional procedure of amplification and multiplication throughout *Orlando Furioso* (which I discuss in my fifth chapter, "Ariosto's Multiple Vision"), the other of the two principal male "characters," Ruggiero, participates in the other aspect of Hercules, the episode of dalliance with Omphale. It is important that Ariosto follows both aspects to the letter. Ruggiero's adventure with Alcina, his surrender to her wiles and drawn-out luxurious servitude reproduce both Senecan and Ovidian versions of that period of the life of Hercules.[10] That well-known paradox expands to contain, in turn, certain aspects of Orlando's amorous plight. In sum, the model of the missing "Ercole" provides an example of the mutual contamination of myths carried out throughout the poem.

The same is true with regard to the pairing of sources. Textual traces of Seneca's tragedy occur at significant moments: like Hercules' *error caecus* (blind error), Orlando's madness is a *cieco error;*[11] and in its throes Orlando shakes off his arms and kills flocks as did Hercules those of Jupiter.[12] Each awakens from fury as from a long sleep. But Ovid's Hercules is ultimately more present in Orlando. *Metamorphoses*, book IX, shows Hercules' being devoured by the fires of Nessus's poisoned tunic. If we consider first the lines Ovid has given to Hercules overcome by pain and later those in which Orlando gives vent to his rage and compare them to Ariosto's treatment of the same material, we find that Ariosto amplifies what Ovid has provided:

> dum potuit, solita gemitum virtute repressit.
> victa malis postquam est patentia reppulit aras,
> implevitque suis nemorosum vocibus Oeten.
> nec mora, letiferam conatur scindere vestem.
>
> (Metamorphoses IX.163–66)

(While he could, with his habitual manly courage he held back his groans. But when his endurance was conquered by his pain, he overthrew the altar and filled woody Oeta with his cries. At once he tries to tear off the deadly tunic.)

> L'impetuosa doglia entro rimase,
> Che volea tutta uscir con troppa fretta
>
> .   .   .   .   .   .   .   .   .   .   .   .
>
> Poi ch'allargare il freno al dolor puote,
> Che resta solo e senza altrui rispetto,
> Giù dagli occhi rigando per le gote
> Sparge un fiume di lacrime sul petto
>
> .   .   .   .   .   .   .   .   .   .   .   .
>
> E quando poi gli e aviso d'esser solo,
> Con gridi et urli apre le porte al duolo.
>
> (XXIII.113.1–2; 122.1–4; 124.7–8)

(Stifled within, the impetuous sorrow stays,
Which would too quickly issue; so to abide

.   .   .   .   .   .   .   .   .   .   .   .

When he can give the rein to raging woe,
Alone, by other's presence unreprest,
From his full eyes the tears descending flow,
In a wide stream, and flood his troubled breast.

.   .   .   .   .   .   .   .   .   .   .   .

And, when assured that he is there alone,
Gives utterance to his grief in shriek and groan.)

Ariosto adapts the cliché of love's fires to complement the topos afforded him by Hercules' burning:

> nec modus est, sorbent avidae praecordia flammae,
> caeruleusque fluit toto de corpore sudor,
> ambustique sonant nervi, caecaque medullis
> tabe liquefactis follens ad sidera palmas
>
> .  .  .  .  .  .  .  .  .  .  .  .
>
> pulmonibus errat ignis edax imis, perque omnis pascitur
>     artus.
>                              (*Metamorphoses* IX.172–75; 201–2)

(Without limit the greedy flames devour his vitals; the dark sweat pours from his whole body; his burnt sinews crackle and, while his very marrow melts with the hidden, deadly fire, he stretches suppliant hands to heaven. . . . Deep through my lungs steals the devouring fire, and feeds through all my frame.)

> Dal fuoco spinto ora il vitale umore
> Fugge per quella via ch'agli occhi mena;
> Et è quel che si versa, e trarrà insieme
> E'l dolore e la vita all'ore estreme.
>
> .  .  .  .  .  .  .  .  .  .  .  .
>
> Amor che m'arde il cor, fa questo vento,
> Mentre dibatte intorno al fuoco l'ali,
> Amor, con che miracolo lo fai,
> Che'n fuoco il tenghi e nol consumi mai?
>         (XXIII.126.5–8; words spoken by Orlando, 127.5–8)

(The vital moisture rushing to my eyes,
Driven by the fire within me, now would gain
A vent; and it is this which I expend,
And which my sorrows and my life will end.

.  .  .  .  .  .  .  .  .  .  .  .

Its sorrow: Love, who with his pinions blows
The fire about my heart, creates this gale.
Love, by what miracle dost thou contrive,
It wastes not in the fire thou keep'st alive?)

Like Ovid's Hercules, Orlando uproots tree trunks while emitting huge groans and tearing off his garments. Again, having hurled a man out into the sea, Hercules at last abandons his arms, a bow and arrows:

> saepe illum gemitus edentem, saepe frementem,
> saepe retemptantem totas infringere vestes
> sternentemque trabes irascentemque videres
> montibus aut patrio tendentem bracchia caelo.
>
> .  .  .  .  .  .  .  .  .  .  .  .  .  .
>
> dicentem genibusque manus adhibere parantem
> corripit Alcides, et terque quaterque rotatum
> mittit in Euboieas tormento fortius undas.
>
> .  .  .  .  .  .  .  .  .  .  .  .  .  .
>
> at tu, Iovis inclita proles,
> arboribus caesis, quas ardua gesserat Oete,
> inque pyram structis arcum pharetramque capacem
> regnaque visuras iterum Troiana sagittas
> ferre iubes Poeante satum, quo flamma ministro subdita.
>                         (*Metamorphoses* IX.207–10; 216–18; 229–34)[13]

(See him there on the mountains oft uttering heartrending groans, oft roaring in agony, oft struggling to tear off his garments, uprooting great trunks of trees, stretching out his arms to his native skies. . . . But while he was yet speaking and striving to clasp the hero's knees, Alcides caught him up and, whirling him thrice and again about his head, he hurled him far out into the Euboean sea, like a missile from a catapult. . . . But you, illustrious son of Jove, cut down the trees which grew on lofty Oeta, built a huge funeral pyre, and bade the son of Poeas, who set the torch beneath, to take in recompense your bow, capacious quiver and arrows, destined once again to see the realm of Troy.)

> Che rami, e ceppi, e tronchi, e sassi, e zolle
> Non cesso di gittar ne le bell'onde,
>
> .  .  .  .  .  .  .  .  .  .  .  .
>
> E stanco al fin, e al fin di sudor molle,
> Poi che la lena vinta non risponde

Allo sdegno, al grave odio, all'ardente ira,
Cade sul prato, e versa il ciel sospira.

. . . . . . . .

Uno ne piglia, e del capo lo scema

. . . . . . . .

Per una gamba il grave tronco prese,
E quello uso per mazza adosso al resto

. . . . . . . . .

Il quarto di, da gran furor commosso,
E maglie, e piastre si straccio di dosso.
Qui riman l'elmo, e la riman lo scudo,
Lontan gli arnesi, e piu lontan l'usbergo,
L'arme sue tutte, in somma vi concludo,
Avean pel bosco differente albergo:
E poi si squarcio i panni

. . . . . . .

Quivi ferien de le sue prove eccelse,
Ch'un alto pino al primo crollo svelse.

. . . . . . . .

E svelse dopo il primo altri parecchi,
Come fosser finocchi, ebuli, o aneti,
E fe il simil di querce e d'elmi vecchi.[14]
                    (XXIII.131.1–2, 5–8; XXIV.6.6; 6.1–2;
              XXIII.132.7–8; 133.1–5; 134.7–8; 135.1–4)


(For he turf, stone, and trunk, and shoot, and lop,
Cast without cease into the beauteous source;

. . . . . . . . . . . .

At length, for lack of breath, compelled to stop,
[When he is bathed in sweat, and wasted force,
Serves not his fury more] he falls, and lies
Upon the mead, and, gazing upward, sighs.

. . . . . . . . . .

He by one leg the heavy trunk in air
Upheaved, and made a mace the rest to bray.

. . . . . . . . . . .

At once desert the field and scour away:

. . . . . . . . . .

The golden sun had broken thrice, and sought

His rest anew; nor ever ceased his wound
. . . . . . . . . . . . .
Here was his helmet, there his shield bestowed;
His arms far off; and, farther than the rest,
His cuirass; through the greenwood wide was strowed
All his good gear, in fine; and next his vest
He rent; and, in his fury, naked showed
. . . . . . . . . . . . .
He of his prowess gave high proofs and full,
Who a tall pine uprooted at a pull.
. . . . . . . . . .
He many others, with as little let
As fennel, wall-wort-stem, or dill, up-tore;
And ilex, knotted oak, and fir upset,
And beech, and mountain-ash, and elm-tree hoar.)

Ariosto shares in the detached contemplation with which Ovid regards his destroyed hero. He adds to it a feigned naïveté, inviting the reader to probe beneath the surface of the text to the drastic emotions it has harmonized stylistically. The poet of the *Furioso* subjects the prior text to segmentation, amplification, and finally, a subordinate place in a new hierarchy over which his own poem reigns.

Ariosto was mindful that the precedents from which he worked represented provisional accounts of classical mythology, that the very notion of an "original" version was itself a myth.[15] That the vicissitudes of contemporary heroes and of ancient ones thus reflect each other reciprocally in turn affects his reading of chronologically prior "versions." The final myth, then, derives from his own text. It is the distillation of multifold comparison and contrast, inclusion and exclusion, collision and collusion.

Certain instances present themselves episodically and almost incidentally. Marfisa, who might claim Virgil's warrior-maiden Camilla as precedent, also possesses features of the very Amazons whose likenesses she is made to confront in battle (XVIII–XIX). Marfisa additionally performs certain story-functions of Athena, particularly that of defending numerous masculine causes[16] from the onslaughts of furious females. The Erinyes (Furies) whom Athena defeats in Euripides have no direct parallel in *Orlando Furioso,* but the women of Lemnos as depicted in Apollonius's *Argonautica* return to temporary power in Marfisa's battles with the homicidal women (XIX.57–110). Thus, the combined traits of a goddess, a warrior, and an Estense lady jostle one another in Marfisa, if we look under the rubric of that name. But if we turn to the categories that cohere in her representation, under the heading "Athene" we also find Logistilla, the half-sister of Alcina. In her role of Minerva Frenatrix or Athena Hippodamia, she teaches Ruggiero how to curb the Hippogryph.[17]

The segmentation of classical myths leads to their transformations and finally to Ariosto's inversion, within a poetic system of value, of the hierarchy of ancients and moderns. Ariosto had before him the constant models of Virgil and of Ovid, but also the medieval and Renaissance allegorized readings of the poets. The new dynast, Ruggiero, bridling his horse under the direction of Logistilla-Athena and directing its wings toward a life of virtue, invites comparison with Aeneas as well as with Hercules.[18] But between the classical and the Cinquecento poet lie miles of Christian allegory and the giant specter of Dante. All are taken into account. On one hand, Ariosto stresses the analogical content of the symbolic myth from which his transmutations draw their primary substance. On the other, he neutralizes that value by imposing hilariously unmatched conditions on the similitude and, finally, by segmentation or fragmentation, as of all the texts he uses. The result is not only that the gods topple from their pedestals but that they are replaced by men in an existential, constantly fluctuating setting. The illusion of an ending—or, in other words, of the fulfillment of desire—dissolves into new and unexpected turns of events. Very much a part of the scheme is the passing of a Hercules-element, say, from Orlando to Hercules and back again, so that each becomes an ad hoc instance of a depersonalized Hercules-function.[19] (These procedures and the transformation of myth are the topic of two of my chapters, "Atlante" and "Perseus and Bellerophon.")

If Ariosto's characters themselves seem like phantoms in a

weightless medium, it is because they represent themselves as moving but framed within the sequences through which they make their appearance. These sequences reveal themselves as analogous to grammatical or stylistic markers. In other words, Ariosto might use a death as a period or colon, a love-idyll as a pair of parentheses, or a meeting as a conjunction. The serial form of the narrative is undercut by parallelism or sudden interruption, encouraging the reader to understand that a repeated action is of the same order as a synonym.

The compositional model used by Vladimir Propp to characterize the *Morphology of the Folk Tale* contains the indispensable concept of function to which I refer here and which enables us to distinguish topical "motifs" from their derivational contexts and to situate them in a narrative grammar. But where Propp himself questioned the applicability of his method to nonfolk literary production, it has been fruitfully utilized to characterize motifs and repeated actions in literary works.[20] The "character" considered as a sign, evident in Saussure's theories of narrativity, appears in terms of his external attributes: his name (if it is a signifying name), his moral characteristics, in short, the sum of characteristics understood as distinct from his immediate environment. Thus may he be returned to the cultural patrimony of Ariosto and clarify it in terms of general, structural properties.

If we did not remain aware of a kind of motif-index as a guide to much of Ariosto's narrative, his operating procedures, clearest when they bear on his use of prior texts, would remain "mystified" or camouflaged by Ariosto's very literalness. The survival of textual form—at a level perhaps more profound and indistinct than that of simple citation or the retention of proper names—confers upon the purloined verse the value of a mediating symbol. The symbol retains the textual function of recalling texts that Plato comments upon in *Phaedrus*. But not every kind of recall harbors an equally compelling trace of the old text. For instance, in the following lines dealing with Orlando's discovery of Angelica's and Medoro's tryst, the reader may or may not discern Dantean traces:[21]

Poi ch'allargare il freno al dolor puote,
Che resta solo e senza altrui rispetto,
Giù dagli occhi rigando per le gote
Sparge un fiume di lacrime sul petto:
Sospira e geme, e va con spesse ruote
Di qua di là tutto cercando il letto;
E più duro ch'un sasso, e più pungente
Che se fosse d'urtica, se lo sente.
(XXIII.122; translation on p. 28)

At the level of stylistic quasi-imitation and decontextualization, such items as Ariosto's recall of Francesca's recital in *Inferno*—"Soli eravam e sanza alcun sospetto" (*Inferno* V)—and of the buffeting winds that hurl the lovers "di qua, di là, di su, di giù" (here and there; up and down) offer themselves but do not insist. So softly do these minute quotations demand their footnote that inventories of Dante material in Ariosto do not take account of them at all to this very day. They accumulate in great mounds throughout the poem, however, and provide the reader who at least intermittently recognizes them with the possibility of heightened enjoyment through the comparisons they implicitly make or invite. Here in the person of Orlando is another buffeted lover, borne on the heavy but persistent wings of desire, who like others before him gives vent to his passion in madness. Such textual detail, particularly in its accumulated wealth, coheres into one gigantic protest against textual authority and finality even as it monumentalizes the old works.

The cult of classical mythology is no exception to the transformatory gusto that imbues Ariosto's inventions with a sense of the already known and makes his poem as much a commentary as a narrative. It is something more complicated than the denigration of ancient gods or the corresponding upward reshuffling of contemporary patrons, more pointed than a vulgarization of classical culture or an implicit reevaluation of modernity over antiquity. Ariosto questions every kind of cult status or uncritical dignification. Otherwise to demoticize the gods could implicitly encourage the deification of the men-gods of his own time. By way of skirting this danger, and in different degrees, his visions and revisions span the distance from the creation or transmission of perfectly fictional characters (Mandricardo, Gabrina, Olimpia) to incidental tales involving mythological precedents (the uprising of Proteus, the prophecies of Merlin), to the accretions of mythicized history (Orlando), to the lavish apotheosis in classical style of the contemporary or near-contemporary (Christopher Columbus, the painter Dosso Dossi, or Baldesar Castiglione or the Polesella victory), to the mock-mythology of the patrons: Ippolito, Ercole, Isabella.[22]

Ariosto inverts the order of Ovidian metamorphosis, as well as reversing its purport. An example would be the transformation of Astolfo into a myrtle, a startling and comical phenomenon that forges together two unlike things, as well as two clearly diverse texts: those of Ovid and of Dante. For we first encounter Astolfo in this adulterated form without explanation, and in the words of *Inferno,* XIII, dilated and sprinkled anew throughout the verses:

> Come ceppo talor, che le medolle
> Rare e vote abbia, e posto al fuoco sia,
> Poi che per gran calor, quell'aria molto
> Resta consunta, ch'in mezzo l'ampia,
> Dentro resuona, e con strepito bolle,
> Tanto che quel furor truovi la via;
> Cosi murmura, e stride, e si coruccia
> Quel mirto offeso, e al fine apre la buccia.
> Onde con mesta e flebil voce uscio
>
> Expedita, e chiarissima favella,
> E disse: "Se tu sei cortese e pio,
> Come dimostri alla presenza bella,
> Lieva questo animal de l'arbor mio.
>
> (VI.27;28.1–4)

> (As in a stick to feed the chimney rent,
> Where scanty pith ill fills the narrow sheath,
> The vapour, in its little channel pent,

Struggles, tormented by the fire beneath;
And, till its prisoned fury find a vent,
Is heard to hiss and bubble, sing and seethe:
So the offended myrtle inly pined,
Groaned, murmured, and at last unclosed its rind:
And hence a clear, intelligible speech
Thus issued, with a melancholy sound;
"If, as thy cheer and gentle presence teach,
Thou courteous art and good, his rein unbound.)

The courteous salutations of souls in the netherworld who beg to be remembered by Dante echo in these lines, in the company of Dante's terrible simile:

Come d'un stizzo verde, che arso sia
    Da l'un de' capi, che da l'altro geme,
    E cigola per vento che va via;
Sì de la scheggia rotta usciva insieme
    Parole e sangue.

*Inferno*, XIII.40–44)

(As a green twig burnt at one end and groaning at the other, creaks because of the wind going through it, so from the broken stem emerged words and blood together.)

This use of transformation can be compared to parallel examples in Ovid and Dante. As in the latter poem, the mutation is what first meets the eye. As in the former, it presents itself in the form of a metaphor (myrtle for Astolfo; or in Ovid, fountain for Byblis; mountain for Atlas). But the individual tale in the *Metamorphoses* or the *Commedia* is the index of a world whose parts easily imply one another and are mutually contiguous, as in the form of each book. Each metamorphosis in Ovid reestablishes a momentarily skewed equilibrium; therefore it occurs at the end of a tale. Once set in motion, nothing in this universe is destroyed. The poet's construction is part of an order of things that causes the newly metamorphosed objects to assume, in repose, their rightful place. The mutation is understood as the completion

and realization of an immanent necessity and as the form of a
new unity. But in *Orlando Furioso* it runs analogously to the
knotted trajectories of ambition and desire. With the clear
understanding that even this end is impermanent, transforma-
tions such as that of Astolfo have no culminating point. Scat-
tering and a new branched series of events ensue. Astolfo, we
are told, will lose his mind again somewhere after Ariosto's
end-stop of his work.

My chapter "Ariosto's Multiple Vision," which consti-
tutes in part a mapping of these trajectories, deals more
purposively with the larger literary collisions that subtend
them. The clashes of codes that form the structural spine of
the work are the source of its comedy. It is this dominant
opposition and interpenetration that for readers since Vol-
taire account for *Orlando Furioso*'s comic mode—indeed,
for its cosmic hilarity. Battles between Carolingian heroic
and Breton amorous matters, Latinity superimposed upon
images in Romance costume, the modern epic confronting
the looming models of antiquity, hyperbolizations of Fer-
rara that enfold their own trenchant critique, apotheoses of
classical mythology that simultaneously dethrone it, a satire
of romantic obsession but also of careless lust: all these
comprise a poem that in Hegelian terms "neither bestows
victory nor ultimately allows any standing ground to folly
and absurdity."[23] Ariosto bridges the chasm between the
chivalric and the epic as the Hippogryph mediates between
the sublunary world and the heavens. Readers have also per-
ceived in it a bourgeois demystification of courtly codes.[24]
Ariosto's unremarkable exponent, Francesco Caburacci, cog-
nized the pervasive and solid base of dialectical thinking
implicit in Ariosto's straddling of genres and hospitality to
contradiction:

> Et venendo le tre specie semplici, cioe la Tragedia, l'Epopeia,
> & la Comedia essere gia note, & trattate da tutti, (Ariosto)
> rivolse l'animo a mescolare tutte le materie loro insieme,
> regolandole però con il modo Epico.[25]

(And since the three basic forms, tragedy, epic, and comedy, had already been treated by many, [Ariosto] turned his mind toward mixing together the material of all of them, measuring them however by the epic mode.)

Caburacci simply assumes the heterogeneity of Ariosto's text without delving into the problem of whether a comical epic can exist at all. What emerges from those Cinquecento defenders of the *Furioso* who grapple with a neo-Aristotelian canon is either acceptance or refusal of its double system of reference and of the ensuing conflicts of norms. Erich Auerbach showed that such clashes go back to the pairing of *armi* and *amori* in medieval narrative, whereas ancient epic had relegated love stories to the "middle" style.[26]

But apart from the relatively stable structural conflicts a fluctuating or flowing conflictual element ensures that new clashes of codes will build new self-destroying problematics. For example, honor supersedes salvation as Ruggiero follows his chivalric duty to his pagan king despite his vows to be baptized. But long before this delay of the baptism Ariosto has bound Ruggiero's decision to become a Christian to the amorous aspect of the poem: his wish to satisfy Bradamante. This secondary (though dynastic) element qualifies the element of religious recantation. At last there can be only a series of temporary love-versus-honor conflicts for Ruggiero, insofar as Bradamante finally constitutes *both* his most enduring love *and* his clearest duty.

It is of course not only on the mimetic level that the parody of the double-system takes place. The ruling literary systems themselves are at war: those of epic and romance, of seriotragic and seriocomic drift, subdividing themselves to accommodate yet another discrepancy or qualification, and thus fragmenting into unrepresentable bits. The smallest unit is one of unrepresentable disorder, a point in labyrinthine space. Voltaire, who commented upon *Orlando Furioso* with regard to his own long narrative poem, *La pucelle d'Orleans,* as well as in his *Essai sur la poesie épique,* thought the work comic precisely because of the clash of codes. His remark prophesies one of the most fruitful ways of looking at our poem! "C'est à la fois l'*Iliade,* l'*Odyssée* et *Don Quichotte*" (It is the *Iliad,* the *Odyssey* and *Don Quixote* together!)[27]

The pattern of bifurcation subtending the poem's action and the chiastic meetings of literary paradigms both disrupt events and link them. Some disruptions seem to freeze the narrative to a halt. Orlando's madness, the reported idyll of Angelica and Medoro, the massing of characters in Atlante's castle all exemplify the binding aspect. The other type of disruption liberates and urges on the narrative: Logistilla's white magic that interrupts Ruggiero's dallying with Alcina, the recovery of Orlando's sanity in a vial. These are the various countermagical magical objects that decree a new dispersion of the characters. So does the narrative create obstacles in order to survive them. Ariosto recounts that the locus of the poem is the Moon. Remembering him, Italo Calvino asks the question "ci dirà se è vero che essa [la luna] contiene il rimario universale delle parole e delle cose" (he will tell us if it is true that the moon contains the universal primer of all words and things). He answers as follows:

> No, la luna è un deserto . . . da questa sfera arida parte ogni discorso e ogni poema; e ogni viaggio attraverso foreste battaglie tesori ban- chetti alcove ci reporta qui, al centro d'un orizzonte vuoto.[28]

> (No, the Moon is a desert . . . from that arid sphere every discourse and every poem originate; and every journey through forests, battles, treasures, banquets, alcoves, brings us back here, to the center of an empty horizon.)

The passage could serve as commentary on the *Furioso* itself. All possible textual fictions are ranged on the Moon. As a lunatic Orlando impersonates all the excesses and shortcomings of identification with fictions. He even retreads old roads, driven to cross Angelica's path without knowing her by the unmitigated power of imagination. He is the instrument whereby Ariosto confronts the excesses and outrages of the world with the excess and outrage of imagination, so as to disrupt climactically, once for all, the madness of a world that supposedly represents a paradigm of reason. Reason is defined here only by what it is not.

As in the text by Giovanfrancesco Pico della Mirandola that I discuss in my chapter "Ecphrasis and Encomium," unbridled imagination is tantamount to unreason. Manifested now as power, now as greed or lust, it is always the sign of a lacuna that needs to be filled or a distance broached. Ariosto's objectification of the imaginary is the Hippogryph, itself a creature of an unstable, hybrid mythology. However, as a deus ex machina, hence as a metaphor for literary relations, the Hippogryph functions as the only stable allegory of the poem. The Hippogryph rescues the journey to the Moon that so comically and thoroughly failed in Ariosto's third *Satira*. Only this magical device can ferry characters obligingly along the boundary between nonreason on earth and its unmasking from "unreasonable" heights.

In a frequently excerpted sequence the Hippogryph plays a leading role. This is the overworked allegory of Ruggiero that runs roughly from canti VII through X and actually constitutes Ariosto's definitive dismissal of naive allegory as a whole. Of the Hippogryph's two riders, Ruggiero clearly suggests the charioteer of Plato's *Phaedrus* gone amuck. His flight, borne on an unmanageable spirit, takes off right into Alcina's arms. The Hippogryph follows the contour of Ruggiero's abandonment to imaginative desire, then deserts him. Ariosto makes of that moment a lure toward allegory that would willingly convert the Hippogryph into a straight analogue of uncontrollable passion, or desire, or imagination. He does this by prefacing Ruggiero's disgrace with patient teaching by Logistilla on the control of the Hippogryph, and then making Ruggiero forget his lesson. Much ink and worry have been expended on this apparently unstable allegory.[29] Ariosto compounds potential confusion by wavering on the stipulation of the Hippogryph's uniqueness. Just when it would be possible to infer that it specifically represents a loss of rationality and control, Ariosto about-faces with multiple comparisons of uncontrollable lust to just any horse: canto VIII finds the old steed of the impotent hermit unequal to his desires; canto XI locates Angelica hidden in a stable for the night among mares; finally in his madness Orlando confuses Angelica with a mare, which he rides to death and ends by tying up and dragging behind him. The Hippogryph will not lend itself even to a distinguished identity among such horses.

Even the implicit comparison of characters to animals bears an extra measure of scrutiny. As parodistic imitation it formalizes an existential crisis of the time, commenting on the Piconian and Ficinian idea of man in an unstable hierarchy between beasts and angels. As a figurative representation in itself, however, it is soon discarded, having led readers into futile allegorizing. Readers become aware that anything that seems so easily penetrable, any allegory so clear and distinct as the sequence in question could not be anything but a mirage in Ariosto's world, where things are never quite what they seem. Rather, like the enchanted arms that pass from person to person, this kind of hackneyed comparison bears the stamp of something recognizable and as such deceptively familiar. Arms are said to be enchanted if they are famous[30] through former ownership or conquest by great knights of the past, like Ruggiero's sword Balisarda, or Marfisa's weapons, or Orlando's Durindana. The epithet of having enchanted weapons conserves a merely allusive value, having reference to a prior glorious or noble lineage.

Again, however, by analogy to the rest of Ariosto's "allegory," here enchantment and invulnerability do not ensure victory.[31] Ariosto even draws the most elementary allegorical forms (such as personification) into service. The Ruggiero-allegory is structured as a symbolic power struggle between Logistilla and her nonpersonified sister Alcina. Owing to the use of traditional imagery, which is arranged in correspondences, it seems to instantiate a hierarchy. That hierarchy, once affirmed by Logistilla's speech, implies a chain of command. But the asymmetry between the two sisters should serve as warning. In the picture of Logistilla each element retains its separate identity with a sharpness that is not maintained in the rendering of Alcina. In Logistilla we recognize a kind of stick figure, but in Alcina the Eternal Feminine, something Ariosto or Ruggiero have not bid farewell. In these early canti the abundance of such verbal signals as personification and linguistic metaphor point to another kind of spurious resemblance, that of subject matter and literary treatment.

Other emblems of recognition taken in and for itself are present: for example, Ruggiero joins battle with a giantess, Erifilla. The educated Renaissance reader might recall that the name is that of a woman, Eriphyle, who was known in antiquity to have assented to her husband's death during the war of the Seven against Thebes in exchange for Harmonia's necklace. On this account Eriphyle was glossed by medieval commentators as a figure of Avarice. Having overcome this monster, Ruggiero shortly afterward succumbs to the sorceress Alcina. The reader seeking allegorical governing patterns would have no difficulty in finding models that would provide similar juxtapositions of Avarice and Lust. One source was the *Aeneid*, which as understood through the filter of Landino posited Troy as Lust and Polydorus (who had been transformed, like Astolfo, into a plant) as Avarice. In this manner one section of the passage alone could show that the poet is concerned with demonstrating that a man who has just overcome lust (Troy) is prone to avarice (Polydorus) by way of seeking recompense for the loss of the prior vice. Ariosto, who knew Landino's work, could be seen as toying with Landino's allegorical reasoning by reversing matters so that Ruggiero, in overcoming Avarice, tumbles into Lust.

This kind of dialectic of vices, however, reveals itself as a poor cousin to the simple mimetic replay of allegory. Although the best of the Ariostean allegorists, Simon Fornari, showed enough "chiaro lume" (clear light; VII.1) to perceive a moral grammar as conveyed through mimetic action, the question of whether such an acute reader is any better off for having perceived it arises. Fornari also identifies the Hippogryph with the horse of the Phaedrus, and views Ruggiero's training in how to control it as reason's taming the sensual nature. In sum, the Renaissance allegorizer falls prey to the lure of recognition, taking the surface textual analogies as signifiers of a kindred interpretative system. If his allegorical reading does not provide him with a stable context in which to situate the events of the whole poem, such a reader is at a distinct disadvantage vis-à-vis the "sciocco vulgo" (misjudging vulgar; VII.1).

Like Ruggiero on the enchanted island, the reader is constantly deceived by appearances. From the first, when he assumes that a myrtle is just what it seems to be, Ruggiero falls prey to the (conceptual) charms of various allegorical figures. "Tal saria Beltà, *s'avesse* corpo, e Leggiadria" (Such would Beauty and Loveliness be if they had a body; translation mine), Ariosto warns (VI.69.7). Just as Ruggiero's victory over Erifilla only leads to his succumbing to Alcina, so the reader is invited to pass through a vain dalliance with allegory. Both the *frutto* (fruit) that the reader may think to gain (VII.2.4) and that which Ruggiero believes himself to possess (VII.25.6) are then discovered to be "putrido e guasto, e non come fu posto", (not what it was, but rotten and decayed; VII.71). The sense of an ending (that the reader may fallaciously supply) belies the continuation of Ruggiero's journey in which his behavior contradicts everything he is supposed to have learned: he forgets his martial duty, tours the world with no thought for Bradamante, nearly rapes Angelica, and loses the Hippogryph. Any reader who subsequently continues to believe in the efficacy of allegory has flouted a whole series of warnings and committed the same error as Ruggiero, mistaking outer for inner and believing in the following precept:

> ben si può guidicar che corrisponde
> a quel ch'appar di fuor quel che s'asconde.
>
> (VII.14)

> (Yet might the observing eye of things concealed
> Conjecture safely, from the charms revealed.)

What Ariosto is doing is inviting the more acute reader to share a confidential awareness of his text, using allegory to activate a process between text and reader that recapitulates that between hero and enchanted island. The so-called *chiaro lume,* especially that *discorso,* turns out to be the counterpart of the *incantato lume* (enchanted light) of Atlante's shield that, when unveiled, precipitates the viewer's fall (IV.21). From this point of departure develops the moral resonance that can be legitimately derived from Ariosto, in the tradition of *serio ludere* (serious play) to which such writers as Ariosto and Erasmus are wedded.[32] Both *Orlando Furioso* and the *Moriae Encomium* concern themselves with the validity or nonvalidity of codes throughout, forcing readers out of pre-fixed patterns of thought and requiring them continually to shift and reexamine viewpoints. Erasmus begins by duping his reader into a false allegorical understanding by playing upon expectations of the nature of Folly. For instance, in chapter IX Folly introduces her attendants and followers, each a "stick figure" of some vice that seems to stand dissociated from the reader. Complacent enjoyment is disrupted when readers find that all too many of their own traits, indeed perhaps their deepest assumptions about the nature of human relations, come to be included among the bevy of these attendants and their attributes. Would any reader wish to do without "Self-Love" (chapter XXII)? In each case the "clarity" of allegory is suddenly extinguished and the reader left in the labyrinth of his own inescapable folly.

Both Ariosto and Erasmus were far too aware of the problems involved in securing knowledge to feel that any single symbolic system was capable of explicating the complexities of any group of things. The *Moriae Encomium* can be read as a process of continual destruction of points of view. This complex flexibility called for by each of the two texts with regard to both the surface of the narrative and the reader's reception of its occult messages ends in teaching the constant recontextualization of everything. The moral seriousness of each consists precisely in showing and advocating that readiness to reverse and rehierarchize data. Each text articulates

the necessity, to the balanced and even the good life, of under-
mining preconceptions. And each text makes itself an object
of perception and reevaluation analogous to the problems
experienced by characters within the text. The book reaches a
degree of self-reflexive irony coextensive with its own being.
If the allegory of the Alcina-Angelica episodes has any retro-
spective signficance it lies in its own allegoresis, or undoing.
The spurious appearance of clarity and distinctness really is
related to the disappearance of allegorical modality as a way
of reading, whether the text at stake be a poem or the world.
Only the understanding that Ariosto is dealing with relations
in themselves reunites under that rubric the detached, frag-
mentary bits of matter that in themselves can form no totality
at all.

Ariosto, then, performs his own allegoresis or "decon-
struction." The critique extends as far as and no further than
his own inability to point the satirical finger and cry out at
the despotic conditions that underlie the composition of his
great poem. The main reason for the elusiveness of the pro-
cess lies in the cardinal reversal and rehierarchization of the
entire narrative: that between literal and allegorical senses.
Reading his book as a metaphor for existence suddenly shows
us the primacy of the letter over any transient "spirit": if we
ever misread canti V through XI it was to miss the "letter" by
attaching too much importance to the "spirit." In an inver-
sion of the old hierarchy that made mimesis the precondition
of textuality, Ariosto transforms textuality into mimesis.
Thus the literal sense becomes a "vehicle" of the old allego-
ries, which are now the "tenor." Even this reversal comports
an awareness that the mimesis is also to be comprehended,
collectively, as the road of successive differentiation that gen-
erates a progressive movement from relative simplicity to
complexity.

A metaphor involves the transposal of features normally
associated with something to a noun (or phrase) that ex-
pressly denotes something else, thereby constituting the rever-
sal or neutralization of a previously extablished hierarchy.
Even a personification allegory approaches metaphorical sta-

tus, although it can run closer to the selection of just one of an arsenal of known properties to signify the whole.[33] But under "radical dispersonification . . . we try to construe the predicate such that its normal meaning is attributed to the 'wrong' noun."[34] For this transposal to achieve success, the words must be taken *literally*. Then, only then, do they generate a mutation or a reversal of conceptual habit. That is the use of Ariosto's title *Orlando Furioso*—in all of its paradoxes, and as the only signpost on an otherwise unmarked road.

# Chapter 2

## Atlante

I t is my intention to show in this and the following chapter that Ariosto implements his own forceful readings of classical myths by embedding their patterns deeply within the structure of *Orlando Furioso*. As often happens in the shifting world of mythographic commentary, the material comes to assume—and finally to embrace—many kinds of differences. Contradictions are revealed as inevitable, and traditions unstable. It is in keeping with the conception of *Orlando Furioso* as "Ariosto's eighth satire" for us to turn from its satirizing power to the treatment of mythographical storytelling as it affects just those discontinuities that, taken together, compose the poem's aerial (though not "airy") view of human events.

To probe the means by which Atlas became Atlante in *Orlando Furioso* is to show that Ariosto's classical antecedents lie at the very heart of that poem's world.[1] The several myths and metaphors of Atlas (Titan, astrologer, ocean, mountain, world) that are recurrently evoked in the course of the *Furioso* define a focus on the following interrelated issues: (1) the confluence (or conflation) of different versions of the Atlas myth in the composite "Atlante"; (2) the idea of "function" as it pertains to Atlante among the various other characters of the *Furioso,* most of whose functions are transferable; (3) Ariosto's cognizance of this relativity of function and his likely parallel interest in a contextually relevant aspect of Petrarch's poetry.[2] Ariosto invokes the spirit of Virgil and Ovid in a number of ways, making use not only of specific works but of preexisting composite types bequeathed through medieval readings of classics to the Renaissance poet as well. The explorations of this chapter thus seek to emulate the successful strategy of iconographic studies in the visual arts.[3]

It is more appropriate to speak here of "influences" than of "sources." The best work on Ariosto's "sources" to date barely glances at the classical material, and not at all with respect to Atlante.[4] Recent scholarship has entered into Ariosto's radical critique of allegorism[5] and documented the more readily recuperable of his tireless decontextualized citations, for instance from Dante.[6] There has been a renewal of interest in Ariosto's readings of Ovid[7] and his demonstrations of mastery over the imposing body of classical literature. At this relatively early stage in the study of Ariosto's interplay with classical literary figures, it seems important to attempt the recovery of both literal and less than literal modes of thought suggested to Ariosto by his readings. To my knowledge, the figure of Atlante has not been studied before in this way.

The first item to be recovered is Atlante's real name, Atlas. This is not an attempt to rehabilitate some original Atlas. Any type once taken up by Ariosto is beyond rehabilitation, so inclusive is his ability to reorder and rescramble whatever he finds and to raise baffling new obstacles that block meaning and deny any finality of interpretation. At the same time, it is evident that even this demurrer has to grasp at a provisional degree of meaning. At some arbitrary point of closure the destruction of meaning must stop short to preserve its communicability. That is how various senses of "Atlas" came to coexist in a composite type.

*Orlando Furioso* is the single text that sets the precedent of demystifying romance even as it adheres to romance's conventions, of demystifying, in fact, every other text that comes its way. That is probably why it was rescued from the bonfire of Don Quixote's discarded books as well as the reason why numerous poets and playwrights accepted Ariosto's invitation to decide Angelica's fate (XXX.16.8). The *Orlando Furioso* is the quintessential open work. It suggests the pleonastic act of killing literature with literature. Ariosto's readings of Ovid, for example, do not produce a renovated, purified Ovid although they recognize the playful side of an oft-interpreted poet. Rather, they demonstrate how no text is safe from contamination by rereading.

Let us assume that Atlante derives in great part from Ariosto's pondering on the Ovidian Atlas and on subsequent interpretations of that Atlas. If this is so, then Ariosto's departures from the composite tradition become clear but do not produce a general cleaning of the overlaid, varnished picture. Instead, the new Atlante becomes understood as a kind of "character-function," overlapping with confreres in the poem but independent of any direct relationship to other Atlases, including Ovid's. On the other hand the sum of Atlantian elements attested in other *fabulae* known to Ariosto clarifies the literary consistency and continued power of signification exercised by the classical heritage.

Knowingly or not, Ovid's medieval allegorizers made use of structural homologies that were historically and culturally quite distant from one another, in order to define their coherences and to cognize patterns held in common. Having internalized this relationship, Ariosto injects just enough confusion into it to display its conceptual limitations. From the allegorizers he retains not only a wealth of literal detail (for the precise purpose of parody) but the freedom to use Ovid and other classical writers in the same way as speakers who use the linguistic systems that are proper to them.

So crowded with references and allusions is the world of

the *Furioso* that piecing them out is like reconstructing a language, and one may well doubt the utility of rebuilding a language that is turned solely to the purpose of destruction. The doubt is aggravated by the appearance of this effort in a literary climate that finds deconstructive criticism, on one hand, and pedantic source hunting, on the other, ideologically opposed but concurrent in their lack of hospitality to structural approaches. The problem may reside in determining the value of nonexegetical criticism, or of the criticism of nonallegorical literature. To the extent that critical approaches to such literature can illuminate both literary and extraliterary worlds, to the extent that reference and allusion become not only dialectical means for writers such as Ariosto but the key to both pleasure in the work and insight into the society that produced the poem, the understanding of structure is nearly synonymous with literary analysis.

*Orlando Furioso* is constructed so as to permit reflection of the generic needs of a nuptial poem (although not written for a wedding and not an epithalamium). For Ariosto to have brought off the double feat of fulfilling the encomiastic purpose regarding Ruggiero and Bradamante and simultaneously providing an epic send-up of their personalities and vicissitudes it was necessary for them to possess markedly "divine" traits along with their human fallibilities. Ariosto effected a rapprochement of the human and divine poles. His poem cannot be thought of simply as a transformation of myth into literature that instantiates a decline in value. Even as Ariosto toys with the legends of gods he raises up a fabulized man and woman. Orlando himself retains the quasi-titanic capacity for obstinacy and physical conflict that the Roland of the *Chanson* turns to his own discomfiture. From a structural standpoint it is really only when he is cured of his madness (not when he falls in love) that Orlando takes leave of Roland. In other words although Ariosto effectuates, through many a textual filter, a transformation or alteration of a previous meaning, a semantic connection remains between that meaning when first encountered and its subsequent transformation. Ariosto is neither encomiastic about literature in his practice nor a respecter of its authority. At the same time he is generous in his praise of poets who shaped destinies, such as St. John the Evangelist (XXXV.28.7–8). Under no condition could it be alleged that he restrains his powers of invention on account of some literary taboo.

Ariosto's work thus acquires a tropological relationship to preceding works on similar subjects, a relation that may be compared to that of the terms in an overarching metaphor. But in tropological relations there can be no trope unless both of its terms are present (the literal and the figural sense).[8] By analogy with the trope, Ariosto's transformations would cease to exist as such without that moment when the "figure" that is the *Furioso* still had its two terms: the *literal,* or the types and modes assimilated by Ariosto, and the *figural,* or his reading of them.

Thus do gods and men meet on new grounds. When Atlas is transformed into a mystery-knight (II) or a wizard of fairy legend (VI, XII, XXIII) or an ailing old man (II), he may be understood as a trope, to be sure, one running downward, counter in valuation to Ruggiero and Bradamante, who move upward.[9] Much of what happens to the titan Atlas in the *Furioso* corresponds to a movement long ago noted by Auerbach: in the world of *cortesia,* feudal elements lost the political function that had governed their usage in heroic epic.[10] But for Atlas the change is not covered by different phases or aspects of medieval thought; its arc is far longer, encompassing early classical antecedents to the allegorism of medieval times, to the dynamiting of exegesis and its demotion to the status of a museum-culture.

For Ariosto Atlante clearly controls a world unto himself. He is already to be found in *Orlando Innamorato* in the character of an old man, a prophet, enchanter, and necromancer whose abode is on the *Monte di Carena,* or one of the Atlas Mountains (II.I.73–76). He has built a garden atop this mountain (II.III.27–28) that is walled in glass, and this wall is in turn encircled with stone. Atlante's function as a pagan and a wizard consists, as later in Ariosto, of protecting Ruggiero and keeping him from conversion and war. Since he appears only in book II it cannot be claimed that he bears the main weight of retarding Ruggiero's destiny, but he is already "Atlante, che giamai non lassa" (Atlante, who never falters; II.XXXIX. 49.4). In Ariosto Atlante remains the bearded necromancer who has brought Ruggiero up from a child and jealously guards him, first in a stable fortress and then by segregating others from him in the "palace of illusions." Being an astrologer and the recipient of prophecy he has long ago learned from his stars Ruggiero's destiny: that he would die a Christian. Atlante's purpose is to keep Ruggiero as his ward and to keep him a pagan. Neither the castle nor the richer, even more seductive palace of illusions provides a central focus. Both are collapsible by Atlante and instantly reconstructable.[11]

Atlante can also enter any disguise in the world; at different times he transforms himself into Angelica for Orlando and into Bradamante for Ruggiero. He lures into his realm of desire and illusion potentially everyone whose efforts will subsequently (we learn) end up as detritus on the Moon. Into that world of credulity and hope and delight enter all engaged in avid pursuit of some single object. But Atlante is subject to deterrents (such as the horn whose sound chases everyone away) and finally to illness and death. His final appearance (XXXVI.59–66) is as a voice from his tomb, ultimately concurring in and abetting the disentanglement of relations between Ruggiero and Marfisa his twin sister, and thus putting the final touches on the union of the royal couple.

From this brief outline it is possible to gather that Atlante is no mere "retarding device" for the action of the poem. Although he does carry on the plot-function that Boiardo had allotted in the *Innamorato* to the two "fairies," Grifone and Aquilante—that of keeping the heroes from their destined death in France[12]—Atlante is a world, the Atlas of a moral geography that the poem sustains on every level. Like King Arthur's court when out of Camelot, Atlante's realm is the center of a domain whose circumference is nowhere. It is the focus of a centripetal movement rivaling that toward Christian and Saracen capitals alike, a prison often beloved and always comfortable for its (distinguished) inhabitants. When freed from it some never want to leave. The patrimony of functions inherited from Boiardo expands and enriches itself in the *Furioso* to the point of divesting itself of anything more than a simple contiguity-relation to the *Innamorato*.

Atlante is the only magus and necromancer, the only old guardian, the only father figure of any note in the poem (aside from the nonspeaking figureheads of Bradamante's father and mother). Although the life of man is curtailed and Atlante dies with his palace, we know that his work will continue in quarters outside the poem. How else could the Moon be so densely piled with so copious a residue? The destruction of the palace in canto XXII hurls the prisoners back into the world of time and death, but it and they must have been preceded by likenesses and are perhaps so at the moment of writing. These supply the Moon not only with what is lost by bad fortune on earth (XXXIV.73.7) but with desired fame and riches never won (XXXIV.80–89), promises and vows and engagements of devotion, treaties and pacts never kept, prayers to God and the saints, gifts and even adulatory poems to princes whose composition remained unrewarded. All are the reified paraphernalia of desire and delusion (with more coming). And the vials of Sanity awaiting their future or forever-lost owners prompt recall of the perpetual "otherness" of the desired object:

> Altri in amar lo perde, altri in onori,
> Altri in cercar, scorrendo il mar, ricchezze,
> Altri ne le speranze de Signori,
> Altri dietro alle magiche sciocchezze;
> Altri in gemme, altri in opre di pittori,
> Et altri in altro che più d'altro apprezze;
> Di sofisti e d'astrologi raccolto
> E di poeti ancor ve n'era molto.
>
> (XXXIV.85)

> (Some waste on love, some seeking honour, lose
> Their wits, some, scowering seas, for merchandise,

Some, that on wealthy lords their hope repose,
And some, befooled by silly sorceries;
These upon pictures, upon jewels those;
These on whatever else they highest prize.
Astrologers' and sophists' wits mid these,
And many a poet's too, Astolpho sees.)

In theory it would be possible for Atlante to end on the Moon with the other *astrologhi,* who give rise in this stanza to the recollection of poets. But this poem has only one poet and only one astrologer. Although Ariosto puts rather severe limits on his supernatural powers (which do not extend to immortality or to keeping the plot going eternally), Atlante is while he lives the custodian of a world of immortal deceptions.

More accurately, one might have said "two worlds": for although Atlante himself is not doubled, he builds first the castle on the Pyrenees in which Ruggiero spends an enclosed youth, then a limited converse of it, the palace of illusions (XII.21) into which knights and ladies gladly pour, the better for Atlante to keep *them* from *Ruggiero.* The first location is a sort of "castle in Spain" for Atlante (though Ariosto does not say so). The second is the more generalized and dominant place, its geographical location indeterminate. Thus whereas the first castle may be the locus of Atlante's illusion (of being able to segregate Ruggiero permanently), the subsequent one is for everyone but Atlante and is potentially all-inclusive, permitting the infinite proliferation of deluded inhabitants.

It is only after his death (XXXVI.59) that Atlante comes to reproduce the plot-function of other prophets, such as Merlin and Melissa, who throughout the poem have been oracles of a positive ending for the Ruggiero-Bradamante alliance. Only then does he speak freely of his past machinations and subterfuges regarding Ruggiero—when he is reduced to a voice in a stone.

Atlante's first and second appearances, described in detail in the same canto, show him on his Hippogryph in flight. On the winged animal he can fly as high as an eagle (II.49.8), and he tears through the air with his spear (II.50.6), subsequently fighting Gradasso and Ruggiero simultaneously from above. He is a *volator* (flier; II.52.11) and a *cavalier celeste* (heavenly rider; II.55.2); finally, he brandishes the shield in Pinabellos's face and stuns him so that no one sees his enchanted flight.

The *castello* Atlante builds for Ruggiero is impregnable (III.67.2; also II.41.8). Ariosto emphasizes its extreme height (III.67.2) and walls of steel (IV.12.2 and 6.3; also II.43), as well as the mountain on which it stands:

> Vi sorge in mezzo un sasso, che la cima
> D'un bel muro d'acciar tutta si fascia;
> E quella tanto inverso il ciel sublima,
> Che quanto ha intorno, inferior si lascia.
> Non faccia (chi non vola) andarvi stima;
> Che spesa indarno vi saria ogni ambascia.
>
> (IV.12.1–6)

> (A rock from that deep valley's centre springs;
> Bright walls of steel about its summit go:
> And this as high that airy summit flings,
> As it leaves all the neighboring cliffs below.
> He may not scale the height who has not wings;
> And vainly would each painful toil bestow.)

When Bradamante challenges him Atlante materializes on the Hippogryph with his book of magic in hand. But Bradamante unhorses him, and he instantly metamorphoses into a pleading old soothsayer. But he can still make himself and the castle disappear (IV.38–39), and he remains a *mago di somma dottrina* (VII.44.3). His second palace encompasses the world of human desire and illusion:

> A tutti par, l'incantator mirando,
> Mirar quel che per sé brama ciascuno,
> Donna, scudier, compagno, amico, quando
> Il desiderio uman non è tutto uno.
>
> (XIII.50.1–4)

(Seeing the sage, all think they see a squire,
Companion, lady-love, or absent friend;
Whatever is each several wight's desire:
Since to one scope our wishes never tend.)

Atlante's final stratagem is to make Astolfo seem to every pursuer the one each is seeking to destroy, be he giant, peasant, or knight (XXII.19–20). And since no one needs to be forced to stay in the palace, a host of warriors pours out of it to chase Astolfo. But as he lifts a great stone under which lies a spirit responsible for carrying out the spells of the palace, Astolfo destroys it with all its enchantments. By that time Ruggiero has spent ten cantos there, and Orlando is about to become mad. And yet Ariosto endows Atlante with magical powers only to have them confront other, decisive astrological influences whose prediction is at last fulfilled. Atlante can dominate only half of the *Furioso* (through canto XXII); at the last he vanishes into the great stone from which he later doubles and amplifies the Ruggiero-Bradamante prophecy.

Atlante is a prime example of Ariosto's functional representation of classical allusion in romance guise. In the transfer of certain functions from the realm of divine to that of human energy, Atlas's character-function, drawn from classical mythology, is turned to the service of a genre, and the heroic myth becomes a romance convention. Similarly the Age of Gold is remembered in the lightly mocking idyll of Angelica and Medoro. The conflict between divine power and human arrogance passes through many a genre to end in Rodomonte; and Atlas, all-seeing astronomer and supporter of the universe, becomes Atlante, the custodian of an illusory world and opponent of stellar prophecies.

Although Ariosto does restore Ovid's sense of play, liberating that poet from the burden of moralizing precedent, he does not thereby deprive himself of the pleasure of scanning the Ovidian myths through other texts and commentaries upon them. His rewriting through the welter of other texts, in fact, mirrors the labyrinthine paths of his characters, their crossings and recrossings, and the whole demoralized map of their *errare*. The *Furioso* is not a work of restoration but of simultaneity and inclusion, a *varia tela* (varied canvas) that "shows" more than it "tells," and is for that reason both hospitable to "iconographic" examination and inimical to the exegete.

Ariosto did go beyond the stage of the mere episode in his acceptance of suggestions from Ovid. The *Metamorphoses,* especially the fourth book, not only dominate the *fabula* (fable) of Ruggiero-Orlando and Angelica, as was noted from the sixteenth century,[13] but penetrate far into the plot-structure of the entire poem.[14] Therefore Ovid's Atlas provides a logical point of departure for a reader seeking to compare meanings and shades of meaning, to perceive unstated relations and implicit ideas and place them at least in a provisional context.

Ovid conceives Atlas both as a man and as a mountain. Each has as a corollary the support of the world. The transformation of man into mountain occupies part of book IV of the *Metamorphoses* and represents a considerable elaboration of Ovid's precedents. Virgil had described Atlas as a giant who had assumed the likeness of a huge snowy mountain commanding the western region of North Africa. Mercury, in flight to Aeneas, sights the mountain:

> iamque volans apicem et latera ardua cernit Atlantis duri, caelum qui vertice fulcit, Atlantis, cinctum adsidue cui nubibus astris piniferum caput et vento pulsatur et imbri; nix umeros infusa tegit; tum flumina mento praecipitant senis, et glacie riget horrida barba.

> (And now in flight he describes the peak and steep sides of toiling Atlas, who props heaven on his peak—Atlas, whose pine-wreathed head is ever girt with black clouds, and beaten with wind and rain; fallen snow mantles his shoulders, while rivers plunge down the aged chin and his rough beard is still with ice.)[15]

Profiting from this amalgam of the toiling giant and the mountain, Ovid draws on the connection between Atlas and Perseus. He imagines that Perseus, returning across Libya with the head of Medusa, was swept here and there by violent and contrary winds that at last drove him back to western Africa and the prosperous fertile kingdom of Atlas. At this time Atlas is still a giant, in human form, ruling over this extreme edge of the west and over the sea but alarmed by Themis's prophecy that one day his famous garden would be robbed by a son of Jove. Perseus, in requesting Atlas's hospitality, describes himself as a son of Jove, and Atlas takes him for the robber, violently attempting to drive him away. Ovid tells of the massive walls that Atlas had built to enclose his orchard and to keep all strangers from it. But his violence is of no avail against Perseus, who at last transforms him into the Mountain with the Medusa head (IV.649–56):

> quantas erat, mons factus Atlas; nam barba comaeque in silvas abeunt, iuga sunt umerique manusque, quod caput ante fuit, summo est in monte cacumen, ossa lapis fiunt; tum partes altus in omnes crevit in immensum (sic, dii, statuistis) et omne cum tot sideribus caelum requievit in illo.

> (Straightway Atlas became a mountain huge as the giant had been; his beard and hair were changed to trees, his shoulders and arms to spreading ridges; what had been his head was now the mountain's top, and his bones were changed to stones. Then he grew to monstrous size in all his parts—for so, O gods, ye had willed it—and the whole heaven with all its stars rested upon his head.)[16]

In a subsequent reference Perseus (*Metamorphoses* IV.772–73) alludes to Atlas only as a mountain, as if this had been so before he procured the Gorgon's head:

> narrat Agenorides gelido sub Atlante iacentem
> esse locum solidae tutum munimine molis.

([The descendant of Agenor] told how beneath cold Atlas
there was a place safe under the protection of the rocky mass.)

The last reference to Atlas in the *Metamorphoses* occurs
in book XV and is of a peculiar relevance to the study of
Ariosto. The speaker is Pythagoras (*Samius,* or man of
Samos), and what he has to say precedes the exposition of
Pythagoras's doctrine of transmogrification. He will sing, he
announces, of hidden, great things from the vantage point of
mountain heights:

> iuvat ire per alta astra,
> iuvat terris et inerti sede relicta
> nube vehi validique umeris insistere Atlantis
> palantesque homines passim et rationis egentes
> despectare procul trepidosque obitumque timentes
> sic exhortari seriemque evolvere fati!
> (*Metamorphoses* XV.147–52)

(It is a delight to take one's way along the starry firmament
and, leaving the earth and its dull regions behind, to ride on
the clouds, to take stand on stout Atlas' shoulders and see far
below men wandering aimlessly, devoid of reason, anxious
and in fear of the hereafter, thus to exhort them and unroll the
book of fate!)

The passage strongly evokes not only the rides on the Hippo-
gryph that at different times provide Atlante, Ruggiero, and
Astolfo with an aerial perspective on the world but the very
stance taken by Ariosto as the poet of the *Furioso*. It needs no
emphasis, of course, that the philosopher unfolding the secrets
of fate is replaced by the poet with his infinite mobility and
capriciousness. The only possible ascent above the world of
unreason and folly is on tbe Hippogryph (which first appears
as an attribute of Atlante).

Superimposed images of Atlas the giant and Atlas the
mountain do occur in the *Furioso*. One instance is embedded
in the same fourth canto that first presents the castle on the
Pyrenees and the winged knight. But like the titanic size
evoked by references to the mountain in Virgil and in Ovid,

these images set topographic limits or convey the notion of hyperbolic space. The king of Scotland promises to Ginevra's champion

> il fior di quante belle donne
> Da l'Indo sono all'Atlantee colonne.
>
> (IV.61.7–8)

> (the sweetest flower of all the ladies fair
> that betwixt Ind and Atlas's pillars are.)

Astolfo's tour on the Hippogryph includes every "province" that lies "tra la marina e la silvosa schiena / Del fiero Atlante" (XXXIII.100.5–6). The "unsayability" topos describes Agramante's army as innumerable. The only possible description would be by one who

> Dirà quante onde, quando è il mar più grosso,
> Bagnano il piede al Mauritano Atlante.
>
> (XIV.99.3–4)

> ( . . . might count as well
> The trees upon its back or waves that beat
> Against the Mauritanian Atlas's feet.)

The vast extent of the desert from "l'Atlante ai liti Rubri" ('twixt the Red and the Atlantic shore; VIII.67) is mentioned as the habitat of serpents, and Astolfo travels "dal mar d'Atlante ai termini d'Egitto" (from the Atlantic to the borders of Egypt; XXXIII.98.4). All of these allusions concur with Ovid's depiction of Atlas as the paragon of height and breadth and as the expression of immense boundaries.

In poets far older than Ovid Atlas stands at the border between heaven and earth and between night and day. Hesiod's *Theogony* (507) already names him as one of the Titans (hence a brother of Prometheus). These collectively and individually personified the agonistic aspect of human nature, and it is likely that Atlas as the epitome of struggle and endurance subsists from Hesiod's characterization. Oppressed by a powerful force on the very limits of the world he upholds the heavens with tireless arms and head (*Theogony* 517–20). Hesiod locates the home of Atlas in the westernmost part of the world, just before the Hesperides ("western maidens") and the House of Night (746–49). "Prudent Zeus" (*Theogony* 520) placed him there, it is understood, as a direct result of the misuse of his strength in the rebellion of the Titans. In Hesiod Atlas clearly constitutes a boundary marker between east and west, day and night.

Homer (*Odyssey* I.52; III.486) saw Atlas as the overseer and caretaker of the columns rooted in the earth and supporting the heavens.[17] Homer also seems to recognize in Atlas the buoyant power of the ocean, for he names Atlas the father of Calypso, whose home is the western Atlantic, and says that Atlas knows all the depths of the sea (*Odyssey* IV.385). For some readers of Homer the columns upheld by Atlas were embedded in the bottom of the ocean, arising out of it to support the clouds. Whereas Homer gave no indication of the connection between Atlas and a mountain, Herodotus (IV.84) mentions an extremely high mountain in northwestern Africa called "Atlas" and "Column of Heaven." Like the columns of a great hall and circling the earth on all sides, the chain of mountains seemed to support the clouds and to maintain the tension and separation obtaining between heaven and earth.

The rich and powerful king who knows the mysteries of Ocean in Homer developed into a seer, and even a mathematician and philsopher as well as astronomer. Virgil (*Aeneid* I.740) says that the singer Iopas, with his golden lyre, had been once taught by Atlas; he has Iopas sing of the voyages of Sun and Moon. Although Ovid does not develop this aspect of Atlas at all, it survives in his allegorizers. Servius's commentary on the *Aeneid* contributes to the tradition.[18]

Before turning to this important legacy of the astronomer Atlas, I will briefly follow a final line of inquiry relating to the classical conception. It is related to the fabled isle of Atlantis, which Plato discusses in the *Timaeus* and at considerable length in the *Critias*.[19] Plato tells of this unusually fertile and rich land beyond the Columns of Hercules, separated by a chain of islands from a further continent. Atlas's people canalized and cultivated the land, but the *Timaeus* emphasized their warlike nature and the vastness of the empire they accumulated, which included Libya, within the Columns of Hercules as far as Egypt, and Europe as far as Tyrrhenia. This people eventually became audacious enough to attack the Athenians, an enterprise followed quickly by the Athenian triumph. But then a series of natural disasters caused Atlantis to disappear into the depths of the sea. As a result, Plato concludes in the *Timaeus* account, the Atlantic Ocean became nonnavigable, for the sinking of the island raised shoals of mud that could not be passed. It was only then that the Columns formed a limit to exploration in a practical sense.

In the *Critias* Plato elaborates a description of Atlantis (110–21). Certain aspects of his account display coincidences with the later story of the king Atlas, so jealous of his orchards. The very existence of Atlantis, Plato explains, arises from the enclosure of its land by Poseidon, who loved Atlas's mother, Cleito,[20] so jealously that he surrounded the hill on which she lived with alternating zones of sea and land (114). Plato then details the greatness of the ensuing empire, of its natural resources, trade, military strength, and the height of its civilization. The city lay in a plain surrounded by mountains that descended abruptly into the sea, mountains "celebrated for their number, size and beauty, far beyond any which still exist . . ." (118).

The Atlantians began as a virtuous people obedient to the divine side of their dual nature (119–21), caring little for the wealth that accrued to them and given to simplicity and friendship; "but when the divine portion began to fade away, and became diluted too much with the moral admixture, and the human nature got the upper hand, they . . . grew visibly debased" (121). The *Critias* ends with a council of the gods called by Zeus (which appears to preface the destruction of Atlantis) and breaks off in the middle of his sentence. Up to this point Plato's description has expatiated on the extreme richness of the kingdom, the palaces, baths, racecourses, and temples and of the cultivation of the vast central plain fed by water from the hills that ringed it completely. Had the Atlantians not extended their empire beyond the "Columns of Hercules," Atlantis proper would have consisted of this territory, entirely surrounded by water except for the seaward gap with its harbor works. It is noteworthy that Atlas is associated with a people inimical to the Athenians besides being simply "eastern." The idea of a realm belonging to Atlas appears, of course, in the *Metamorphoses,* where it is also described as unusually prosperous and fertile. But in the myth of Atlantis the kingdom extends itself to become a small world. Its location near North Africa would argue well for the possibility that Atlantis contributes to the aggregate of suggestions to Ariosto about a fabled though not always virtuous enclosed "universe" of pleasure and eventual delusion, and "Moorish" in conception.

Of course neither Plato's nor Ovid's Atlas has much relation to the titan, astronomer, and habitué of the ocean who eventually gives rise to the *mago Atlante.* This side of Atlante was in all probability bequeathed to Ariosto by the allegorizations of Ovid mentioned earlier. These pervade the intricately woven fabric of the *Orlando Furioso.* Allegorizations of Ovid, such as that of Petrus Berchorius (Pierre Bersuire), Petrarch's good friend who figures among the last in a long medieval tradition of mythological exegesis, continued to go through many printings in Ariosto's time.[21] Their purpose was to show how myths could be taught for moral purposes and the exposition of Christian doctrine and historical truth.

Berchorius's text is representative of allegorized readings of Ovid and was followed by others well into the sixteenth century. Among those myths that best display the success of his method he adduces that of Atlas and Perseus.

> Quod etiam in fabulis aliquando lateat veritas historica patet in fabula Atlantis. Perseus enim dicitur Gorgoniam occidisse et cum (capite) eius Atlantem maximum gigantem in montem qui Atlas dicitur convertisse quia s. Perseus miles strenuus orti regis, qui in insulis meridionalibus que Gorgone dicuntur regnabat, occidit et vicit Gorgonii filiam, et caput eius i.

divicias, regnum et substanciam tulit, cum quo exercitum con-
gregatit, ita quod Atlantem regem Affrice superavit ipsumque
in montem figere coegit. Et quia postea non comparuit, in
montem mutatum poetica garrulitas ipsum dicit.

(That sometimes historical truth is hidden in fables is shown
by the fable of Atlas. It is said that Perseus killed the Gorgon
and transformed the great giant Atlas with it into the moun-
tain called Atlas, because the sturdy soldier Perseus killed the
king of the orchard over the southern isles called "Gorgon,"
who reigned and conquered, and killed the Gorgon's daugh-
ter, and by taking her head is meant that he took the kingdom
and wealth with which he called together an army that tri-
umphed over Atlas the African king and forced him to flee to
a mountain. And since Atlas himself did not reappear, poetic
garrulity said that he turned into the mountain.)[22]

But Atlas has several more possible meanings:

Athlas rex ulterioris Hispanie ita erat magnus. . . . Vel dic
quod Athlas signat altos et subtiles theologos et philosophos
qui s. celum videntur attingere in quantum de celestibus
consueverunt sciencialiter disputare. . . . Vel di quod iste
Athlas est Dei filius.[23]

(Atlas was the great king of outermost Spain. . . . Or say that
Atlas denotes high and subtle theologians and philosophers
who are seen to attain to heaven in that they were used to
disputing celestial things scientifically. . . . Or say that Atlas is
God's own son.)

Berchorius draws substantially from Fulgentius[24] in his narra-
tive of the myth. Other interpreters, including the poet of the
*Ovide moralisé,* combine Atlas the king with the philosopher
and astronomer.

—Athlas fu rois de grant noblesce
Et sorabondans en richesce.
Mestres fu de philozophie.
Tant sot l'art d'astronomie,

Qu'il sot de tout le firmament
L'ordenance et le mouvement
Et des etoiles la nature
Et la chalour et la froidure
Et la cause dont ce venoit:
Pour ce dist l'en qu'il soustenoit
Le firmament desor sa teste.[25]

(Atlas was a king of great lineage, superabundant in riches. He was a master of philosophy. He knew so much of astronomy that he knew the order and movement of the entire firmament and the nature of the stars and the causes of heat and cold; that is why it is said that he sustains the firmament on top of his head.)

Note the displacement of Atlas as upholder of the heavens to that of conserver of knowledge about them. The *Ovide moralisé* poet goes on to explain the allegorical meaning of the orchard: it is the *cuer* of Atlas, wherein is cultivated the art of *philozophie,* signified also by the golden tree. According to this account, Perseus and Hercules, whose myths are conflated, are recognized as having important features in common, for Atlas feared Perseus as the robber of his golden fruit (although the thief was to be Hercules). Both Perseus and Hercules, the author says, are above all devoted learners and imitators of Atlas, and the serpent Atlas set to guard the apples seems to represent the difficulties of study. But both triumph over it and take the fruit:

Perseus, li filz de Iovis,
Et Hercules, ce m'est avis,
Furent desciple d'Atlantis,
Qui moult estoient ententis
Come il peussent l'arbre embler,
C'est a dire Athlas resambler
En sens et en discretion.
Moult misrent lor entencion
En aprendre philozophie,
Et le serpent, qui signifie

L'estuide et l'arbre a a garder,
Vainquirent, et lors sans tarder
Orent l'arbre a lor volente
Qu'Athlas avoit au cuer plente.

(6322–35)

(Perseus, the son of Jove, and Hercules, as I see it, were both
disciples of Atlas, who were very determined to rob the tree;
that is to say, to resemble Atlas in wisdom and judgment.
They put their minds to learning philosophy, and they van-
quished the serpent of studies who guarded the tree, and then
without delay they had the tree at their pleasure, which Atlas
had planted in his heart.)

Boccaccio in the *Genealogia deorum gentilium* follows
Fulgentius as far as Berchorius does but adds to his analysis
of Atlas Augustine's acknowledgment[26] of the Titan's astro-
logical powers. He also points out that Pliny attributes the
invention of astrology to Atlas, "et hinc, ob sudores ex arte
susceptos, celum humeris tolerasse dictum est" (And so be-
cause of the sweat drawn by the practice of his art, he is said
to carry the world on his shoulders).[27] Boccaccio's account,
then, conjoins the aspects of kingship, arcane wisdom, and
forbearance that compose the figure of Atlas in varying de-
gree throughout the Ovidian allegorizations. It is not so far to
the gloss of Atlas as a Christ-figure in Berchorius and in the
*Ovide moralisé* as God the Father. I cite from the apposite
portion of the *Ovide moralisé* the lines that mesh with the
characterization of Atlas as a wise man:

Cil cria ciel et terre,
Si fist le soleil et la lune
Et les estoiles. De chascune
Sot le nombre et quel force elle a,
Et per lor noms les apela.
Cil porte tout le firmament,
Et donc a tous soustenement
Par la vertu de sa parole.
C'est li maistres de bone escole,

Qui a toute science enclose
En soi seul: le texte et la glose.

(6424–35)


(He created heaven and earth, and made the sun and moon
and stars. He knew the number of stars and the force each
has, and called them by their names. He carries the entire
firmament, and thus the virtue of his word sustains all. He is
the master of the great school who contains all knowledge in
himself alone: both text and gloss.)


The master of *clergie* who composed these medieval lines
recurs naturally to the old metaphor of the book of the uni-
verse. And here the strength of the Word upholds the world,
reinforcing the idea of Atlas as the repository of knowledge.

Whether as Creator, sage, or powerful king of a fabled
domain, Atlas remains throughout these varied medieval char-
acterizations the summation of a world. He is a composite
type whose single outstanding trait is that he can include
everything. This vastness of compass is retained as a feature
when the ocean and mountain named for him are mentioned
in classical and in postmedieval writings.

But it is a domain tinged in medieval accounts with a
certain kind of negative (or at best, ambiguous) value. As
guardian of the golden tree Atlas placed a wall around the
garden (*Metamorphoses* IV); as a mountain range he shut
them in. If in several allegorical readings that tree symbolizes
*philozophie*, then the surrounding walls variously represent
study, with its attendant obstacles; or in another quite late
reading (that of the Spanish scholar Enrique de Villena, cited
by Aldo Bernardo),[28] "the order and principles within which
wisdom is enclosed." But the fruit is also reminiscent of the
other, forbidden tree of knowledge. And the location of Atlas
at either end of the Atlas Mountains, and/or near the fabled
Lake Tritonis in Libya, should make it unnecessary for Ari-
osto to have to emphasize the "paganness" of Atlante. He is
"Mauretanian" or "African" partly because that is the loca-
tion of his mountain. In the composite of allegorizations,

whether a king, sage, or magus, Atlas represents a world that only bounds on the known world. Beyond the limits of the "Columns of Hercules" (or Atlas Mountains) he enjoys a ubiquity based on the unknown *ultima tellus* (ultimate land).

Embodying a power that straddles accustomed boundaries and mediates between heaven and earth (as between night and day), Atlas is a brilliant choice for the forebear of Atlante. No longer a symbol of physical force or tension, Ariosto's elegant magus travels easily between earth and sky on the wings of the Hippogryph. Of course he is able to read prophecies in the stars, because of his reputation as an astronomer-astrologer; and like his namesake in Ovid, he opposes the prophecy of what will be taken from him. Ovid's Atlas mistook Perseus, whereas Atlante makes no mistake about the source of his eventual deprivation. But each stands uselessly against the gods or the people of the gods. Although Atlante has absorbed the arcane knowledge Atlas possessed, it seems similarly available to anyone who captures his magic book (as Ruggiero does and later, Astolfo).

Atlante's knowledge of stellar and marine mysteries, his jealousy of Ruggiero that corresponds to Atlas's concerning the golden apples, his mediating power between heaven and earth as expressed in his flight of the Hippogryph (which enables Atlante to fight in the guise of an armed knight from a lofty position), and his beautiful, wealthy, and "African" domain of illusions, so like the fabled realm of Atlas, clearly recall the anterior composite type. But two of these features are transferable—the knowledge, portable in his book, and the Hippogryph. They atrophy to little more than functions that temporarily define Atlas by opposition to other characters, who are "personnages-signes,"[29] acting in relay as vectors of one and the same message.

Ariosto's reassignment of these functions—riding the Hippogryph, reading the magic book, crossing and recrossing the same labyrinthine paths—underscores the illusory aspect of all of his geographical and concrete paraphernalia, all the props that, rather than being moved about, come to move the characters. If I am correct in the supposition that the characters themselves are "plot-functions," largely present in order to be pushed and pulled about by the mischief inherent in their reified natures, it is also true that they are assigned natures and objects of desire just as some get horses (often runaway ones),[30] and others get veils and skirts. Atlante's desire to remain a world unto himself also finally is exposed as a delusion, for his world can not only be moved but also collapsed—and not only by Atlante but by any reader of his magic book. How better to show the malleability of all poetic matter? The giant turned forever to stone and the magus sent to live under his tombstone as a voice are in this respect one: the medievalized fairy-model faithfully echoes his petrified antecedent. It is appropriate, therefore, for Atlante the Moor to meet the punishment suffered still by Atlas the giant.

The ubiquitousness of the character-sign in the *Furioso* is one of Ariosto's means of setting texts free from anterior contexts and challenging the possibility of any kind of final textual authority.[31] His own, he says, is partially an open book, too. Ariosto's catholic treatment of the composite types assembled from classical myths and their medieval and Renaissance allegorizers provides yet another means. I have shown that Ariosto does not strip the layers of "later" exegesis but exploits them; and not, by far, for the sole purpose of ridiculing medieval readers. For the state of blinding desire and pursuit, he shows, is indeed common to human beings at any time. Ariosto's implementation of suggestions from classical literature is itself eclectic, and it might not be excessive to venture that he perceived—as anyone working with the contradictory, episodic, syncopated, partial renderings of classical myth would do—that these too present a tangled and mysterious picture. Given the difficulties of separating out any strand of this skein one might ask whether it is at all possible to detach the "classical" from the "medieval" aspects of his retelling. Paradoxically, this can be done only by careful philology and point-by-point comparison of *all* the "authorized versions" of his stories. Such work may be the only way out of the realm of illusion Ariosto created for his readers.

Like that realm Atlante's lies on the boundary of the known world, not beyond it. The very invention of a palace of illusions may have taken wing from a known precedent established in Petrarch's poetry. How does the kingdom of Atlas become transformed into a palace of illusions? I would like to suggest a kinship between Ariosto's brilliant innovation and the presence of a possible realm of Truth in Petrarch's *Africa*.

Although this epic poem was largely neglected in its own time, it was published and republished in Venice early in the sixteenth century (1501 and 1503). It is not farfetched to suppose that Ariosto might have known *Africa*. A (now-missing) Mantuan codex has been indicated by its most thorough editor,[32] in addition to the Codex Urbinate in the Vatican Library. *Africa* recounts the victories of Scipio (Africanus), following closely the account in Livy. Petrarch's return to Roman history for the substance and inspiration of his epic, his Herculean efforts to revive classical Latin language and style, and his perception of the spirit of *Romanitas* distinguish this work from major efforts of other medieval poets and prompt Morris Bishop's apt observation that "*Africa* should rightfully be seen as the earliest Renaissance epic rather than as a medieval artifact."[33]

In his important book, *Petrarch, Scipio and the Africa*[34] Aldo Bernardo analyzes the meanings of Scipio Africanus in Petrarch's poetry. His analysis emphasizes the portrayal of Scipio as embodiment of "the humanistic ideal of the supreme man of action" and Petrarch's concomitant self-designation as the poet "who will sing so worthily of Scipio that, like Scipio, he will merit the laurel crown."[35] Thus by celebrating the victor over Hannibal and the savior of Rome Petrarch fuses together the images of poetry and of glory, "and this fusion, encompassing as it does not only the triumph of Scipio and Ennius on the Capitoline but also the reflections on poetry that echo all that is finest in the classical tradition, truly summarizes the total drama of Petrarch and his views as a man of letters—his lifelong dream of achieving in a literary work a fusion of the truths of philosophy, history and poetry."[36]

In addition to this work of renovation Petrarch's Scipio was to exemplify a reconciliation of classical and Christian ethical ideals. Scipio could easily be upheld as exemplary of both warlike and civilized traits, in the line of succession of authorities from Cicero to Macrobius and into the Middle Ages. It is in any event within that tradition that the *maga* Melissa designates Scipio to Ruggiero as one of the models he should be emulating together with Alexander and Caesar (VII.59.3). Long before the creation of Ruggiero in Boiardo's *Innamorato* Scipio had been viewed as a figure (according to Auerbach's definition)[37] and as an instrument of historical fulfillment in time. *Africa* goes so far in the depiction of fulfilled prophecy, and its chief character so clearly instantiates the intrinsic superiority of the conquering Romans, that *Africa* provides an apt term of comparison for subsequent Italian epics.

In *Africa* the titanic aspect of Atlas the man-mountain emerges at several points. Two of these are connected with exhortatory purposes. When Scipio's father meditates on his imminent death and the African iniquities and urges Scipio to a life of combat, he invokes their desired punishment in an *adynaton* or impossibility-figure:[38]

> ... Num periure denissimus Atlas
> Telluris clipeus, mundi tutela nefandi,
> Cedet sponte loco radice revulsus ao ima,
> Serpentumque acies montesque immittet harene
> Ardentis, facietque viam spirantibus Austris?[39]
>
> (III.58–63)

> (Affronted by such sins
> shall not great Atlas, shield and guardian of an abominable
>   world, uproot itself
> from out of the depths of earth and so make way
> for swarming vipers, hiss of burning sand,
> and yield free passage to the scorching blasts borne from
>   the south?)

Again, the image of Atlas juxtaposes the two views in a sweeping period:

. . . Huc olim Argolici finxere poete
Convenisse deos, potuque ciboque refectos
Ethiopum cum rege gravis duxisse sub umbra
Athlantis placidam tranquillo numine noctem:
Quod fictum est ideo quia numina magna putabant
Sidera, que liquidis primum vescuntur in undis,
Ethiopum quas litus habet, mox fessa videntur
Vergere ad occasus, ubi maximums eminet Athlas,
Ultima terrarum qui possidet: ille paratus
Excipit ac magno venetia contegit antro.

(II.377–86)

(There once the gods convened
(so feign the Aeolian bards) and took their rest
refreshed with meat and drink, and passed a night
of tranquil ease beneath the shade of Atlas
in converse with an Ethiopian king.
So might they fable because they believed
the stars were great divinities who first
rose from their dwelling in the waves that beat
on Ethiopia's shores and then, grown weary,
seemed to turn westward where great Atlas strains
bearing aloft the last of lands. He waits
to take them as they come and shelter them
in his vast cave.)

This is again Ovid's *ultima tellus,* and Petrarch follows
the boundary of that outer world from a beginning in "Ethio-
pia" in East Africa to the extreme west. Atlas the astronomer
comprehends both the setting and rising of the stars through
the allegorization of geography. In Petrarch's characteristi-
cally anthropomorphic reading of nature, the stars them-
selves become weary of their journey, and here Petrarch links
this kind of reading to the *prisci poetae* (originary poets).
Closer to the Petrarch of the *Canzoniere*, even, is the version
of Atlas he gives, of his transformation into a mountain. With
reference to Scipio a minstrel sings to him and his men of one
who has dared to pass the Columns of Hercules:

. . . sed nuper ab Ortu
Vesanus veniens iuvenis convollere metam

Est ausus, nomenque ideo mutare nequivit
Herculis auctoris, Libie cui rara tenenti
Longevus nimioque Atlas sub pondere fessus
Deposuit celum ac stellas; sic ipse quievit.
Nec sibi longa quies, nam mox dulcedine captus
Heu miseratque oculos ausus vidisse Meduse
Vertitur in scopulos. Nunc stat quem cernimus ipsi
Magnus et ingenti tellurem contegit umbra
Immensoque iacet spatio porrectus et astra
Vertice tangit adhuc. Illum nix hospita semper
Et nimbi atque aure quatiunt et fulmina et imbres.

(III.400–412)

(But newly, from the east, a savage youth
has dared to spurn such limits yet has failed
to change the name they bear since Hercules
defined the frontier, he to whom old Atlas,
lord of all Libya's kingdoms, wearying
of his great burden, gave in trust the stars
and lofty heavens while he took his ease.
Nor did the wretch repose for long; bewitched,
he turned to look upon Medusa's face
and so was turned to stone. Behold him now:
darkening the world with his vast shade he stands,
far reaching into space and with his head
touching the highest stars. Eternal snow
enshrouds him and he towers for all time,
harassed by thunder, wind and cloud and storm.)

The final lines of this evocation are derived from the Virgilian description. Ovid alludes briefly to the episode in which Hercules assumed the support of the heavens from Atlas ("hac caelum cervice tuli" [Upon this neck I upheld the sky]; *Metamorphoses* IX.198). But the narrative emphasis falls upon the transformation of Atlas by Medusa, which Bernardo designates as the Medusan transformation most frequently mentioned in Petrarch's poetry as a whole.[40]

In the sequence of Ovid's account it is clear that by the time Perseus displays the Medusa head to Atlas it is already

wreathed with serpents.[41] But at the end of the fourth book
Perseus explains why Medusa, alone among her Gorgon sis-
ters, has snaky hair: once beautiful, she was loved and ravished
by Neptune, and to punish this deed Athena changed Medu-
sa's hair to serpents (*Metamorphoses* IV.794–801). The dou-
ble aspect of Medusa, beautiful and terrible, was recognized in
medieval allegorizations.[42] Petrarch's allusions to Medusa in
the *Canzoniere* are bound up with the idea of restlessness. His
desire, as well as *folle, fero,* and *vago,* is "fermo," and since
this aspect of it could find its appropriate symbol in the face of
Medusa (CLXXIX.10), she becomes the image whose appear-
ance in *Vergine bella* (CCCLXVI) is the extreme expression of
Petrarch's revulsion from his own desire.

Petrarch begins one poem with the comparison of Laura
to Daphne and her dazzling power. This leads into his regret
that he cannot transform himself into his beloved or into
stone; for the eyes of Laura have narrowly missed doing so:

> E s'io non posso transformarmi in lei
> Piu ch'i' mi sia (non ch'a merce mi vaglia),
> di qual pietra più rigida s'intaglia,
> pensoso ne la vista oggi sarei,
> di diamante, o d'un bel marmo bianco
> per la paura forse.
>
> (LI.4–10)[43]

(And if I cannot transform myself into her more than I have
[and no begging for mercy avails me], I would wish to be of
that most rigid stone ever cut, of diamond, or perhaps,
through fear, of beautiful white marble.)

Following through the Medusan subtext, Petrarch seems to
concur with the gloss (derived from Fulgentius)[44] that the
*Ovide moralisé* provides for Medusa, which is fear:

> Gorgon l'orible signifie
> Paor, qui fet home enfredir

De sa pensee et enredir,
Et met en orible freor.

(5777–80)


(Gorgon the terrible signifies fear, which makes man become stiff and horribly cold.)


The link with Atlas penetrates well into the fabric of the poems. Laura has the same power over him as


. . . nel vecchio mauro
Medusa, quando in selce transformollo.

(CXCVII.6–7)


(Medusa, when she transformed the ancient Moor into stone.)


That fear and fixity are deeply fused together in the mountain itself is substantiated by Bernardo's observation that even the previously cited description of Atlas in the *Aeneid* (the most direct antecedent of Petrarch's in *Africa*) is itself an extension of that image, the "projection of Aeneas' fixation on Dido."[45] And Petrarch's evocation of serpents and burning sands of Libya actually describes the Libyan terrain wet with Medusa's blood. As Perseus flew over the sands, bearing the head, those drops on the earth changed into serpents (*Metamorphoses* IV.617–20)

*Orlando Furioso* contains no overtly presented Medusa figure. Yet Orlando's obsession with Angelica constitutes an outstanding example of a Medusan love fixation. It freezes the lover out of his function as a warrior and is expressed in the terms of Petrarchesque devotion. It is difficult to mark precisely those stylistic peculiarities in Orlando's love laments that derive from Petrarch directly (without the overlay of his less distinguished successors), but the presence of another subtext insinuates itself more directly. It is composed of a nexus of Virgilian-Ovidian-Petrarchan plot elements and concepts and is hospitable to their glosses. The *Ovide moralisé*, for example, goes on from the characterization of Medusa as fear to explain the three kinds into which it is divided: one weakens the heart, the second makes it sink, and the third hardens it:

> Si qu'il ne puet apercevoir
> Qui soit menconge ne qui voir.
>
> (5780–81)

(So that it cannot distinguish lies from the truth.)

*Enfredir, enredir,* and *endurcir*: these three verbs characterize the effect of the third kind of fear. They result in a loss of judgment, in other words, in the lack of just that feature needed in *Orlando Furioso* for the negotiation of the labyrinthine world. And yet when the lover in Petrarch expresses the wish that he too had been petrified, he sees the transformation as freedom from the state of eternal desire:

> e sarei fuor del grave giogo et aspro,
> per cui i'ho invidia di quel vecchio stanco
> che fa co le sue spalle ombra a Marrocco.
>
> (LI.12–14)

(And I would be free of the harsh and bitter yoke which makes me envy that tired ancient who makes shade for Morocco with his shoulders.)

The resonance of this weary Atlas in that other of the *Africa,* "sub pondere . . . fessus" (tired beneath the heavy weight) and in the very stars as described therein conveys the notion of a tired world dutifully supporting the heavens. May we not also perceive some wordplay in that *giogo* (yoke), a word also applied to a chain of mountains? At any rate, Petrarch deplores in these lines a yoke comparable to that of the giant, once again a salient example of Atlas doubled into mountain *and* man. It seems as if the plurality of references to Atlas in the *Canzoniere* could account alone for any direct Petrarchan influence upon Atlante in the *Furioso.*

As we continue to examine the readings of Atlas available

to Ariosto from Petrarch, however, the explanatory force of
*Africa* potentially exceeds anything available in the Italian po-
ems. I refer to the detailed depiction of a palace and its sur-
rounding domain, accepted by a number of scholars as the
palace of Syphax, a Libyan king[46] to whom Scipio sends
Laelius for the purpose of an alliance. The passages occur in the
third book of *Africa* after a brief textual lacuna. They chiefly
concern the wealth and ornamentation of the palace and the
sculptures disposed throughout it that figure the gods. The
creator of the palace was Atlas, and his work reproduces the
physical and moral universe of man. Not only are the heavens
themselves represented but also the life-controlling forces of
the constellations and the planets, drawn in precious tones:

> . . . Ibi ceu lumina septem
> Que vaga mundus habet, septem faber ordine gemmas
> Clauserat ingenio, nondum lapis, optimus Athlas.
>
> (III.115–17)

> (And there with craft, ere he was turned to stone, had Atlas
> set
> seven gems to ape the seven spinning stars.)

Although this is a description in pagan terms, the dazzling
montage contained in the golden palace constitutes an at-
tempt to sum up the entire gamut of moral and intellectual
virtues with which the epic hero was to be imbued. The *orbis*
formed by the precious stones represents the heavenly orders,
and at its very center stands a huge carbuncle, representing
the Sun, as two other bright lights represent Venus and the
Moon. Beyond these appear the twelve pagan constellations
(111–36), followed by fourteen pagan divinities to whom
Petrarch alludes as gods and heroes (138–39); then a series of
mythological creatures such as Pegasus, the Gorgons, and
Perseus. These descriptions occupy some 125 lines (138–242)
and are followed by a representation of the underworld. Fi-
nally, two more lines explain that what Scipio has seen so far
represents earth, heaven, and hell.

Bernardo in his book on *Africa* argues persuasively for the symbolic value of this representation. He concurs with the theory advanced by Festa that the passages represent a misplacement of lines that originally belonged in another section of the poem and constituted a representation of a Palace of Truth. Bernardo finds the journey to this realm of Truth complementary to Scipio's earlier dream. According to this symmetry Petrarch intended to have Scipio travel to the palace in order "to come in contact with human and divine wisdom (just as in the first books the dream transports him directly to heaven and makes him understand the moral order of the world)."[47] Three arguments (first presented by Festa) to the effect that this is indeed a realm of Truth refer to matters contained within the text: that the descriptions of the astronomical bodies have moral force, that they are misplaced in a purely decorative context, and that the creator of the palace is Atlas.

The fourth argument advanced by Festa concerns a reference that Petrarch made elsewhere to such a realm. In the *Secretum*, the lady Truth introduces herself to Franciscus as follows:

> Illa ego sum—inquit—quam tu in *Africa* nostra curiosa quadam elegantia descripsisti; cui, non segnius quam Amphyon ille dirceus, in extreme quidem occidentis summoque Atlantis vertice habitationem clarissimam atque pulcerrimam mirabili artificio ac poeticis, ut proprie dicam, manibus erexisti.

> (I am the one whom in your *Africa* you depicted with loving elegance; the one for whom with wonderful art and, as it were, with poetic hands, you built, no differently than Theban Amphion of old, a most splendid and beautiful abode, in the extreme west, on the loftiest peak of Mount Atlas.)[48]

Nowhere else in Petrarch's epic poem is such a description to be found. Festa concludes therefore that since it is natural to expect the creation of Atlas to be replete with wisdom, and since the truth value of its parts is affirmed in a

number of features (such as the carbuncle, which is a medi-
eval symbol of truth), this palace is where the *Secretum* lo-
cates the realm of Truth.[49] Bernardo notes that the forced
landing of Scipio described by Livy, on an island off the coast
of Carthage, harmonizes not only with the location of the
domain in Africa but also with the distinct references both in
the *Secretum* and in the description itself, and with the facts
that the palace was to be found on the highest peak of Mount
Atlas and that Atlas had made its wonders.

Such a journey to Truth would echo similar journeys by
ancient epic heroes and cohere at the same time with Chris-
tian symbolism (possibly entering into a dialectical relation to
the journey of Ulysses in Dante's *Commedia*). It fuses in turn
with classical legend as inherited by medieval readers and
with the idea of Mount Atlas as the place where *prisci poetae*
imagined a resort of the gods, with the entire conception of its
privileged height and depth, and with the conception of Atlas
the astronomer. These conceptual aspects of the realm of
Truth would not themselves contend with the geographical
belief in Atlas as the westernmost boundary of the known
world. Indeed, it would carry out the idea that he signifies the
limitations set on knowledge.

The arguments of Festa and Bernardo are so convincing as
to establish that the realm of Atlas described in *Africa* is indeed
that of Truth. Otherwise the mythological representations con-
tained in the palace are not allegorized, and Bernardo points
out that Petrarch successfully avoids the euhemeristic interpre-
tation of the gods that had enjoyed so considerable a vogue
throughout the Middle Ages.[50] It is arguable that since here
Petrarch abstracts the pagan divinities from possible demotion
to mere mythologized human beings, the Palace of Truth (if
such it is) also offers a purified philology in honor of the classi-
cal precedents. And the marriage of Mercury and Philology
that is celebrated in the relevant passage of *Africa* seems a
persuasive echo of that effort.

Petrarch does not appear to draw any moral effects di-
rectly from a consideration of the pagan myths. In that con-
nection, Bernardo remarks on the double focus provided by

pagan and Christian viewpoints, that "while in his dream
Scipio sees Truth as willed by an Almighty Creator, in the
palace he sees Truth as conceived by the pagan mind."[51] A
bifocal view of Truth is at least implied, though Petrarch does
not refer to internal contradictions. Is it not possible that the
Truth Scipio sees in the palace, which reinstates the pagan
gods in roles divested of medieval allegorizing, is of a chiefly
philological kind? Then the lady Truth of the *Secretum* would
remember it as incomplete and the Franciscus of the *Secretum*
have more reason to wonder whether he should continue the
*Africa* to its end.

Not only Truth seems doubled here. Curiously, Petrarch
seems to have effected the same kind of overlapping repre-
sentation of Atlas that Ovid produced in the *Metamor-
phoses*. On his way to Atlas's domain Perseus had already
rested in the shade of the Mountain. And in the realm of
Truth, Atlas, who made it, is already represented as a
*marmoreus senex* among the various figures, including the
Gorgons and Pegasus. Ariosto continues the doubling pro-
cess by representing Atlante the magician and Mount Atlas
with the same simultaneity.

It is tempting to conjecture a realm of illusion constructed
in *Orlando Furioso* by express opposition to the realm of
Truth in *Africa*. The idea of a fabled domain distinguished by
riches and an isolated location furnished by Plato's extended
account of Atlantis seems complicated by the fact that Plato
expresses belief in its actuality. Plato casts no suspicion on the
previous existence of Atlantis; its truth in *Timaeus* and
*Critias* is to be taken at face value. This is not the case with
Petrarch's invention, which stresses its cosmological impor-
tance and makes claims for comprehensive knowledge. If
Festa and Bernardo are correct (as I believe they are) in their
assumption that Petrarch built a realm of Truth on Mount
Atlas and at that textual locus, then the suggestive potential
of such a creation for Ariosto's *palazzo* of illusions would be
self-explanatory.

But Ariosto's reading of the mythological Atlas seems to
differ in at least one major respect from Petrarch's. Whereas

Petrarch does indeed restore the pagan giant to something resembling his grandeur in Ovid, Ariosto recurs instead—and with new vigor—to the medieval allegorizations. To say that he debunks these readings is only part of the story; it is more accurate to say that he deconstructs them only so far as is necessary for him to create meaning, for deconstruction alone is a negative having by itself nothing to do with the creation of new meaning. Atlante contains many old euhemerized meanings of Atlas that have to coexist with the Atlas of Homer, of Virgil, and of Ovid. Ariosto really seems to add—along with the sadly comical transformation of Atlas into a fairy-wizard and then an ailing old soul—little more than the fact that Atlante dies.

And what could be more "euhemeristic" than the death of Atlante? His end extends and expands the old Petrarchan awareness of the caducity of all things, their fluctuations and inevitable metamorphoses. It coheres perfectly with the idea that gods themselves are of their very nature impermanent—or with the idea that literature can arrogate to itself the ability to destroy them. In the context of literature gods can also be no more than mortal. So if Atlante in *Orlando Furioso* can be viewed as a degenerate trope, according to the downward trajectory taken from Atlas to Atlante, remember that Ruggiero and Bradamante are taking the opposite, upward course, buoyed up to their human limitations by their poet. Somewhere on their contrary journeys they meet on neutral ground.

Atlas the mountain and ocean, the marker of outermost limits, the giant, the astronomer and seer, the king, the "Moor," and the ad hoc allegory of God the Father, Atlas's orchard with its golden trees of *philozophie,* all find their place somewhere in the nexus of interpretation that constitutes truly an atlas of meanings. Ariosto decided that the female of the sorcerer's kind, Alcina, was to live forever against even her own will (X.49–55), in accordance, perhaps, with precedents that affirm that Medusa, or the Eternal Feminine, or its negative effects will perdure in the world. But Atlante is only a man, singular, himself a metonymy for his own illusionary world. It is that world that will survive him,

recreatable in other places and times, void of center or circum-
ference, at the pleasure of other demiurges. The precedents do
not foresee his demise, and by breaking from them Ariosto
shows the autonomy and the ubiquity, in the mind of the
builder, of worlds of delusion where happiness is exclusively
pursued. Far from destroying Atlas, the new poetic context
reinterprets his totality as a literary sign with painstaking
literalness as a guide. Finally, Ariosto reads into the simultane-
ity of the giant and the mountain a tribute to literary petrifica-
tion, Medusa's tallest monument.

# Chapter 3

## Perseus and Bellerophon

We turn now to an entwined pair of myths whose adaptation by Ariosto exercises a crucial influence on the dynastic aspect of his poem. Whereas the raison d'être of Atlante can be determined chiefly through his participation in the task of *representing* the magic of the storyteller and his world of illusion, that of Ruggiero and Astolfo pertains more directly to the skeleton of the work: its own enactment of the vicissitudes attending those characters who are to repeat and revise the ancient adventures.

Since the sixteenth century, commentaries on *Orlando Furioso* have recognized the derivation of one of its most famous episodes, that of Ruggiero and Angelica, from the rescue of Andromeda by Perseus in Ovid's *Metamorphoses*.[1] Early scholars also acknowledged other implied analogies and imitations with a provenance in classical mythology throughout Ariosto's poem. Giambattista Pigna, who identified its very title as an allusion to Seneca's *Hercules Furens*,[2] also pointed the way to a structural interpretation, construing

*Orlando Furioso* as a proposal to read old myths in new ways:

> Essendo che come ad Hercole gli antichi tutte le stupende cose tribuivano; così i nostri fanno intorno ad Orlando & se quelle infinite forze e fatiche accettate si sono, & via passano per vere o al vero prossime; così è stato & tutta via meglio sarà nei fatti d'Orlando. Rinaldo poi Brandimarte & altri paladini sono a guisa di Theseo, di Giasone, & d'altri Heroi.[3]

> (Just as the ancients attributed to Hercules all sorts of stupendous things, so do moderns for Orlando; and if Hercules' infinite strength and labors are accepted and pass for true or near to the truth, so it has been and will be for the deeds of Orlando. Rinaldo, Brandimarte and other knights are like Theseus, Jason and other heroes.)

These remarks, which bear mainly on the question of the verisimilitude of the poem and far less on the presence of a substructure based on classical mythology, still represent the closest effort to date toward an understanding of Ariosto's manifold uses of the legacy of antiquity. Apart from reconsiderations of the Perseus imitation in canto X,[4] very little has been added to the store of sources amassed by Pio Rajna, and the whole matter still calls for analysis.

A general understanding of the functions of interrelated myths in *Orlando Furioso*, particularly those of Perseus and Bellerophon, begins with the knowledge that these (historically paired and often scrambled) myths, like those pertaining to Atlante in the preceding chapter, become semantic components of Ariosto's discourse that confer upon the poem an internal structure that differentiates it perhaps more than any other constitutive element from other narratives too often grouped with it under the rubric of chivalric poetry. The meanings of myth are not equal to immediately given segments of speech in *Orlando Furioso* and are not to be extracted from citation. They form a structure that pervades the work as a whole.

In the comparative movement between variants of classical myths and the narratives of *Orlando Furioso* one may discern the components of the poem's radical critique of authority and concomitant lack of formal structure, compensated by a highly developed sense of plot- and character-functions. At times the voice of a capricious narrator is heard, announcing the supersedure of an old runner by a new one.[5] This disposition of events, however, is simultaneously enacted in diverse narratives to be kept in mind while one or two are still running. Amid the welter of such narratives two are to be distinguished, not least of all because one of them especially concerns Ruggiero, founder of the house of Este and an important raison d'être for the poem. The clues to a sustained parallel between Ruggiero and Perseus lie close to the surface and include patent references. Another, less direct, relationship rewards more persistent investigation: that between Bellerophon, rider of Pegasus, and Astolfo, whose voyage to the Moon restores Orlando's sanity and makes possible a Christian victory.

The embedded presence of ancient myths in new ones in fact provides an important means of emphasizing the distinctions asserted throughout the poem between "Christian" and "Saracen." It has often been noted that these distinctions tend to become obscure, that the distribution of positively and negatively valued elements is approximately equal, and that as foreshadowed by Boiardo's *Orlando Innamorato* the Christian-Saracen opposition is absorbed into other common interests that thrive among the dramatis personae or into their inner conflicts. It is as sheer opposition taken in the abstract, however, that the Christian-Saracen dichotomy is most active: an aprioristic statement of "otherness" that expands or seeps into many other kinds of opposition and is perhaps most closely relatable to the mixed lineage of epic and romance genres that subtends Ariosto's poem. The application of classical mythology as a substructure for the plot of a romance and its function as a symbolic framework for literary elaboration largely determine Ariosto's contribution to the generic aspect of the development of Italian narrative poetry.

Ariosto's son Virginio claims in a letter that his father was

not a man of many books.[6] The Greek myths that underlie the
stories of Ruggiero and Astolfo were assimilated essentially
through Latin poetry, and the great library that stood at
Ariosto's disposal was also importantly supplemented as a
source by the sheer immediacy and ubiquity of pictorial art
observed by Ariosto both in Ferrara and beyond it.[7]

Ariosto is justly known as a deallegorizer and unmasker
of pretensions to originality and uniqueness.[8] This characteris-
tic is revealed and emphasized by a pervasive pattern of repeti-
tion in *Orlando Furioso*—of characters, events, paths, motifs
(see Chapter 5). What happens twice, or more often, shows
itself subject to still further doubling or imitation; once may
be tragic, as Hegel remarked; twice must be comic. In addi-
tion, Ariosto makes positive critical use of the medieval accre-
tions of allegorized readings of ancient myths. The case
against uniqueness points in both directions, forward to the
new heroes and backward to the Greek heroes themselves.
Their myths come under the dominance of the idea that sto-
ries are there to be reread and retold and reinterpreted. There
can be no question of simply divesting them of exegetical
accretions to reveal the untrammeled originals. Fulgentius,
Boccaccio, Bersuire, *Ovide moralisé*, especially in the many
reprints issued during the sixteenth century, live in the ex-
ploits and careers of Ariosto's paladins. Perhaps the poet saw
fit to comment on the curiously structural homologies ad-
duced by medieval and Renaissance allegorizers or included
their readings within the comprehensive purview of his cri-
tique of authority in order to level the very notion of logical
priority to the ground.

The various medieval disguises through which the new
myths of Ruggiero and Astolfo must pass function as screens
and occasional mystifiers and as implementation of the con-
stant wandering (*errare*) that climaxes in the account of
Orlando's madness. They are comparable as well to an argot
spoken within the confines of an entire language, that of
classical mythology. Since the edifice of culture is built from
language, and a culture's *total* mythology may be said to
comprise its entire language edifice, I believe that the allegoriz-

ing accounts are to be considered a part of the totality that
enables Ariosto's poem to comment convincingly on a world
that is always his own, but invariably at one remove.

## Astolfo

Astolfo is presented as the cousin of Ruggiero (on whom
destiny has conferred an exemplary status). But he appears
first as transformed into a myrtle plant by the hand of the
sorceress Alcina, whereupon he recovers human form and
begins to share in his cousin's useful patronage. At that
point the fairy Melissa enables him to recover his enchanted
spear and to travel to the realm of Logistilla (VIII.16), where
he arrives undisturbed (X.64). Accompanied by Andronica
and Sofrosyne, armed further with Logistilla's gift of a book
full of counterspells and with a magic horn whose blast
drives away all who hear it, Astolfo kills the giant Cali-
gorante (XV.49) and the monster Orrilo (XV.87) and hurls
the enemy warriors Grifone and Aquilante to the ground
(XV.118). Arriving at the City of Women (XIX.57), with a
blast of the horn he disperses the Amazons (XX.87) and
eventually uses the horn again to destroy the palace of the
African magus, Atlante (XXII.23), when the book of coun-
terspells does not avail him. Thereupon he takes over the
winged steed, the Hippogryph, and on this swift transport
undertakes a leisurely world tour (XXXII.96;101;114). In
the fabled Ethiopian kingdom of Senapò he is able to save
that distressed king by dispersing the Harpies who oppress
him by stealing his food. In subsequent canti he carries the
baton of Destiny into Inferno itself; to the Earthly Paradise,
where he is received by St. John the Evangelist; and finally
to the Moon (XXXIV.4;48;68). There among the debris of
earthly hopes and efforts Astolfo recovers the vial contain-
ing the sanity of Orlando, together with his own, presum-
ably lost in the foolish Alcina days. Again by heavenly de-
cree it is Astolfo (XXXVIII.24–29;33;XXXIX.26;57) who
raises the army necessary to besiege the Saracens at Biserta,
Astolfo who raises the vial of sanity to Orlando's mouth,
and Astolfo who at last releases the Hippogryph (XLIV.23).

The magic horn ought to be easily recognizable as a reversal of the tragic horn of Roland—that which was blown at last and too late, in order to recall the Christian rear guard and win the war for the faith in the original "version": the *Chanson de Roland*. The power to drive away and disperse all hearers, in direct opposition to that of assembling and uniting them, is the function now reversed and reassigned to a relatively minor paladin. Like Roland's Oliphant, though, it works when nothing else will, and the horn takes precedence over all other enchanted paraphernalia carried by Astolfo. Indeed, there would seem to be little room here for fruitful comparison of the hero in question to a warrior of Greece. Examination of the Astolfo tradition in poetry before Ariosto, however, yields considerable support for just such a confrontation.

From the first, Astolfo, or Estout in the French *chansons,* appears a frivolous and rather unstable kind of knight, especially given to boasting and joking, and likely to get into trouble with both enemy warriors and superiors on his own side.[9] The early *Historia Karoli magni et Rotholandi* simply links him to Roland and Oliver,[10] and in the *Chanson d'Aspremont* he is mentioned as a courageous fighter.[11] But in the transformations effected by later, Franco-Italian, poems the personality of Estout assumes distinctive traits. In Niccolo da Padova's *Entree d'Espagne* Astolfo acquires unusual physical beauty and a burlesque wit.[12] Roland there chides his companion sarcastically for talking too much and fighting too little:

> Perduz avoit en grant proz en parlant.
> Por quoi diables vos ales menaçant?[13]

> (You have lost a good deal speaking; why the devil do you go about threatening people?)

Although Estout uses his proximity to Roland to ward off attack and exalt himself before other knights, he earns the contempt of the enemy:

Dist Feragù: "Se Rollant vos sentance
A metre vos in la prime bobance,
N'e da reprendre, car bien a connoissance
Qu'il puet en vos avoir feible sperance;
Par itel gent segnor trop no avance."[14]

(Feragu said: "If Roland thinks of putting you in the first
rank, he should be reproached, for he well knows he may have
precious little hope of you: through such as you no lord gains
much.")

In the fourteenth-century poem *Li fatti de Spagna,* Astolfo is
called *buffone* and gives himself up to Ferraù without a fight,
certain that Orlando will come to his rescue. Astolfo's willing-
ness to flee danger appears there as a kind of leitmotif,[15] one
perhaps interpretable to subsequent generations as Prudence.

In Pulci's *Morgante maggiore,* Astolfo appears as a kind
of skeptic with a secular and also a discursive inclination that
lead him to defend earthly morality against some of the more
sour pieties of passionately devout companions. To a group
of monks who exhort him to allow some thieves to go
unpursued, trusting in divine justice, Astolfo responds:

. . . A cotesta mercede
Non intend'io di star del mio destriere,
Ch'io so ch'io me ne andrei senz'esso a piede,
E'l Signor vostro si staria a vedere;
Questa vostra speranza e questa fede
A me non dette mai mangiar né bere.[16]

(For such mercy I have no intention of staying off my horse,
for I know that without him I'd go on foot and your lord
would just stand and watch; that hope and faith of yours
never got me any food or drink.)

Pulci's ribald portrayal of Astolfo, suggesting the Brother
Jean of Rabelais's *Gargantua,* adds to his store of characteris-
tics a detachment that interposes a screen of playfulness be-
tween this knight and his warlike profession.

Francesco Bello's *Mambriano* presents lightheaded, womanizing Astolfo; and in *Orlando Innamorato* he lacks aggressiveness entirely, restricting his exploits to boasting. It is noteworthy in view of the approaching comparison with Bellerophon that he is also famous for his unusual handsomeness:

> Signor, sappiate ch'Astolfo lo Inglese
> Non ebbe di bellezze il simigliante;
> Molto fu ricco, ma più fu cortese,
> Leggiadro e nel vestir e nel sembiante.
> La forza sua non vedo assai palese[17]

> (Lords, know ye that Astolfo the Englishman had no peer in beauty; he was very rich but even more courtly, handsome in appearance and dress. His strength I think does not show much)

Boiardo plays on the divergence between Astolfo's promising appearance and his reputation for reluctance in battle:

> Stava molto alto sopra dello arcione,
> E somigliava a cavallier soprano;
> Ma color tutti che l'han cognosciuto,
> Diceano:—Oh Dio! deh mandaci altro aiuto.[18]

> (He sat tall and looked like a supreme knight, but everyone who recognized him said, "O God, send us other help!")

When Astolfo succeeds in unhorsing Grandonio he can hardly believe it himself.[19] From no less an enemy than Gano di Maganza he recovers the epithet *buffone*.[20] Later Carlomagno calls him *paccio*.[21] In a practical joke on his sovereign, Astolfo announces himself converted to Islam.[22] Thus Boiardo develops the hint of madness already shaded into Astolfo's character. Together with good looks and ready wit, the touch of the irrational contributed to Astolfo in *Orlando Furioso*. One episode of *Orlando Innamorato* in particular seems to emphasize the connection of Astolfo with *pazzia*. Brandimarte, housed in Monodante's castle, pretends to be Orlando. Astolfo, having heard that Orlando is in the castle, demands to see him. In fear of discovery, Brandimarte attempts to depict Astolfo as a *paccio palese,* an obvious fool-madman; and indeed Astolfo appears mad once he hears what the presumed Orlando has to say about him. The amusing scene that follows points toward Ariosto's eventual decision to make Astolfo the paradoxical savior of Orlando's sanity:

> E Brandimarte allor molto contento
> Diceva al re:—Per Dio lascianlo stare,
> Perché ponerà tutti a rio tormento:
> Poco da un paccio si può guadagnare.
> Adesso in tutto è fuor di sentimento:
> Questo è la luna, che debbe scemare;
> Io so com'egli è fatto, io l'ho provato:
> Tristo colui che se gli trova a lato!

(And Brandimarte then, satisfied, said to the king: For God's sake let him alone, he will just bother everyone. You can't get much out of a madman. He's completely out of his mind now; that's what the moon is like. I know what he is, I've found it out; woe on anyone who comes near him!)

Carlomagno then commands that Astolfo be captured and tied up as a lunatic.[23]

The sum of characteristics transmitted to Astolfo by the traditional composite type includes unusual good looks, wit for its own sake, and imperturbable mediocrity as regards the knightly profession. Astolfo takes his calling lightly, profiting from his close relationship to Roland. This lightness of mind will enable Astolfo to suggest himself to Ariosto as the most likely rider of the Hippogryph when it is not in use by Atlante or Ruggiero. It also suggests a detail that Ariosto touches upon with apparent casualness but perfect clarity: Astolfo, who recovers his own sanity together with Orlando's on the Moon, will lose it again.

This account of Astolfo's direct antecedents ought already to have suggested comparison of the composite type with the knight who journeys to the Moon. Ariosto retains for his poem the important contrast between Astolfo's extra-ordinary adventures and his intrinsic qualities. The latter are supplemented to a crucial degree by a number of supernatural gifts and charms, of which the magic horn is only one. These have appeared to Ariosto scholars as simply the legacy of romance and its realms of "enchantment." I hope to show that they also function as a means whereby Ariosto juxta-poses or intertwines features of romance with his rereading of classical myth: as a means, finally, of semantic integration.

Astolfo appears linked to Bellerophon by certain common features that emerge immediately from the segments of narra-tive that comprise their myths. The two traits of unusual handsomeness and wit, the abundance of supernatural gifts received by the two heroes, the concrete nature of those gifts, and the mediocrity of character and ability are shared by the two heroes. The following narrative of Bellerophon, com-posed from various sources available to the Renaissance reader, will indicate these and other correspondences be-tween them, as well as additional resonances of the Bellero-phon myth in *Orlando Furioso*.

## Bellerophon

The *Iliad* (VI.155–210) contains the earliest known ex-tended account of Bellerophon. According to Homer he was the son of Glaukos of Ephyre, but in Hesiod's *Theogony* (319–21) he is the son of Poseidon, brother of Zeus, who was the father of Perseus. Bellerophon left his home in Cor-inth under the cloud of having murdered his brother or another man[24] and arrived as a suppliant at the court of Proetus, king of Argos. There he found himself compelled to repulse the advances of Anteia (or Stheneboeia), Proetus's wife. Homer then relates that the enraged queen denounced Bellerophon to Proetus for attempted rape. Not wishing to kill Bellerophon by direct means and incur the vengeance of the Furies for killing a suppliant, Proetus sent Bellerophon to the court of Anteia's father, Iobates, king of Lycia, with a sealed letter instructing Iobates to kill the bearer. This king, too, forswore direct means and instead sent the hero to his expected death in the fight against the Chimera, a three-natured monster breathing fire. Homer tells that Bellerophon slew the Chimera (*Iliad* VI.183), but it is Hesiod (*Theogony* 319) who says that Bellerophon attacked it from above on the winged steed, Pegasus. According to Hesiod, Pegasus was given to Bellerophon by Poseidon, his father.[25] Pausanias[26] adds to this account that Athena provided Bellerophon with a golden bridle for the taming of Pegasus. Other versions state that Poseidon gave Pegasus to Bellerophon already bridled.[27]

Far from rewarding Bellerophon for the slaying of the Chimera, Iobates next sent him against the warlike Solymians and their allies the Amazons (*Iliad* VI.185–86). These too he conquered, by soaring above them on Pegasus and dropping huge boulders on their heads.[28] Subsequently Bellerophon beat off a band of Carian pirates in the Lycian plain of Xanthos. As Iobates continued to show no gratitude, and even sent the palace guard to ambush Bellerophon on his return, Bellerophon dismounted Pegasus and prayed that as he advanced Poseidon would flood the Xanthian plain behind him. The floods rolled forward as Bellerophon approached the king's domain. No man could force him to withdraw, but one solution worked: the women of Xanthos hoisted their skirts to their waist and came rushing at Bellerophon, who finally retreated, followed by the waves.[29] Convinced at last of the falsity of Anteia's accusation and Proetus's judgment, Iobates begged forgiveness of the hero, gave him his daughter Philonoë in marriage, and made him heir to the Lycian throne.[30] He also ordered that as reward for the resourcefulness of the Xanthian women, in future all Xanthians would reckon their descent matrilineally.[31]

But at the height of his good fortune, Bellerophon on Pegasus undertook the doomed flight to Olympus, as if he were an immortal. Then Zeus sent a gadfly that stung Pegasus under the tail, making him fling Bellerophon to earth. Pegasus alone completed the flight, whereupon Zeus decided to use him as a pack beast to carry his thunderbolts. Bellerophon wandered the earth mortal, lonely, and cursed, "eating his heart out" (*Iliad* VI.201–02) until death took him.

Even on the most superficial level of factual comparison no connection has, to my knowledge, been made between the myth of Bellerophon and that of Astolfo in *Orlando Furioso*. And as I have noted, there is much in the Astolfo tradition itself to be discovered as part of the knight in *Orlando Furioso*. But the astonishing new uses Astolfo serves, his voyage through the supernatural realms, and his designated privilege of restoring Orlando to the Christian cause have no precedent in medieval or Renaissance poetry. Ariosto's implementation of the substance of classical myth, just as in the Ruggiero-Perseus parallel, makes the knowledgeable reader do the work of interpretation. In concert with and sometimes by means of the more overt suggestions from the Perseus myth, the lineaments of the related myth of Bellerophon emerge with a clarity deriving from factual matter and an import transcending it.

On both levels of fact and of symbol the link between the myths of Perseus and Bellerophon is Pegasus; for Ruggiero and Astolfo it is the Hippogryph. Since Ariosto works on both levels, limiting oneself to establishing analogies would be inadequate to the analysis of his use of myth. For historically, myth is apparently an embryonic form of all verbal imaginative creation, and therefore the conceptual space where room should be found for a theory of narrative may be appropriately located in relation to myth-analysis. In accordance with such an aim one may conceive of the Hippogryph simultaneously as an analogue of Pegasus but also as a transformation and even more of a hybrid creation, one that directs the reader's imagination to follow the flights of human desire. For it is imagination and desire filling a void that provide for the "characters" in *Orlando Furioso* the illusion of progress, or that of ascent.

Ovid is Ariosto's chief classical source in *Orlando Furioso,* and the lack of any extended account of Bellerophon is notable in the *Metamorphoses*. Whereas this work contains the longest known narrative of Perseus, the absence of the related myth creates a void that is compensated by Ovid's intervening readers. Not Ovid himself, but his allegorizers and mythographers discuss Bellerophon at a length similar to that of their glosses for Perseus, and often just in such glosses. *Ovide moralisé*, for example, follows its exegeses of Perseus immediately with those of Bellerophon. Ariosto would find not only that the myths are intertwined through ancient precedents, but also that previous interpreters of the distant past were mindful of the relationship. In the diverse and often contrasting accounts of Bellerophon he would note how the mystery and tragedy signified by one version could turn into chaos and fiasco in the next, or into joy and feasting. Ariosto would not have had to turn to the medieval allegories to uncover confusion or experience a recognition of other unreliable narrators. A case in point is the widespread and very early conflation of Perseus and Bellerophon arising from its assumption that both were riders of Pegasus.

Besides Pegasus, Bellerophon received a number of other magic gifts. Like Bellerophon, Astolfo derives nearly all of his power from such gifts, not only the Hippogryph but the horn and the dazzling shield, which recalls that of Perseus. Just as Bellerophon received a bridle for Pegasus and instructions on controlling him, Astolfo receives from Logistilla instructions on the taming of the Hippogryph. An Athena-surrogate, "Logistilla" represents a drop (*stilla*) of the goddess's wisdom.

Astolfo flies on the Hippogryph to Ethiopia, where Senapò is helpless against the monsters sent by divine wrath. The Harpies are dual-natured, as Bellerophon's Chimera was triple-natured. When Astolfo tries the power of his sword against them he accomplishes nothing until he uses the Hippogryph to fly above them and the horn to drive them off. As in the *Aeneid* (VII.255) the Harpies are the agents of divine vengeance. But whereas the Trojan attempt to stop their work meets with the punishment of wandering and starvation, Astolfo's magic goes unpunished by God or Providence. Perched on the Hippogryph he soars to the Terrestrial Paradise and ultimately to the Moon, where he receives not only the vials of sanity but also valuable guidance for the further waging of the war against the Saracens.

In addition to the evident recollections of the Bellerophon myth to be found in these exploits of Astolfo, other resonances of this myth make themselves felt in comparatively nondynamic areas of Ariosto's poem. For example, the episode of the Xanthian women and their upraised skirts is evoked by that of Marganorre and the City of Women. For the misogynous king Marganorre, the cutting of the women's skirts is a fit punishment *for* women, namely those not of his city; those who do belong to it are generally killed or imprisoned. When Marfisa, Bradamante, and Ruggiero defeat Marganorre (XXXVII.117) they award home rule to the women. This event is counterbalanced by Astolfo's encounter with the Amazons, which also constitutes an explicitly Bellerophonic anecdote.

Framed within the voyage of Astolfo to Inferno and the Moon is the story of Alceste of Thrace, which furnishes another corollary to the Bellerophonic aspect of Astolfo. The tale is told by Lydia, the only character Astolfo addresses in Hell. Having tied the Hippogryph to a tree and descended knee-deep into the odoriferous shadows, Astolfo hears her complaint. He is encumbered by the smoke (not the fires) but hears her out with some impatience. In what appears to be a reversal of Dante's Infernal system, Lydia is condemned to the punishment due an ungrateful beloved. Alceste has fallen in love with her and accomplished great feats to win her, but her ambitious father has refused the match, and Alceste first goes to serve an enemy king against him, then returns to wage war on the father's side, restoring his kingdom to him. For this and a succession of similar enterprises there is no reward but rebuke and further death-dealing errands—greater by far, Ariosto says, than those accomplished by Hercules for Euristheus (XXXIV.39). But Lydia is firm in her hatred of Alceste, who eventually languishes and dies.

This apparently non-Herculean ending could be viewed as merely an analogue to the madness of Hercules as depicted in Ovid. And the series of labors enjoined upon Alceste link his story not only to that of Bellerophon but to that of Hercules, and thence to Orlando himself. But the particularities relating to Bellerophon are especially clear. Like Bellerophon, the Thracian is a foreigner in Asia Minor. This simple synonymy is set off by the near homonymy of *Lydia* with Bellerophon's *Lycia*. Both heroes contend for the hand of a king's daughter; both are sent on missions intended to kill them. Both repeatedly emerge succesful, to the consternation of the sender. Both end unhappily in the fullness of time (if we follow the unhappy ending for Bellerophon).

The Homeric ending to the story of Bellerophon could have been underscored for Ariosto by Cicero in the *Tusculanes* (III.63) or their derivatives, where Bellerophon provides an example of extravagant grief. In Petrarch's investigation of his own melancholy, the *Secretum*,[32] Augustinus cites Cicero on the example of Bellerophon. But a happy ending, which actually seems to be the one preferred by Ariosto (for the poem does not expatiate on Astolfo's relapse into folly), could be found in a host of precedents following Apollodorus, who closes with the slaying of the Chimera and Bellerophon's marriage. The allegorizations of the positive aspect of Bellerophon are typical of late medieval sources drawing from Fulgentius, such as Boccaccio's *De genealogie deorum gentilium,* where Bellerophon emerges as the triumphant hero in whom virtue is finally rewarded, who though falsely accused and compelled to carry his own death warrant wins safety and fame, mounted on his wondrous steed.

The myth of Bellerophon invited reinterpretation in the Middle Ages through the prism of knight-errantry. *Ovide moralisé,* glossing Perseus with Bellerophon (II.5892–6209), dwells on the hero's personal traits far more than on the narrative of his exploits. The author of this text explicates the name of Bellerophon in two alternative ways: some commentators, he says, derive it from *fontaine de biauté* or *des beaux* (fountain of beauty; 5935–36), referring to the great beauty of the hero, while others derive the name from *sages conseillerres* (wise counselors; 5939), because of his outstanding wisdom. Bellerophon is even allegorized as Jesus on account of this trait: "C'est Jhesus, sages conseillierres" (It is Jesus, the wise counselor). Bellerophon the wise tames Pegasus (5897), and the "fable" section ends with horse and rider "par l'air volant" (flying through the air; 5995), followed by the allegories. The comparison to Christ links Bellerophon's gloss again with that of Perseus, who is allegorized in exactly the same way. No word of Bellerophon's attempt to scale Olympus or of his subsequent fall or wandering is given. The entire section on Bellerophon, occupying far fewer lines than the section on Perseus and inserted within its compass, appears present, *for explanatory purposes,* as a support for the Perseus allegory and narrative. In much the same way Astolfo's career often seems a branch of Ruggiero's in *Orlando Furioso.*

Although both Perseus and Bellerophon are depicted in *Ovide moralisé* as strong, wise and kind, only Bellerophon is singled out for his good looks, noted as far back as Homer. And not only is Bellerophon wise like Perseus, but this wisdom is contained in his name. The two features of handsomeness and wit are outstanding for Astolfo in representative works before Ariosto. Now in *Orlando Furioso* Astolfo, as he presents himself in myrtle-form to the surprised Ruggiero, stresses this feature of handsomeness:

> Leggiadro e bel fui sì, che di me accesi
> Più d'una donna.
>
> (VI.33.7–8)

(I was so handsome and beautiful, that more than one lady burned for me.)

As he goes on to relate his meeting with Alcina the aspect of wisdom seems doubtful at best. But the tradition of Astolfo-

Estout exhibits just this characteristic, sometimes disguised as ironic joking, or subject to mad exaggeration, at other times revealed in his clear statement of some difficult or uncomfortable truth. Zingarelli remarks of the traditional knight that he retains throughout "un fondo di buon senso che spesso i più insigni cavalieri di quei romanzi non hanno" (a basic good sense that the most heroic and distinguished knights of those romances do not possess).[33]

There seems no reason to suppose knowledge of the ancient Bellerophon on the part of so many medieval authors, but every reason to assume it for Ariosto. He could also have interpreted the medieval accounts ambiguously, so as to emphasize Astolfo's mediocrity or his unusual good looks and wit, fusing them with the Astolfo-Estout tradition. These possibilities merge with those presented by the Bellerophonic interpretations of texts such as *De genealogie,* which underwent eight editions between 1472 and 1532. There too Bellerophon appears as a handsome man and a wise counselor, but Boccaccio follows Fulgentius, not an Ovid tradition, when he etymologizes the Chimera: "Chimeron cio è fluttuatione d'amore" (fluctuations of love).[34] This version, too, ends with Bellerophon's triumph. For Ariosto the allegorization of the Chimera as "fluctuating love" may well have contributed to Astolfo's amorous dalliance with Alcina, even if we take into account that she is a Circe figure and also a Morgan-la-fée!

In *Orlando Furioso* Astolfo retains from the tradition of this knight a good humor and ability to take fortune lightly. Although much of his travel is initiated by the Hippogryph itself, the pleasure in the fortuitous flight is Astolfo's own choice. It instantly outranks the ancient bond between horse and knight, even though Astolfo's own horse whom he abandons, Rabicano, is miraculous also (XV.40–41). To the Ethiopians Astolfo seems an angel (XXXIII.114.5), but his heroics have an extraneous origin; his sword proves less effective than the horn. Sometimes his fortuitousness masquerades in the welter of magic trappings; at other times it emerges as Providential. San Giovanni explains to Astolfo that he has achieved

the Earthly Paradise "per voler divino"; and in this speech the
"wise counselor" seems to make an ironized appearance:

> Venuto meco a consigliar ti sei
> Per così lunga via, senza consiglio.
> Né a tuo saper, né a tua virtu vorrei
> Ch'esser qui giunto attribuissi, o figlio;
> Che né il tuo corno, né il cavallo alato
> Ti valea, se da Dio non t'era dato.
>
> (XXXIV.56.3–8)

> (With me to counsel, hither are conveyed,
> Who without counsel from such distance speed.
> But, son, ascribe not you the journey made
> To wit or worth; nor through your winged steed,
> Nor through your virtuous bugle had ye thriven,
> But that such helping grace from God was given.)

These words of San Giovanni play on the term *consiglio*
to contrast the man of wisdom with the *homme moyen
sensuel* who brings to the profession of knighthood no out-
standing qualities of heart, mind, or arm. Astolfo's wading in
the marshes of hell and his reception by San Giovanni, to-
gether with many a stylistic detail of the text, appear more as
direct ironic commentary on the Dantean supernatural.[35] But
Ariosto does not long dwell on this aspect; it is rather
through the filter of ancient myth that he views the subse-
quent voyage to the Moon.

Astolfo finds his own vial of sanity, but

> . . . uno error che fece poi, fu quello,
> Ch'un'altra volta gli levò il cervello.
>
> (XXXIV.86.7–8)

> (Till other error [as he says] again
> Deprived the gentle baron of his brain.)

Although it is Turpino, a figure for Ariosto of the unreliable
narrator, who alleges that Astolfo falls back into folly, the

statement leaves room for two endings. The fall into insanity would correspond in function to Bellerophon's last flight, mad flight as it was. But this conclusion is balanced by an alternative one: just as Bellerophon might have remained content with his kingdom and his princess, Astolfo might have remained sane. Perhaps no one who understands the scope and variety of classical myth could remain content with any single form of it, especially a poet pledged to variety and given to interlacing. Ariosto found a way of representing both possibilities within the text by borrowing, transforming, and displacing elements from many versions as well as other myths.

If my reading of the Bellerophonic elements in *Orlando Furioso* is cognitively and genetically correct, then Bellerophon may be said to double not only Perseus but himself: twice he flies on Pegasus and twice deals death to the Chimera (the Orca is wounded once, then killed). The flight of Astolfo to the Moon is both succesful and unsuccessful, and the literal, Providential event is allegorically unmade. It pleased Ariosto to undo the literal by the allegorical sense, thereby turning inside out the hierarchy of interpretative means that came down from the medieval glosses. Ariosto's solution to the problem of superannuated allegorical method is to interpret allegory on the level of *fabula*, the literal sense. And in the case of Ruggiero-Perseus, by this sort of interpretation he can return to the action and imagery drawn directly from the text of Ovid.

## Ruggiero

The brilliant allegory begun and developed in canti VI through X of *Orlando Furioso* tells how Ruggiero, swept away by the Hippogryph, falls captive to the beautiful enchantress Alcina; how the good fairy Melissa acting on behalf of Bradamante uses the magic ring of Invisibility to free Ruggiero from Alcina's garden of delights; and at last, how Ruggiero, having conquered a small army sent against him by Alcina, joins forces with Logistilla, who then instructs him in the bridling and management of the Hippogryph. In broad outline the allegorical parallel seems obvious enough: a young man of promise and marked destiny allows his vagrant passions to carry him away into a life devoted exclusively to the enjoyment of sensual pleasures. Meanwhile he forgets his responsibility to the better half of himself (embodied, again partially, by his intended bride). Only through the goodwill of benefactors can Reason enter to make him see the degradation of his condition. But once aware, he submits himself to the instructions of Wisdom and learns to control his desires. This is an edifying outline, quite in harmony with the allegories applied to classical myths throughout the Renaissance, such as those of Hercules and of Perseus. But it is not yet over.

Ruggiero soars from Logistilla's palace on the newly bridled Hippogryph, only to find the beautiful Angelica chained naked to a rock, where she is waiting to be devoured by the ravenous Orca. Ruggiero adroitly rescues her, then whisks her away to the nearest lonely spot. There he fails in an attempt to rape her only because he cannot free himself from his armor before she outwits him with the ring and vanishes. With a magnificent gesture Ariosto bursts the bubble of his allegory and frees himself from the constraints of the Perseus myth: Angelica will not marry Ruggiero. His attempted violation of her vitiates his previous instruction by the Athenasurrogate. Angelica, not Ruggiero, takes possession of the magic charm of invisibility, using it to escape. Indeed, the distance that separates the universal myth from the particulars of Ruggiero is so important that the myth cannot be invoked directly but has to be reconstructed through analysis.

It is this section that contains the greatest concentration of mock-Perseid elements. At its conclusion, in canto XI, Ariosto moves to the diversion of several subplots (those of Mandricardo, Isabella, and Zerbino, of military clashes, the presentation of a long encomium to the female Estensi) before Astolfo picks up the baton and the mythological succession turns principally to Bellerophon. Not until the final canti that resolve the epic aspect of the poem does Ruggiero again so dominate it. An account of the Perseid elements follows here.

## Perseus

The birth of Perseus (like that of Ruggiero, son of Galaciella), is the result of a seduction. An oracle had told Acrisius, king of Argos, that his daughter Danäe would give birth to a son who would kill him. He therefore shut her in an underground chamber, but nevertheless she bore a son. In one version of the myth, the father was Acrisius's twin Proetus, who was also host to Bellerophon.[36] The second and more widely diffused version makes Zeus the father, recounting that he appeared to Danäe as a shower of gold.[37] Disbelieving this account, Acrisius threw Danäe and the infant Perseus into an ark on the sea. They were washed ashore and encountered another pair of brothers: Dictys, a fisherman, and Polydectes, king of the island, in whose house Perseus was reared. Polydectes attempted to force marriage on Danäe but was prevented by Perseus, now quickly grown to manhood. Then Polydectes took up Perseus's boast of fearlessness and bid Perseus to get for him the head of Medusa.

Now Perseus received assistance from several sources: from Hermes he had the gift of a sickle with which to behead the Gorgon;[38] from Athena, a shield; later the Stygian nymphs gave him winged sandals; the cap of Hades, which (like Angelica's ring) made the bearer invisible; and a wallet in which to carry the severed head. Perseus flew to the Gorgons, and using Athena's shield as a dazzling mirror, was able to deflect with it the glance of Medusa, which turned any direct gazer to stone. He cut off the head and, protected from the other Gorgons by the cap of Invisibility, set off for his home, only to stop in Ethiopia for the rescue of Andromeda. He was subsequently welcomed by Andromeda's parents as the husband of their daughter. Among the beings that had been engendered from the remains of Medusa was the winged horse, Pegasus. But Perseus in Ovid and in the earliest Greek accounts used his winged sandals, not Pegasus, to fly to Ethiopia. On the way, he alighted near the palace of the Titan Atlas. As punishment for

Atlas's inhospitality, he showed him the Medusa head, thus transforming him into a mountain.[39] Perseus received the throne of Ethiopia, but according to Ovid rejected it to return to Argos. Some mythographers say that he reigned afterward at Tiryns; Ovid has it that Perseus at Argos turned the usurping ruler Proetus to stone and reigned over the whole of Argolis until Proetus's son Megapenthes avenged his father's death by murdering him.

The medieval determination to uncover edifying meaning wherever possible in the Perseus myth finds evidence in Fulgentius and also in a host of commentators on Ovid, as well as in Boccaccio, the chief link between the mythology of the Renaissance and that of the Middle Ages.[40] Ten centuries after he composed his mythographies Fulgentius was still echoed by Renaissance interpreters.[41] I cite one of these at length because he is typical of the authors who established a three- or fourfold allegorical analysis of Perseus. It is Leone Ebreo (Giuda Abarbanel) in his *Dialoghi d'Amore,* where Perseus is glossed, as usual, as the very image of moral virtue:

> Il senso *istoriale* è che quel Perseo, figliuol di Giove, per la partecipazione de le virtù morali che erano in lui, over per genealogia d'uno di quelli rè di Creta o d'Atene ovvero d'Arcadia, che furono chiamati Giove, amazzò Gorgone, tiranno in la terra; e per essere virtuoso, fù esaltato dagli uomini fino al cielo. Significa ancor Perseo, *moralmente,* l'uomo prodente, figliuol di Giove, dotato de le sue virtù, il qual, amazzando il vizio basso e terreno, significato per Gorgone, salì nel cielo de la virtù. Significa ancor, *allegoricamente,* prima che la mente umana, figliuol di Giove, amazzando e vincendo la terrestreità de la natura gorgonica, ascese a intendere le cose celesti, alte ed eterne.[42]

(The historical sense is that Perseus, the son of Jove, through the participation of the moral virtues he possessed, or through the genealogy of one of those kings of Crete or Athens or Arcadia, who were called Jove, slew the Gorgon, who tyrannized the world, and because he was virtuous was exalted by men to the heavens. Perseus signifies further, morally, the

prudent man, son of Jove, gifted with his virtues, who in
slaying base and earthly vice, which is signified by the Gor-
gon, ascended to the heaven of virtue. He signifies further
allegorically, [first] that the human mind, son of Jove, in kill-
ing and conquering the earthliness of Gorgonic nature, as-
cended to the understanding of heavenly, high and eternal
things.)

Two other allegories follow in this commentary, of an
evidently neo-Platonic derivation, termed by the author *celeste*
and *teologale,* both dealing with the liberation of human and
angelic nature from the burdens of materiality. Otherwise this
characteristic specimen of Perseus allegory stresses just those
qualities of human nature that the educators of Ruggiero in
*Orlando Furioso* are doing what they can to bring out in him: a
general moral superiority, prudence, self-control.

For Boccaccio the Perseus myth is to be taken literally as
the account of an actual happening; morally, as a symbol of
the wise man's ascent to virtue after his conquest of sin; and
allegorically, as a symbol of Christ triumphant rising toward
his father.[43] *Ovide moralisé* also glosses Perseus as a figure of
Christ (5605) and is followed in this by the later *Ovidius
moralizatus* of Pierre Bersuire (Petrus Berchorius), in which
the myth becomes an allegory of salvation. In the Ovid com-
mentary of Arnulf of Orleans the sea monster had already
become a figuration of vice: "Monstris i. viciis . . . Perseus i.
virtus . . . Monstra maris interfecit i. extirpat vicia." (The
monster is the vices . . . Perseus virtue. . . . He destroyed the
sea monster, that is, he extirpated vice.)[44]

These glosses for Perseus indicate a composite type that
may well have nourished the imagination of the poet who
recreated Ruggiero—a new, somewhat flawed Perseus. The
secondary senses attached to the glosses—virtue slaying vice
with the help of divine gifts, the triumph of man's better
nature, the savior of a people—all contribute to the heroic
destiny of a Ruggiero. The comic aspect of *Orlando Furioso*
that is built around him depends largely on the contrast be-

tween the intrinsic role-functions of Ruggiero and the typological demands to be made upon him.

It should be noted, however, that certain of the ambiguously heroic attributes of Ruggiero are already contained within the type of Perseus: for example, the wealth of external gifts. When Ariosto's hero refuses the expedient of using Atlante's shield he fares less well then usual:

> Se di scoprire avesse avuto aviso
> Lo scudo che fu già del negromante
> (Io dico quel ch'abbarbagliava il viso,
> Quel ch'all'arcione avea lasciato Atlante),
> Subito avria quel brutto stuol conquiso
> E fattosel cader cieco davante;
> E forse ben, chè disprezzò quel modo,
> Perchè virtude usar volse, e non frodo.
>
> (VI.67)

> (If he had thought the magic shield to show,
> [I speak of that the necromancer bore,
> Which dazed the sight of the astonished foe,
> Left at his saddle by the wizard Moor]
> That hideous band, in sudden overthrow,
> Blinded by this, had sunk the knight before.
> But haply he despised such mean as vile,
> And would prevail by valour, not by guile.)

Again he feels shame when he makes use of the shield against Grifone, Aquilante, and Guidon Selvaggio in a "vittoria poco gloriosa" (a victory worthy little praise; XXII.90.3–4). However, the fact remains that like Astolfo Ruggiero would not meet his obligations without the constant aid of enchanted apparatus and good connections. When he throws away the shield (XXII.91), the Perseid stage of his story is nearly complete.

The Orca, or sea monster, is not slain by Ruggiero. This task (in the allegories of Perseus, analogous to the extirpation of vice) is relinquished to Orlando, betokening a comparison of Ruggiero to Perseus in which the former falls short. In both narratives the sea monster represents a destructive force sent by the sea god for purposes of revenge. In the Perseus myth, Cassiopeia, the mother of Andromeda, had claimed her beauty superior to that of Poseidon's daughters, the Nereids. When they complained to Poseidon he retaliated with the virgin-devouring monster.[45] Ariosto's adaptation of the myth displaces two elements: this time it is the marine god Proteus who unleashes the monster; and it is for his own revenge against the king of Ebuda (who had killed his own daughter, whom Proteus had loved, together with her unborn child). A reminiscence of the Perseus myth may reside in this offshoot of the story: the banishment of Danäe and the infant Perseus.

The medieval accounts stress the slaying of Medusa and of the sea monster as well as Perseus's ability to fly. They attributed to these features the conquest of vice, the saving of the soul, and sometimes triumph over death and the devil (*Ovide moralisé* 6915;6970). Through this association the monster comes to be identified or connected with the world of the infidel, a trope that returns us to the most clearly "medieval" aspect of *Orlando Furioso:* the survival of chivalrous love and the communal battles of the Christian knights against the Saracen enemy.

"Africa" in Ariosto's poem often represents the total aggregate of its non-Christian elements, and the African terrain a nebulous realm, with the exception of Ethiopia, depicted as a partly Christian kingdom. Agricane, the instigator of the great battles of Boiardo's and Ariosto's poems, is "king of Africa": Atlante is a Moorish sorcerer, and Angelica, though a princess of "Cathay," is part of the Saracen arsenal. Of most immediate interest here is that Africa is also a meeting ground for the myths of Perseus and Bellerophon, as for those of Ruggiero and Astolfo. It is the scene of the rescue of Angelica by Perseus and the slaying of the Chimera by Bellerophon, and in some accounts, of the decapitation of Medusa.[46] In Ovid, Perseus wins Andromeda as princess of Ethiopia (*Metamorphoses* IV.753–64). In *Ovide moralisé*, Medusa is Libyan

(5884), and there Libya is also the birthplace of Bellerophon and Proetus, his father, a Libyan prince (5900–02).

Ethiopia had long been depicted in Greek literature as a paradise on the edge of the world, when the Perseus legend existed in its prototypes. It belonged to a conception formed from exaggerated and fantastic reports of India, Arabia Felix, and the fertile lands to the south of Egypt.[47] The fabled realm of Atlantis is often located as a broken portion of Africa.[48] And in a geographically interesting passage of *Orlando Furioso*, Andronica, showing Astolfo around the world, tells him that all lands but those of Africa are surrounded by Ocean, but even Neptune cannot pass beyond Ethiopia (XV.19–21). Only new explorers, future Argonauts, will transgress those limits and create new boundaries for the known world.

It is appropriate that this nexus of connections suggests in *Orlando Furioso* two complementary notions of "paganism": the classical, mainly pre-Christian one, and the medieval one comprising the Saracen world. Ethiopia, literally a border zone between Christians and Saracens, contains the sinning emperor Senapò (Prester John), who had been baptized by fire (XXXIII.102). The episode of Astolfo, Senapò, and the Harpies belongs to both pre-Christian and Saracen universes of discourse. Again, a character like Rodomonte, who possesses certain traits of Virgil's Turnus, is therefore a "pagan" twice over; and Ruggiero's twin sister Marfisa, though drawn in part from Camilla of the *Aeneid* and in part from Athena, emerges as a Christian like her brother, devoid of any Saracen local color. Ariosto does not often favor the pejorative or barbaric coloration that Boiardo (for example) uses to display the Saracen-Christian polarity.

But the kinship of different Africas serves as a corollary to the near-doubling of the myths of Perseus and Bellerophon in *Orlando Furioso*. Ariosto has literalized this fabled realm, depicted it as a geographical entity subject to dispassionate curiosity and exploration. It is the Africa of Agramante, to be sure, but also that of Atlante (or Atlas), and of the Ethiopians who witness Astolfo's miracle (as once they did that of Perseus).

Although on occasion, as in the Ethiopian episode, Astolfo's tale may assume certain features of the Perseus—not the Bellerophon—myth, in essentially structural ways Astolfo follows Bellerophon and Ruggiero Perseus, more so if the medieval interpretations are taken into account. But the two myths have much in common. To begin, in the variant that makes Poseidon the father of Bellerophon, the two heroes are kinsmen. Both benefit from the instrumental gifts of the gods, particularly Athena. Both are mortals who are either transformed into or contiguous with a transformation into stars: Perseus into his own constellàtion, Bellerophon's Pegasus into another (to say nothing of Andromeda). One hero achieves his destiny of kingship, the other (in most accounts) that of failure and wandering. And if the composite of the myths and their allegories is considered in the mass, both are interpreted as riders of Pegasus.

Ruggiero and Astolfo, by analogy, are kinsmen. Both complete their tasks with the indispensable gifts of Logistilla. Both slay monsters with the help of winged transport. Both are mortal in their qualities and defects as well as in status. Both ride the Hippogryph. One ends a king, the other a fool.

All four heroes share the property of personal mediocrity. So far as Perseus is concerned, this trait is noted by Philip Slater, who points out that Perseus is no exception to the general run of well-endowed young heroes, dependent upon Athena for the achievement of his outstanding victories. Slater refers to him as a member of what he calls the *superman genre:* "An apparently weak or helpless individual has or obtains supernatural powers with which he defeats his many enemies and amazes the crowd. The most significant and dramatic power, however, is the ability to fly."[49]

One might say much the same of Bellerophon. Although handsome and a "wise counselor" he has no virtues or capabilities commensurate with his accomplishments. Each of the two "lacks the intensity of an Achilles or the suffering of an Oedipus or the cleverness of an Odysseus or the strength of a Prometheus or the urbanity of a Theseus."[50] What each has is the ability to do as he is told and to use in an obvious way the tools he is given. Perhaps the "Golden Mean" best describes a characterization of their Renaissance counterparts.

As a result of mythographical commentary and summary, as well as of their similarities, confusion developed early between Perseus and Bellerophon.[51] It focused on the very intermediary without which they might not be "supermen." The substitutionary instrument is Pegasus, the winged horse.

### Pegasus and the Hippogryph

Ariosto's "Narrator" carefully informs readers that the Hippogryph is no fictional creation but a natural animal, sired by a griffin and mothered by a donkey, like its father in front and its mother behind (IV.18). A number of iconographic forebears, however, contribute to this composite beast. One of these is the Christian legend of St. George and the dragon.[52] The horse ridden by St. George and the dragon he slays before the eyes of the rescued princess are combined here into one being. It is possible that Ariosto viewed the Perseus-Andromeda episode through the filter of this one; but in any case he was certainly familiar with representations of griffins—part lion and part eagle—in ancient art.[53] A suggestion provided by Virgil's eighth *Eclogue* goes on to connect the hybrid mating of griffin and horse with the entire notion of hyperbolic impossibility made present by unrequited love:

> Mopso Nysa datur: quid non speremus amantes? iungentur iam grypes equis, aevoque sequenti cum canibus timidi venient ad pocula dammae.

> (To Mopsus is Nysa given: What may we lovers not expect? Griffins now will mate with mares, and in the age to come the timid deer shall come with hounds to drink.)[54]

The context of hopeless love is similar to the presentation of the same emotion in *Orlando Furioso*, not only in the case of Orlando but in that of the "Narrator" himself.

Since a griffin already combines two natures in one, it may be noted that Ariosto has further divided the nature of his Hippogryph. The double-natured Griffin appears in the allegorical procession of Dante's *Purgatorio,* where the pilgrim is about to be united with Beatrice. There two griffins, denoting the double nature of Christ, human and divine, are reflected in Beatrice's eyes as she focuses her glance on Dante. And it is at that moment that Beatrice is first presented to her lover in a new light, one that permits a renewal of his previously impossible love. But Ariosto makes no direct reference to this passage, choosing a different place in Dante's *Commedia* that recalls another precedent of the Hippogryph: the monster Gerione in *Inferno,* with its own roots in the myth of Hercules. Gerione, the image of Fraud and the means of transportation used by Dante and Virgil to enter Malebolge, carries them on his back, wheeling downward in a series of wide circles ("rote larghe"; *Inferno* XVII.98). The Hippogryph alights in the same way when he is first sighted ("larghe rote"; IV.24.8).

Although the classical Geryon may also inhere in Ariosto's conception of the hybrid beast, Dante's particular representation of Gerione as Fraud claims a special importance. Heralding the arrival of Gerione, Dante prepares the reader for something unbelievable, remarking on the incredible appearance often assumed by truth: "Sempre . . . quel ver c'ha faccia di menzogna" (Always . . . that truth which has the face of a lie; *Inferno* XVI.124). Ariosto echoes and extends this observation in the opening of canto VII:

> Chi va lontan da la sua patria, vede
> Cose da quel, che già credean, lontane,
> Che narrandole poi, non se gli crede,
> E stimato bugiardo ne rimane.
>
> (VII.1.1–4)

> (The traveller, he, whom sea or mountain sunder
> From his own country, sees things strange and new;
> That the misjudging vulgar, which lies under
> The mist of ignorance, esteems untrue.)

Since Gerione is a trope for Fraud in Dante's *Commedia* the recollection of Gerione in *Orlando Furioso* provides yet another example of Ariosto's literalization of old allegories and his leveling of the hierarchy previously acknowledged in Dante between the literal and allegorical senses of a text. The suggestion of a direct connection of the Hippogryph with Fraud, however, occupies a relatively modest place by comparison to its most important literary correspondence: with Pegasus, who sprang from the blood of Medusa when she was decapitated by Perseus. A blow from Pegasus's hoof then produced the (Hippocrene) spring of the Muses.[55]

It is clear that Ariosto drew far more on classical mythology and its allegorizations than on his immediate predecessors for his conception of the Hippogryph. The Renaissance precedents are generally insignificant. Boiardo couples "grifoni e pegasei" (gryphons and pegasi) as beasts of the chase, thereby indicating their relationship.[56] The continuation of *Orlando Innamorato* by Niccolò degli Agostini contains a reference (discussed later in this chapter) that links the *griffo* to an idea of poetry as a whole. But even the classical myth of Pegasus itself is represented, so far as direct reference is concerned, by exactly one stanza of *Orlando Furioso:* it is a comparison of Pegasus not with the Hippogryph but with Frontino, Ruggiero's horse, considered superior to "Pegaso, Cillaro e Arione":

> Avresti a quel destrier da invidiar poco
> Che volò al ciel, e fra le stelle ha loco.
>
> (XLV.92.7–8).

> Shouldst have to envy him, so highly graced,
> Who soared to heaven, and mid the stars was placed.

As usual Ariosto does not underscore the fact that *historically* his creation takes its precedent from myth. Like any other connection of an historical nature, reference (if any) is veiled. Another example of such a disguise is constituted by Ariosto's several references to Mount Atlas, a distant echo of the story of Atlante.[57]

Nor does the poet dwell on the known connection between Pegasus and one of *Orlando Furioso*'s important topics: literary fame. In fact the drift of allegorical exegesis traceable from Fulgentius on through Boccaccio and his Renaissance followers reads Pegasus as a figure for Fame, whose power is borne on wings: "From [Medusa's] blood Pegasus is said to have been born, shaped in the form of renown; whereby Pegasus is said to have wings because fame is winged."[58] Thus Fulgentius, followed by Boccaccio: "Perseo guidato dal cavallo Pegaso dimostra l'huomo guidato dal desiderio della fama" (Perseus guided by the horse Pegasus demonstrates man led by the desire for fame).[59] *Ovide moralisé* shows that the Ovid tradition agrees on this point with other medieval allegories:

> Par Pegasus est entendus
> Bon renons, qui est espandus
> D'aucun home par sa proesce,
> Par son sens ou par sa noblesce.
>
> (5808–11)

(By Pegasus we understand a good reputation, which is spread by the prowess of a man, his good sense or his nobility.)

Fulgentius's etymology for Pegasus may draw on the contiguity of the winged horse with Bellerophon: "a horse which is none other than Pegasus, for *pegaseon*, that is, an everlasting fountain. The wisdom of good counsel is an everlasting fountain. So, too, is Pegasus winged, because he looks down on the whole nature of the world with a swift perception of its designs."[60] The notion of Bellerophon as a wise counselor lives in this passage. And the panoramic view Pegasus takes of the world is in keeping with the fact that in none of the ancient and medieval accounts does the horse appear moved by preference for a particular rider; he is above it all and flies for the hero who can control him. Like Ariosto's Hippogryph he tours in leisurely fashion; unlike him, he does not choose his riders. But

when ridden by Astolfo the Hippogryph carries a "wise coun-
selor," for Astolfo on the Moon is shown the world's designs.

The trope of Pegasus as fame should be extended in the
case of Ariosto to *poetic* fame or renown as transmitted by
the poets. The link is that between great actions and the
means of transmitting them, or in other words, a contiguity
relation. Boccaccio has it that Pegasus stands for good repute
earned by deeds well judged—a fame in the keeping of the
poets. And a parallel contiguity-association between Pegasus
and the Muses' spring furthers the tropological coupling of
poetry and fame.

Ariosto, again, does not discard these medieval accretions
of interpretation but (as in the cases of Perseus and of Bellero-
phon) uses them to endow his poem with increased complex-
ity. Precursors of the *Furioso* point the way: Niccolo degli
Agostini's continuation of *Orlando Innamorato* explicitly as-
sociates Pegasus with the "griffo" and does so with Pegasus
as a secondary symbol of poetry:

> Non perch'io creda al Eliconeo fonte
> Tuffar el Griffo mio ne le sacre onde
> Et con rime fiorite, terse & pronte
> Cingermi al capo de le aurate fronde
> Ne con Apollo al bel Pegaseo monte
> Seder con le sue muse alte, & feconde
> Che essendo come io son di poco peggio
> Salir non spero a sì sublime seggio.[61]

(Not because I hope to bathe my Griphon in the spring of
Helicon, or to wreath my head with golden fronds through
my flowering rhymes, so terse and flowing, or to sit with
Apollo and his exalted and fecund Muses upon the beautiful
mountain of Pegasus; for being of little worth, I do not hope
to ascend to so sublime a perch.)

Ariosto made a similar explicit connection between poetry and
fame through Pegasus. In one of his *Satire* he remarks that his
father had compelled him to study law although he was fit for
the *pegaseo melo*—the melody of Pegasus, or poetry.[62]

The discourse pronounced by San Giovanni to Astolfo on the interwoven relations between poetry and fame (XXXV.18–30) extends Ariosto's discussion of this theme and displays its cardinal importance to the very function of his poem. San Giovanni reverses the poetic fame of epic heroes to show a result parallel to the "reversal" of Moon and earth experienced by the voyager:

> E se tu vuoi che 'l ver non ti sia ascoso,
> Tutta al contrario l'istoria converti;
> Che i Greci rotti, e che Troia vittrice,
> E che Penelopea fu meretrice.
>
> (XXXV.27.5–8)

> (Yet—would'st thou I the secret should expose?—
> By contraries throughout the tale explain:
> That from the Trojan bands the Grecian ran;
> And deem Penelope a courtezan.)

In other words, reversing the poetic statement will produce a history opposite to that now assumed to be true through the influence of canonical texts. Even Christ needs his Evangelist, that personage tells Astolfo; and we may also comprehend without being told that Ruggiero and Bradamante need their chronicler. But in the course of time the fame of a text may undergo erosion and dispersion, for reputation is as ephemeral as the words that create it. So pliant is history that it can be created and recreated, and the fame that rests upon an accretion of texts drives history now in one, now in another direction. This view embraces all writing and poetic composition. The ancient poets were themselves interpreters; so are the medieval allegorizers with their search for edifying meaning. The original "version" is not to be found; rather, fables multiply and diversify, variety for singleness.

Even the Hippogryph provides only an arbitrary vantage point for the universal panorama of jumbled significance. It is as if Ariosto had studied the Petrarchan (and Petrarchesque) type of the fluctuating human individual and enlarged it to include all of humanity in one simultaneous narration. Everywhere the instability of desire is illustrated and bodied forth in action. The single exception, the desire of Orlando for Angelica, is distinguished not only for its degree but its constancy. But even this love would ultimately find its way to the Moon with the others when he is returned from his foray into madness.

The Hippogryph is (like poetry itself) still an indispensable means of transport into the "other realms" of poetic inspiration. Beyond his resemblance to Pegasus as a physical being and as a representative of poetic fame, the Hippogryph also serves to link the Ruggiero-Astolfo pair; and this pair, in turn, with Perseus and Bellerophon. Due to the persistence of interpretation across the ages, the two Greek heroes came to share Pegasus just as Astolfo and Ruggiero share the Hippogryph. Through a tradition originating in ancient times but flourishing particularly in medieval mythography, Perseus actually supersedes Bellerophon on the winged horse.

The earlier antique rider of Pegasus was not Perseus, the savior of Andromeda, but Bellerophon, who slew the Chimera from his perch on Pegasus. In Ovid, Perseus flies only on his winged sandals.[63] As a result of mythographical summary and commentary, the two heroes came to be confused. In a twelfth-century manuscript Bellerophon is declared to be identical with Perseus: "Bellerophon qui e(s)t Perseus."[64] Boccaccio does not identify them but states in his section on Pegasus that the winged horse had carried each rider on an exploit,[65] Bellerophon against the Chimera, Perseus when he traveled to the land of the Gorgons. The *Ovidius moralizatus* of Bersuire places Perseus on Pegasus immediately after the slaughter of Medusa. Diverging from Ovid, Bersuire relates that Perseus then climbed on the horse's back and was carried far and wide through the air.[66] Bersuire otherwise follows Ovid, their major difference in *fabula* being that Perseus riding the air on his winged steed has supplanted the Ovidian figure of the hero on winged feet. The verse *Ovide moralisé* does not differ from Ovid on this point and mentions only Perseus's ability to fly on footwings.[67] But a prose *Ovide moralisé,* probably composed 1466–67, contains a lengthy description of the aerial travels of Perseus on Pegasus.[68] These mythographical sources were well known to Ariosto's time. And once securely established, the flight of Perseus on Pegasus came to captivate the imagination of sixteenth-century poets.

One reason surely was that the hero riding to the rescue of the beautiful maiden had obvious and direct appeal to those nurtured on the conventions of courtly love—romances. At the same time Bellerophon's exploit lacks chivalric and amatory overtones. It may have seemed less appropriate an occasion for the use of Pegasus. Bellerophon's tragic fall from Pegasus when he attempted to scale Olympus made him a conventional symbol for ambition and overweening arrogance, as well as for excessive hope.[69]

The tradition of mounting Perseus on Pegasus, originally(?) Bellerophon's steed, provided perspicacious readers of classical myth with a ready-made example of displacement and redistribution. The case could not only have inspired the idea of a winged steed (already suggested in part by a previous *griffo*) but provided more powerful ammunition for the fight against the idea of an authorized version for any myth, any *fabula.* It so happens that the "vehicle" dashing between the variants is the image of (poetic) fame, or Pegasus. The Hippogryph functions analogously in *Orlando Furioso,* transporting heroes from place to place in the mind of the poet, neatly avoiding any slavish, compartmentalized reading. For just as the structural homologies between ancient and medieval accounts of the myth might have suggested to Ariosto a continuation of that comprehensive doubt of the single reading, as well as an apparent similarity, the Hippogryph is different from Pegasus—the more so if other, corollary interpretations are taken into account, such as that involving the Platonic "horses" of the human soul.

And indeed Ariosto may well have found in that notion, too, support for the conception of an "almost-Perseus" (Ruggiero), one pushed by destiny and gifts to supersede him-

self and become mythic. Medieval readings in which Perseus
figures Virtue, the Medusa Vice, and Bellerophon's Chimera
a near double of that Vice, join the multiplicity and variety of
Ariosto's comment on reading.

In an age of skepticism and fragmentation, one haunted
by many little myths of empire and conquest, the rapproche-
ment of Ferrara to Hellas through the many screens of read-
ing could certainly provide humor via comparison and con-
trast. But at the same time that juxtaposition could screen the
negative aspects of the new Perseus himself, facilitating the
happy flow of encomium in Ariosto's poem and the flourish-
ing of its theme of praise. The *partial* ingathering of threads
from various derivations works toward the constitution of a
new, *partial* myth of origins for the Estensi, one that could
cloak any cynicism Ariosto might have experienced regarding
his noble patrons.[70] This poetic procedure also comports the
discovery, however, that even the antique myths (as San Gio-
vanni states) are themselves freer and more multiform than is
often realized by poets.

The ancient myths that hover over Ariosto's text also
provide him with further means of articulating the stylistic
and epistemological distance between diverse ideas of "other-
ness." It can be expressed by the opposition between pagan
and Christian or between "Saracen" and Christian, or even in
the title of the poem itself: *Orlando Furioso*, which incorpo-
rates the maddened Hercules into the canon of the Christian
warrior. "Africa," which Ariosto has literalized from the do-
main of sheer mystery and otherness, becomes a tourist attrac-
tion far from the Saracen territory where only the lions of
ignorance are to be found. It is the ground of Agramante, but
also that of Atlante, of Atlas, and of the Ethiopians, who
appear in the poem as Christians but in a secondary sense, as
the witnesses of Perseus's victory.

These turnings from one to another universe of discourse,
facilitated by the mythological adstructure, constitute a po-
etic manipulation of time and history as well as an examina-
tion of stylistic discontinuity. Ariosto's frequent reminders to
the reader that time is moving on, at the ends of canti or in

other announcements of a coming change of topic, are supple-
mented and ultimately validated by the total epic framework
of the poem, which narrates the temporal development of a
war, a victory, and the founding of a dynasty. Although ele-
ments from different literary genres and sources often con-
tend for pride of place and sometimes appear to contradict
one another in purport, the contention finds its *formal* resolu-
tion in the nuptials of Ruggiero and Bradamante, which put a
stop to the flow of time in the poem. *Orlando Furioso* is full
of seers—Atlante, Melissa, Logistilla—who foretell that end.
Its text is already prewritten, ready during the poem's unfold-
ing. It is an end foreseen by hindsight, a historical or quasi-
historical past turned into a textual future. But the reader
may still conclude that since there is no ultimate textual au-
thority there is neither uniqueness nor permanence in the
founding of the Este dynasty, formal ending or not. The im-
plicit comparison of the new to the ancient myths may yield
emphasis either on their similarities or repetitions, as in the
ancient, cyclical conception of time, or on their respective
uniqueness, as in the Christian, or linear, conception.

The melee of displaced elements so variously derived
contributed to the confusion on the part of neo-Aristotelian
readers of the poem.[71] Even awareness of the structures remi-
niscent of classical myth would have provided no panacea. If
as Aristotle claimed, "Myth [plot] is the first principle
and . . . the soul of tragedy,"[72] how does it produce comedy
for Ariosto? The reshaping of a Ferrarese myth, or plot, of
origins with the aid of classical suggestions is not humorous
in itself (for instance in Boccaccio's *Ninfale fiesolano,* which
domesticates a classicizing repertoire). The answer may lie in
Ariosto's outlining of opposites, nearly deprived of clear ar-
ticulation, and in the fact that the reader has to interpret
these in order to bring them to life. Ariosto's strategy is not
one of organic incorporation but of distantiated inclusion.
So considerable are the resemblances and the differences be-
tween versions that their myths cannot be invoked directly.
They are no longer plainly accessible in themselves but have
to be reconstructed as a *forma mentis* from earlier embodi-

ments, all held at arm's length by a fastidious poet who rarely if ever declares an actual source.

Myth coupled with chivalric romance finds a comic resolution in *Orlando Furioso*, all the more so in that "myth is the imitation of actions near or at the conceivable limits of desire,"[73] and it is here accommodated to the scrutiny of comment. The poem is a quest-romance abetted by mythology, not only for Orlando (who exhibits the full hyperbolic extent of desire) but also for Bradamante, who seeks Ruggiero, and for Ruggiero, who seeks his destiny. Translated into ritual terms, Frye's definition of quest-romance is enacted by their nuptials and the preceding search: "the victory of fertility over the waste land. Fertility means food and drink, bread and wine, body and blood, the union of male and female."[74] *Orlando Furioso* is a poem that touches on the limits of desire, simultaneously celebrating and destroying it. Therefore its semantic basis is oxymoronic, its solution purely formal in nature. Every fool in the poem is ruled by desire and every survivor disillusioned. Only those desires that are aligned with the nuptial myth can subsist in it. Even the explicitly Christian formulation of Frye would find its echo in the triumph over the infidel, but only an echo. The nuptial myth is the poem's stable anchor and its link to extratextual necessity.

That necessity may help to explain the Hippogryph as the device of poetic fame. If the winged steed represents Fame procured by poetry (represented largely by the encomiastic aspect of the poem), the entire myth of Perseus and its adaptation, and the Bellerophonic diversion from it, can function as a shield with which to screen the unbearable view, grotesque beyond words, of despotism and broken desire. Kenneth Burke suggests this function when he remarks that the shield of Perseus corresponds to style in literature and considers the story of Perseus and Medusa as a parable of art. Looking into the mirror of his shield, Perseus could view her whose sight turned other beholders into stone. For Burke, the poet's style is the mirror, "enabling him to confront the risk, but by the protection of an indirect reflection."[75] That enchanted mirror, figured by the shield that passes to Ruggiero, having belonged to the magus Atlante, combines both the properties of the Medusa and of the shield that helped Perseus to slay her. Not only does this shield dazzle the beholder, deflecting by its brilliance the image to which it nevertheless points, but like Medusa herself it petrifies every *other* sense besides the visual one. It is only when Ruggiero forgets or declines to use the shield against the monsters he fights before Alcina's realm (VI.67) that the shield's power begins to bifurcate, and the "petrifying" half is transferred to Alcina, the Medusa of the early canti (or Circe, or Omphale).

The secondary sense of that shield, the sense of "style" that guards the light touch for the most profound of topics, is what carries fame, *la vaga fama,* through the world of knights-errant, and it is forgotten only just before *Orlando goes mad* (XXII.93–94).

For a poem that challenges established meaning, *Orlando Furioso* would appear to have acquired a number of new ones in this analysis. But the lack of an authorized version does not betoken the lack of a text. The mythologically oriented reading of Ariosto (and by him) helps to define the status of *Orlando Furioso* as apart from that of all other *poemi cavallereschi;* it provides an explanation of Ariosto's handling of the encomiastic and dynastic aspect, veiling the brute force of events in Ferrara; it functions also as a way of cognizing the unknown, making it the terrain of exploration; it judges and distances diverse reading processes, exposing their common fallacies; it furnishes a way of dealing humorously with analogy and opposition on many levels. Through Ariosto's combinatory process the reader may come to understand a semantic system of universal connections, this amid the mass of data and intermediary meanings that seem to call for a diagnosis of "pure irony." But Ariosto's implementation of diverse readings of Perseus and Bellerophon furnishes a case in point of his reservation of meaning, and evidence that pure irony exists neither in this poem nor, perhaps, in all of literature. "Pure" irony and nonreading would be best expressed by a blank page and the final, nonfigurative release of Pegasus, or the Hippogryph.

# Chapter 4

## Madness and the Writing on the Wall

Just as Ariosto's reader has to keep in mind the entanglements of pairs of tales rather than the one unified myth, so Orlando on the brink of madness has to read not one but two sets of writing: first the names on the trees, then the inscriptions on the wall of the cave in which Medoro and Angelica became lovers. For Orlando at the crucial moment, downfall will take place not because of his ability to read, or because of the linguistic capacity he displays in the course of translating the inscriptions, but because his seemingly infinite resourcefulness breaks down against Fortune so as to obscure from him the binary form of accurate understanding.

The entwined names carved on the trees of their favorite grove, Orlando immediately recognizes, are in Angelica's hand. He sees them in "cento lochi," "con cento / nodi legati insieme" (a hundred places, bound together with a hundred ties), but the byways through which he first evades their full sense are "mille" (XXIII.103). Medoro's celebratory poem written on the cave is another story. First Orlando sees the entwined names, all over the inner and outer walls. They are inscribed in chalk and charcoal and carved by knifepoint, multiplying exponentially the comparatively discreet signs on the trees. It is when Orlando reads Medoro's poem that the dissolution of chivalry (that Hegel perceived as the subject of *Orlando Furioso*) suddenly crystallizes in the undoing of its most legendary representative.

It is appropriate for this reason that Orlando's fury also summarizes all the literary madness that belongs within Ariosto's conception: Tristano's brought on by a letter from Isotta in the *Tavola Ritonda* version;[1] the bouts of insanity of Lancelot and Yvain; and at the same time and no less, that of an earlier Orlando. In Pulci's *Morgante maggiore* Carlo Magno believes Gano's slanders against Orlando, who thereupon leaves the Paris court alone, "e scoppia, e impazza di sdegno e di duolo" (and bursts into madness from grief and pain; I.16). When Alda comes to embrace him Orlando, "che smarrito avea il cervello" (who had lost his mind), and "come colui che la furia consiglia" (like one counseled by madness), tries to deal her a blow on the head with his sword (I.18). Like his later namesake this Orlando is blinded to the reality of the woman who stands before him.

But Ariosto's new version faces the literary future more directly than the past. Orlando's is a madness of vain presumption, a madness of desperate passion, a madness of romantic identification with a world of values that are those of another age, art, and morality. In fact, it is a metamorphosis largely due to Orlando's self-attachment to an outdated view of the world. Ariosto makes madness a judgment on Orlando's quest for the "angelic" beloved, but more, even, on the chivalric code in both of its (conflicting) aspects of love and of war. The reader should exercise care before deciding that the characters of *Orlando Furioso* are generally mad: if others are, it is in notably varying degree and with differing rates of recovery. The chosen madman is Orlando alone, *not* a figure of a deranged cosmos but a characteristic of the times. Viewed from the Olympus of a Narrator who is out of danger, this madman awaits his answer and completion in *Don Quixote*'s unhinging by a similarly poetic and private truth.

The decline of chivalric codes in concert with crucial change in the modes of actual warfare does help to explain the quandary of the paladin displaced from his medieval context. But the isolation proper not only to the "poetic" fury but to the warrior as a character plays no small part in the background of Orlando's madness. He becomes a collection of the disorders, confusions, and formlessnesses that any "culture" would strive (without ever being fully successful) to banish to the sphere of "nature."[2] Ariosto must engage in this process so as to order all chaos behind the screen of a *bello stile*. Turning the canvas round, we see the knots and cut endings of threads, the juxtaposed clashing colors, perhaps even the residue of dropped stitches, among which is the scattered raw material of Orlando's preparation for madness. Of course the heroic ideal he embodies appears on the outside of the canvas, but Ariosto allows us to feel the texture of difficulty in the warrior-knights' common plight. Each is both the representative of collective expectations, responsible for the army's well-being, and at the same time an individual for whom the purpose of life is his own personal glory, who values his own exploits above everything else. He embodies the heroic ideal shared by everyone but can only realize it by entering into a world of blood and defilement that excludes and isolates him from his fellows. The hyperbolization of this conflict alone could serve as a fertile ground for madness.

The exemplary value attached to chivalric life provides yet another stimulus. Self-knowledge, the requirement and beginning of individual transcendence in the neo-Platonic paradigm of the Renaissance, cannot suffice a knight. Isolated as Orlando may often be, his acknowledgment by society is essential to his identity. He is without the certainty that according to Augustine (in quite a different paradigm) defined true knowledge. This feature of the knight's life also supports and particularizes, for his literary status, the notion of the Golden Mean. If the knight needs to be known ("recognized") by others of his kind, he must never be other than what they can know; this condition threatens in turn the very identity it was intended to preserve.

Somewhere among the subdivisions of the "lone" aspect of knightly life, the hyperbolized love for Angelica was allowed free rein in Orlando's mind. Significantly, the madness occasioned by this love defines the only important episode of Ariosto's poem that takes place in the mind of a character without supernatural or external aid. Orlando's love is also a more urgent cause of his isolation, tied not only to the thematized errantry of his quest but to eventual exclusion from the society of other knights. Like the medieval leper, or the heretic, the madman here accomplishes his salvation through exclusion.[3] The Renaissance madman dies to the world around him. As in the treatment of the theme of death, "what is in question is still the nothingness of existence, but it is no longer considered an external, final term, both threat and conclusion; it is experienced from within as a continuous and constant form of existence."[4] Imaged as a wanderer, a literary account reinforced by the actual practice of sending madmen out of local jurisdiction to wander, the Renaissance literary madman is a passenger par excellence.

The analogy with the leper, or with the heretic, stands in virtue of the exclusion of all three from the larger society. But whereas the leper bears witness to divine power through his affliction, the other two draw nearer by comparison in that they are perceived as especially involved with the Word, or words, alone. Heresy, too, is exclusion from the body of believers, and it concerns (in the view of believers) an inability to see the unlikeness between the word of man and that of God. Not too far from this discursive judgment of the heretic one might locate that of the Narrator and his proliferating, free imagery loosened from the bounds of allegory and explicability, capable of being amused by his own madness. Like Orlando's antics in his fury, that Narrator's image gravitates self-sufficiently toward its own madness, calling for no gloss, leading nowhere. This very liberation of the madman's image for itself derives, as will be seen more clearly in

Ariosto's choice of signs, from a proliferation of meaning, a multiplication of significance that weaves a sign-system so intertwined, so rich, so numerous, that it can be disciplined only through the self-knowledge of tragedy (here unattainable). Those signs become loaded with attributes, allusions, references—all unnamed—hence free from the control of form. Orlando does not "know himself," but he can interpret the writing on the wall since he knows Arabic. Three, four, six times Orlando rereads Medoro's poem, interpreting each time more clearly until he no longer sees the writing, just the cold stone of the cave itself.

> Era scritto in arabico, che'l Conte
> Intendea così ben come latino;
> Fra molte lingue e molte, ch'avea pronte,
> Prontissima avea quella il paladino.
>
> (XXIII.110.1–4)

> (In Arabic was writ the blessing said,
> Known to Orlando like the Latin tongue,
> Who, versed in many languages, best read
> Was in this speech; which oftentimes from wrong.)

Orlando's madness ensues upon his translation of the poem, and it is more decisive of his fate than the entwined names of Angelica and Medoro. It is this graceful icon of the embraced lovers that reveals itself as a preeminent power that comes to permeate his mind as word and as image. For this purpose Ariosto's choice of Arabic script is not only fortuitous or merely traditionally motivated.[5] Indeed, this choice draws Medoro's little poem nearer to the core of unbearable excess, the very pervasiveness of its calligraphy no accident but the feature Ariosto most neatly distinguishes as the mark of the endlessly proliferating written sign. The moment of textual revelation tells Orlando the truth by means of his translation ("interpretation"). Rather than return the reader to some idea of encompassing deception in language, its function in the story is to erase all doubt as to its authority.

Such a result is fully compatible with the debunking of textuality in other parts of *Orlando Furioso,* such as the long speech by San Giovanni Evangelista to Astolfo or the recounting of literary debris on the Moon. Here Orlando's knowledge is turned to the service of delusion and mad vitality; the writing is the "pre-text" for an examination of the multiple relationships in the poem between recognition and forgery—of ideas, of human relations, of sexual roles. That these have to be unearthed by reader-interpreters is a part of the poem's structure, for Ariosto is a "secret" poet, and his ecological recycling of old narrative materials explicates internal bonds between the author and his world. The Narrator mentions no source by name other than "Turpino," the fictionalized chronicler of the Roland song.

The entire sweep of his sources is made synchronic via sheer aesthetic strategy. Throughout the poem Ariosto has emphasized the flowing quality of both writing and the content it represents; everywhere his use of sources has recognized temporariness, mutability, and the split between word and deed implicit in decorous discourse. His interpretations of the ancient gods decontextualize them so as to elicit again and again a redefinition of the "ground." But Medoro's tribute to his enjoyment of Angelica is unambiguously true within the poem's fiction; nor does the reader have to specify what has been left out of any source or fill any hole in this text with any other sense. Orlando's reading of the poem is not a demystification of reading or of interpretation, as critics have sometimes alleged;[6] nor does his understanding of it vary from fact. If anything besides the information contained in it conspires in his insanity it is the ubiquitousness and endless replication of the message.

So secret a poet was Ariosto that his working methods, traced by Santorre Debenedetti and by Gianfranco Contini, are known to have suppressed from edition to edition "evidence" of physical or geographical import as well as dialectal forms. This process resulted in a writer who, as Contini put it, thought in prose but wrote in "un linguaggio obbliga-

toriamente poetico."[7] Ariosto's poetic education had pene-
trated his writing habits to so great an extent that he did not
make prose sketches of parts but narrated directly in verse.
Although the "oral tradition" of telling the Carolingian and
Breton stories survives in some of the conventions mocked in
*Orlando Furioso*—notably in those used to break off story
lines, such as a plea for rest or a defense of variety—we do
not find in Ariosto even the insistence upon the illusion of
public recitation that is still pervasive in Boiardo's *Innamora-*
*to*.[8] Techniques of delay and deferral, the Narrator's caprice,
and the whims of sudden change all appear in the service of a
comprehensive textuality. If there are privileged points to be
discovered beyond the poem's confines, these are usually de-
rived from other texts or copies of texts. For readers still
confined in this life ("questa assai più oscura che serena vita
mortal" [this moral life more gloomy than serene]), poetic
vision can be glossed finally only in the terms provided within
the self-enclosed universe of the work itself, and closure, or
ending, can only be formal, not semantic. This largely ac-
counts for the persistence of repetition and doubling, for the
progression of enchantment and disillusion is reversed con-
tinually as the cycles turn, so that as in the case of Astolfo's
foolish mind, a first step once transcended can still be re-
mystified.

Nor is linear temporality necessarily respected in the po-
em's construction: the time of narration and that of discourse
are discrete. Scenes change without respect to their chronol-
ogy. Orlando arrives at Rodomonte's bridge (XXIV.14), for
example, before Rodomonte builds it (XXIX.33). In fact, Ari-
osto moves toward the literary tour de force of closure in his
last five canti, only to see Rodomonte walk away with anticli-
mactic, muttering exit lines. Ariosto's wealth of literal cita-
tion embraces even Orlando's breakdown, rendered in Petrar-
chan lines: "Conven che'l duol per gli occhi si distille" (Let
my grief fall in drops from my eyes; LV); "a le lagrime triste
allargai il freno" (I loosened the reins of my sad tears; XXIII);
"e non lascia in me dramma / Che non sia foco e fiamma"

(and leaves in me not a dram but fire and flame; XXV).[9] The poem's entirety sums up the mendacity of all literary models taken in themselves.

So much citation and stylistic evocation is devoted to Dante's *Comedy* that the reader is compelled to remain mindful of the medieval poet as a principal point of contrast. Whereas Dante adopted the Augustinian analogy of temporality and syntax, wherein the center to which the whole poem tends is simultaneously the end of the pilgrim's quest and that of the narrative statement, Ariosto's poem seems to constitute and end in itself. He can send readers to other texts not for a vision (such as that of the Apocalypse of St. John to which Dante alludes in *Purgatory*) nor to show the mediate nature of his poem, but only to remind them that books, like Logistilla's when Astolfo tries to destroy Atlante's palace with spells, may not "work," and that he has entered a contest with his source that neither can win.

Ariosto's "secrecy" consists mainly, perhaps, in the avoidance of naming. He is poetically most energetic and most evocative of the gods when relieved of their classical names. His reconstructions of lacunae in older texts carry the weight of Petrarchan philology (that of the poet himself, not his successors!) onto the plane of narrative just as his characters play out the dramas of Fluctuating Man sketched in Petrarch's lyrics. Those demoted gods, now fashioned into decor, remain uncommitted to any single context. Ariosto is sure to blur his reminiscences. He may recall the rhythm of a passage and pay strictly literal attention to what he is reconstructing—the status of the words as a specific verbal configuration—but it takes only a small deviation from translation, or a quick turn into a new one, to alienate his own text from old certainties. What remains is the literary symbol, which subverts some of its implied meanings to yield to others. The slavish copying of old texts seems then a response primarily to moments of verbal *grazia* vouchsafed by others rather than to any structures of stable meaning. Reading "with an open notebook"[10] pours into the continuous mold of an open structure a sinuous and flexible form. Ariosto's avoidance of designation makes possible a recognition by the reader that an experience he is describing simultaneously etches out an absent but virtual other version of itself. When the texts *Orlando Furioso* evokes have metaphysical import, such as Dante's, Ariosto's is the letter that kills. What remains then is the old text joined to the new as a mediating symbol.

A few examples of the procedure may suffice. In the *Aeneid* the Trojan attempt to arrest the divine vengeance wrought by the Harpies (VII.255) met with the punishment of enforced wandering, suffering, and starvation. Conscious of the Virgilian lesson, even Dante's pilgrim in his early phases makes no attempt to pity and help Pier delle Vigne (*Inferno* XIII). In direct contrast, however, to these texts and carefully informed that the Harpies are emissaries of the gods' anger, Astolfo still agrees to deliver Senapò from them (XXXIII.95), an act he quickly accomplishes. Astolfo's visit to the tar pit of hell is motivated not by direction of his will but by simple touristic curiosity (XXXIV.48.6). When Dante's pilgrim undertakes an "altro" *viaggio* the poet is referring to the whole descent into Hell and the laborious ascent of Purgatory (*Inferno* I.91). For Astolfo, the "other voyage" (XXXIV.67.1), the journey proposed is made via the comfort of Elijah's fiery chariot, normally in use for trips to Paradise (XXIV.68). Before Astolfo blows his horn to drive away the Harpies he orders Senapò and his attendants to stop their ears, as Odysseus had done against the enticements of the Sirens (*Odyssey* XII.140–90). But whereas the Sirens signified, across the ages of interpretation, resistance to temptation, Astolfo's order simply warns against the loudness of the horn. It is no accident that Astolfo's voyage proves a nexus of such inner displacements, for it is the most explicitly anti-Dantesque section of the poem. The disarray of earthly detritus to be found on the Moon warns, in its truth, against striving for any single object. Obsession is blind, whereas vision accepts confusion and multiplicity by definition.

Fragmenting and dividing, parceling out, shifting and repositioning—these are the actions implied in Ariosto's treatment of his "sources." All of these motions display a concern with space rather than with time or tradition, a scrutiny of human motives applied to situations or roles. All imply an awareness of reality as prismatic, fractured, decisively disjointed. The shifting and manipulation of texts are analogous to the method of collage in visual art. It is in disposition (not invention, or even elocution, or memory) that Ariosto proves decisively original. The matter to which his poem tends, and whose critique it most effectively divulges, is that of publicity, or publication—the process whereby the poem becomes an object and a factor in the world of other poems. It is in this interest that Ariosto has his Narrator spin out texts and literary signs in so great a profusion that he surpasses his descendant, the Cervantes of *Don Quixote,* in the prolixity of that much derided literary world now gone amuck.

Like Don Quixote's, Orlando's is a madness engendered in part by and through literature. Orlando's lamentations (and Rodomonte's, and Bradamante's) are conducted with an ear to Petrarch. Astolfo's voyage is a contrary of Dante's. The various tributaries leading out of lost myths into garbled allegories are all faithfully evoked. Pastoral is no exception; *Orlando Furioso* is studded with decadent and illusory *loci amoenae* such as Atlante's castle and Alcina's garden. Most clearly pertinent to the pastoral realm, however, is the discovery of Medoro and Angelica's cave.

The scene of the lovers' meetings has all the most conventional details of pastoral romance landscape. It is very much the usual place of harmony and repose celebrated from the Golden Age forward, linked to human love by Theocritus, praised for its leisured freedoms by Horace, a place whose sacred associations stretch from Statius's grove that reached heaven through Dante's Terrestrial Paradise, particularizing itself for Italian letters in Poliziano's backgrounds for Simonetta. Everything promises pleasure but is not, for Orlando, what it appears to be or ought to be. It remains only a subject of art: Medoro's epigram and Ariosto's poem.

Like the surrounding Nature, Medoro's writing seems to fulfill the expectations of the pastoral. He is indeed a shepherd, singing, having disported himself in a refuge from convention and royal goings-on. For Medoro, despite the directness with which he reports the carnality of the lovers' meetings, this is a sacred place of healing and love:

Liete piante, verdi erbe, limpide acque,
Spelunca opaca, e di fredde ombre grata,
Dove la bella Angelica che nacque
Di Galafron, da molti invano amata,
Spesso ne le mie braccia nuda giacque;
De la commodità che qui m'è data,
Io povero Medor ricompensarvi
D'altro non posso che d'ognior lodarvi;

E di pregare ogni signore amante,
E cavalieri, e damigelle, e ognuna
Persona, o paesana, or viandante,
Che qui sua volontà meni o fortuna;
Ch'all'erbe, all'ombre, all'antro, al rio, alle piante
Dica: Benigno abbiate e sole e luna,
E de le ninfe il coro, che proveggia
Che non conduca a voi pastor mai greggia.
(XXIII.108–09)

(Gay plants, green herbage, rill of limpid vein,
And, grateful with cool shade, thou gloomy cave,
Where oft, by many wooed with fruitless pain,
Beauteous Angelica, the child of grave
King Galaphron, within my arms has lain;
For the convenient harbourage you gave,
I, poor Medoro, can but in my lays,
As recompence, for ever sing your praise.

And any loving lord devoutly pray,
Damsel and cavalier, and every one,
Whom choice or fortune hither shall convey,
Stranger or native—to this crystal run,
Shade, caverned rock, and grass, and plants, to say,
*Benignant be to you the fostering sun*
*And moon, and may the choir of nymphs provide,*
*That never swain his flock may hither guide!*)

Medoro's little poem within a poem is worth citing in full because it could serve as an epistemological model for the whole of *Orlando Furioso*. It seems to fulfill the expectations of the pastoral and of the grateful shepherd. But the analogy, as in the texts consumed by the whole Ariostean work, breaks down. Any reader who cannot perceive the play of identity and difference performs as Orlando does, taking things for what they are not and people for one another. The similitude to a simple pastorale is deceptive. Like the poet of *Orlando Furioso*, Medoro is repaying a beneficent patron (in one case Ippolito d'Este, Nature in the other) for the "comfort" (*commodità*) vouchsafed him, and in his only coin, poetry. This pastorale ends in a rejection of pastoral fiction, a prayer that no shepherd may ever soil the sparkling landscape with such things as flocks. Medoro's poem clearly echoes the exordium of Ariosto's:

> questo che vuole
> E darvi sol puo l'umil servo vostro:
> Quel ch'io vi debbo, posso di parole
> Pagare in parte, e d'opera d'inchiostro.
>
> (I.3.3–6)

> (Hippolitus, to smile upon his pain
> Who tenders what he has with humble heart.
> For though all hope to quit the score were vain,
> My pen and page may pay the debt in part;)

Both poets have made monuments to their debt and obeisance to opportunity. Each adheres sufficiently to the conventions of genre—Ariosto to epic, Medoro to pastoral—that the rupture between their works and the preexistent body of such works may command recognition. The writing on trees and cave walls seems to speak a language of distant provenance and long lineage—that of lovers in pastoral and elegiac literature. And no one more appropriately than Angelica and Medoro can remind readers that rustic songs cause no less delight than learned verses composed by humanists. It may serve as warning to comparatists, though, that here the customary elegiac note is no longer present: the carvings celebrate present joys. Medoro's epigram (on a greatly diminished scale) finds adequacy in the banal, is gladdened by the satisfaction of a perfectly conscious and commonplace desire. The external convention is thus displaced inwardly, and the classical virtue of moderation turns from moral discipline to aesthetic strategy.

*Orlando Furioso* hastens slowly over the varied familiar terrain of global textual survey, just as the Hippogryph displays to Ruggiero and Astolfo the geographical plan of the world. The displacements are effectuated in a literary shorthand that actually constitutes a type of writing all its own. It is decorative as well as monumental in the most "literal" sense, for in this poem textual forms outlive their content. The old texts thus continue to exist as mediating symbols, bearing the function of "recalling" that Plato commented upon in *Phaedrus*[11] and conferring another measure of posthumous life on the "originals." Ariosto's is a monument more lasting than precious metal, because it is more ductile. *Con miglior plettro* (with a better plectrum; my translation), he says, another may succeed him also. If Ariosto found no one whose continuation of *Orlando Furioso* could rival his own development of the *Innamorato,* this fact testifies (as he might well acknowledge) more to the mysterious, missing component of individual genius than to the lack of contenders.

As the motifs in Medoro's little poem continue to repeat themselves in Orlando's native language, as they gradually take over his consciousness to exclude all possibility of contradiction, they are fetishized by the larger poem. The moment engages the very totality of art as writing and writing as art. The Arabic writing, in its multiplicity, its continuity, its decorative fluidity placed before Orlando a wealth of shapes to be interpreted. All cohere in one meaning, one set of names, and for the successful translator the tour de force of style has yielded up its meaning. Whereas the Roland tradition had held him to be multilingual with the goal of fitting him into the supreme position in texts of any language, here his translating takes on the superannuated quality of any textual symbol no longer bound to an expressive telos and no longer supposing any putative value.

Even the entwined names of Angelica and Medoro, present to all viewers, cannot provoke madness as does the poem, the writing to which the reader supplies the names. His act of translation (divorced from the ancient context of omniscience once accorded to Roland) argues the fact that all procedures of expressive articulation and interpretative reception are in some sense translational. For translation is the perpetual, inescapable condition of signification, and the meaning of any linguistic sign is its translation into some further one.[12] If language is "a necropolis of dead metaphors,"[13] translation must be considered as exponentially metaphorical, involving *two* equivalent messages in *two* different codes, each already weighted with old metaphor. The translator's need to recreate the previous message with his own leads him to imitation in its most paradoxical degree, since the two messages are related to each other only by an imputed similarity. The rule of convention regarding translation specifies that the two messages—or texts—make practically equal representations of the same semantic purport, the difference being chiefly one of linguistic vehicles. The translation is assumed by readers (especially those who do not know both languages) to be as close an imitation as possible, therefore dependent on its original. But considered as a practical linguistic tool (as in Orlando's mad scene) for the recovery of information, the translation takes precedence over its original.

This hierarchy does not betoken any incoherence or deception in the written words themselves. Although it is quite frequent for two speakers not to mean the same thing even when they use exactly the same terms, even if there is no conceivable way of demonstrating the homology where it might exist, even though no complete and verifiable act of communication can be documented and all discourse (to say nothing of translations) is in some way fundamentally idiolectic, these commonplaces do not prevent Orlando from understanding and translating what the inscriptions say, enough to find out what he has to know. He has done it word for word, substantiating thereby the efficacy of the imitative model for learning. The words communicate far more than simply themselves. They are therefore not void of substance.

The notion of having Orlando translate the critical text reveals itself as a skillful parallel to the myriad examples of doubling and multiplication and imitation rampant throughout *Orlando Furioso* (compare Chapter 5), and not least of all to Orlando's own re-creation of a thwarted Petrarchan lover trapped in the body of a thwarted Carolingian warrior. The translation he makes is concentric to his whole metaphor, the translation of his character by Ariosto. The name of metaphor, *translatio,* contains a model of understanding and of the entire potential of statement.

From the metaphoric power inherent in translation derive the creative transpositions effectuated by Orlando in his madness, as later by Don Quixote in his own remaking of knighthood. In the context of imitation as a whole, the role of translation is enlarged in both books from yet another masking device (concealing authorship) to an epistemological pillar. *Don Quixote* turns on a translation from Arabic into Castilian, and its chronicler, Cid Hamete Benengeli, serves as Narrator. This personage resembles Ariosto's Narrator in numerous ways whereby he evokes or openly asserts the truth of an obviously fictional story: he flatters the audience by assuming its intelligence, he interweaves the story with contemporary *faits divers,* he even introduces Don Quixote to a duchess who has already read all about him in the printed Spanish version of the ancient Arabic account. The panoply of humorous pseudodocumentation in Cervantes' novel achieves hyperbolic status, as does the convention of translation, as yet only cued and marked in Ariosto. Already in the earlier poem the crucial ontological dependence on a previous text undergoes a critique that questions historical causes. Ariosto, before Cervantes, probes the roots of the determinism that underlies the recursive structure of chivalric, pastoral, and amorous codes. Accumulated pressures from the past already suffice to form perhaps the last important commentary on madness expressed by silence.

The sign of Tristan's madness was silence. Well after the Tristan cycle had become lexicalized and melted down into the chivalric code, madness was still signified by the loss of the faculty of speech. This topos could gain new resonances in the sixteenth century, with its heightened awareness of the vast number and diversity of languages occasioned by travel and exploitation. The madman would then exhibit himself as one unfit for membership in any society, not only his own, by speaking no language at all. At the same time, the Renaissance recognized a new proliferation of the linguistic sign divorced from a clear and present referent. The variety of human languages contributed to this detachment between word and thing; so did the vast enlargement of literary divulgations of texts due to the discovery of printing. Now the words could be perpetually fixed in type and released on a mass scale. Publication was facilitated by the increased standardization of European languages (in which Ariosto's own reelaborations of his poem into a Tuscanized Italian play their part). Languages themselves could be more easily studied as objects in nature. The constituent analogies could be visualized by dedicated Realists between terms and referents challenged by the argument—among many others—of linguistic multiplicity and diversity.[14]

The breakdown of research in logic during the Renaissance, in concert with a decline in syllogistic reasoning, helped open unlimited conceptual space to the profusion of signs, taken in itself and cut off from interpretation. The pun achieved much of its popularity as a concomitant of this development. No figure reveals better than homonymy the fortuitousness and randomness of which linguistic signs are capable, or the specious character (if the user wills it) of phonetic resemblance. From here it is often an easy step toward doubt in the capacity of language to render content adequately at all.

More in practice than in theory, the Italian Renaissance

(well before the French seventeenth century at which Foucault locates the great divide) challenged the notion of resemblances embedded in the correspondence between words and things. To the extent that it is part of the poet's work to restore the sense of resemblance, this function juxtaposes him to the Renaissance madman. In "the Renaissance world, writing has ceased to be 'the prose of the world'; resemblances and signs have dissolved their former alliance; similitudes have become deceptive and verge upon the visionary of madness."[15] Magic, or we might interpose, medievalistic etymology, "which permitted the decipherment of the world by revealing the secret resemblances beneath its signs, is no longer of any use except as an explanation, in terms of madness, of why analogies are always proved false." Foucault, in the discussion from which these phrases are drawn, takes Don Quixote to be the victim of such analogy; Orlando is another. Note, however, that it is not a misreading of discursive content in either case that prompts the errors of each knight: it is a *misapplication* of the book, its signs taken as form and as content together, to themselves, the interpreters, and thus the completers of the sign.

That is why Logistilla's book does not "work" for Astolfo when he tries to find the right spell to destroy Atlante's palace. Had it done so, the reader of the book and of Ariosto's poem might rightly conclude that there is no difference of configuration between the marks set down in books denoted by authority and the marks stamped upon the earth that point to its innermost secrets. The image of the world (containing the discrete microcosm of Illusion) as a concatenation of secret syllables underlying the rent fabric of human languages refuses to yield up the appropriate formulaic permutation. Astolfo has the presence of mind to turn to the horn for results. But Orlando had read into the Petrarchan, or Stilnovistic, or courtly texts for the knightly lover a crushing similarity to himself, "load[ing] all signs with a resemblance that ultimately erases them."[16]

The poet, on the other hand, although he approaches in some respects this role of madness (acknowledged by the sometimes mad Narrator), differs from him in a crucial way. True, his is the role of discovering resemblances among distinct things and in their interplay; he must transcribe a language of similitude—more comprehensively, of metaphor or *translatio*. Colligating his discussion of poetry in canto XXXV with the preceding one of madness, both having their place on the Moon, Ariosto takes cognizance of their common properties. The Narrator declares that he can no longer "star su l'ali in alto" (XXXV.31.1), exploiting perennial description of poetic creativity. And the lunar landscape is composed precisely of the concrete images corresponding to the types of folly general-ized on earth: poems for flattery, love letters for amorous hopes, eagles' claws for military authority, ruins of forts and cities for broken treaties. San Giovanni Evangelista explains it to Astolfo (with echoes of Matelda's lesson to Dante in the Terrestrial Paradise):[17]

> Tu dei saper che non si muove fronda
> La giù, che segno qui non se ne faccia.
> Ogni effetto convien che corrisponda
> In terra e in ciel, ma con diversa faccia.
>
> (XXXV.18.1–4)

> (There moves no leaf beneath, thou hast to know,
> But here above some sign thereof we trace;
> Since all, in Heaven above or Earth below,
> Must correspond, though with a different face.)

The matching of the two "faces" of expression constitutes a tropological or poetic relation. Tenor and vehicle are found on earth and on the Moon, respectively, but the Moon is the place where the images crystallize—the place of *translatio*. This is to say that only the trope for madness is on the Moon; the actuality is all on earth, and the lunar dwelling is reserved for poets and their figures. It is the meanings or causes of lunacy that are located on the Moon, which thus becomes a locus of neutrality, even sanity. But if madness is definable— as in *Orlando Furioso*—only as the absence of reason with all its concomitants, names, and subordinate definitions, then the Moon is also its virtual home. For madness would then encompass, or collect into itself, all the lost names for reason. The proper names or abstractions to which the piles of debris refer remain floating signs completed by interpretation of their palpable counterparts (*segni*) on the Moon, from which all proper names are missing. This distribution defines poetry, not madness, and clarifies Ariosto's choice of the Moon as the storage house of "sanity."[18]

Ariosto's concretization of the written sign does not differentiate it notably from the spoken sign in respect of truth value, verifiability, deceptiveness, or unreliability. It would be difficult to claim any evidence that the Narrator intends to compare the two to the disadvantage of speech. Orlando, translating the Arabic poem, ends with his own text (as any reader must). But the poet does give us cause to remember the permanence of the written sign and to distinguish between recitation and writing insofar as writing confers corporality and exponentially increased publicity on words.

An important means whereby Ariosto joins the signs of writing to the aesthetic realm in which his whole poem belongs is the interlace structure in which the threads of his plots and subplots are entwined. This complex narrative method, which has been recognized many times as that of the French prose romances (some of which are sources for Ariosto),[19] actually adheres to an aesthetic of medieval times, a mode of perception that appears in diverse creative spheres and assumes various artistic forms in literature, the plastic arts, and religious writing.[20] Eugene Vinaver, who gave the term *interlace* currency as a way of describing the French romance, takes it to refer to narrative lines woven throughout an entire cyclic work.[21] A character may engage in one adventure and in pursuing it be sidetracked by another; or he may meet other characters whose adventures are related first. The elaboration of this process may continue for several hundred pages before the narrative resumes the first adventure. The resulting complex structure may involve several characters engaged in several different episodes all taking place concurrently and interrupting one another in the narrative. The rendition of action differs from that in visual art chiefly in respect of the temporality of language; if we say that the movements of characters take place on a vast map we are not taking account of their two contrasting methods of timing: within the story (entwined) and the discourse (linear). We have seen that Ariosto is carefully attentive to the passage of time on both levels, orchestrating action so that paths in the labyrinth cross and repeat or just miss one another, and also recording the fictional time of recitation frequently though irregularly. There is every reason to assume that he was aware of interlace forms and had special reasons for constructing his poem on such a design.

The condition of the knights-errant of romance may be viewed in itself as an interlacing—an entry into and exploration of labyrinthine depths—and the adjective *errant* that helps to define their lives carries a sense of their wandering in a world that is prone to error. The meaning of wandering rejoins that of misbehavior, particularly in a context that assumes that all men wander *in media vitae* seeking the right path to God and avoiding if they can the path of sin, in the *silva* of the world's vices. This context is made ready for Ariosto by the earlier Italian versions of the romances, in which the moral and spiritual meanings attached to the quests are gravely attenuated. But the later knights still have missions to accomplish and, in contrast to the successes of their predecessors, often remain lost on erroneous paths. Ruggiero never quite heeds the counsel of his advisers, nor does he do penance after his "conversion." Few resist temptation in any steady way. Most remain essentially limited to the forest of their own mixed nature or live out their potential madnesses.

Whereas errantry connoted two levels of meaning, one moral and one physical, in *Orlando Furioso* these entwined significances persist only in scattered texts. Events cannot proceed along a continuous spatiotemporal axis, so that episodic readings are invited, and in turn apparently continuous discourse is created only by means of juxtaposition or symmetrical placement of episodes. Viewed from an aerial perspective the agglomeration of episodes can be comprehended as an account of knights and ladies wandering on forest tracks that form a complex interlace design, like that of a huge illuminated letter in the *incipit* of a literary work. And the patterns entwined in the letter not only adorn it but reflect a feeling that they are to be contemplated, not merely read. The medieval use of elaborate interlaced initials to decorate commentaries and treatises, which continued into the Renaissance, showed the presence of figures amid the twisting lines and coils. These inhabited texts frequently symbolized as artifacts the struggles of man against matter and the vices of the world.[22] In the prose romance, as Vinaver puts it, interlace displays "the art of perceiving the infinity of the great and the infinity of the small." In other words, the poem as artifact and symbol invites interpretation without forcing it, the key to the treasure being the treasure itself.

The notion of ornamental writing and the many variants it assumed during the Middle Ages brings to mind Ariosto's dialectical view of the recent past, his incorporation of medieval allegories into the ranks of the challenged mythological reading, his use of multiplication, doubling, and entwinement, the better to question their teleology or accelerate them to a pitch at which they must cease or change. Decorative calligraphy provides another way into the contemplation of the Other, whether it be an alien age or an alien culture such as the "Saracen" one that in his poem signifies sheer Otherness. Medieval Christian writing had made of itself the geometric intersection of the activities of body and mind. Zumthor writes of the composers of visual poems in the shape of their object, a kind of early *Calligramme:* "Ces hommes du livre cherchent la clef perdue d'un langage où le graphisme comme tel ferait sens: ils tentent, maladroitement, de dépasser, en le forçant, la limite arbitraire que l'on fixe d'habitude à la corporéité du poeme: versification, syntaxe, mots, images: pourquoi pas la position du copiste, le poids de l'encre, le format des caractères?" (These men of the book search for the lost key of a language in which graphism as such would make sense: they attempt clumsily to surpass by force the arbitrary limits normally fixed for the corporality of a poem: versification, syntax, words, images: why not then the posture of the copyist, the weight of the ink, the format of the letters?)[23]

This sort of extreme position taken toward writing for aesthetic pleasure characterizes Arabic writing as much as the "visual poem" (some written to God in the form of a kneeling man). In the Islamic world of Ariosto's time and the centuries immediately preceding it writing was fundamental. All the most important things had to be put down, and a suit of armor would be viewed as more impenetrable if it had writing on it.[24] Intensely wrought language held primacy in the decorative interlaces of the Quran, a holy text that is still itself a claimant for the Muslim standard of literary eloquence.

Not only in its presence but in terms of its interlaced design, Arabic script was ubiquitous and given pride of place on all kinds of objects, things of everyday use as well as entire wall surfaces, the interiors and exteriors of mosques, tombs, and of Al Kabah, Islam's most famous sanctuary. It was a frequent practice in medieval times for Western artists to reproduce in stone, wood, enamel, and paint bits of Arabic writing as an ornament on the borders of their own works without consulting the possibly un-Christian sense of these inscriptions. They were excerpted from Moslem objects, mainly textiles and ivories, on which the letters form either an inscribed text (often with invocations of Allah), or a stylized, repeated pattern of two letters of the holy name.[25] Teeming with clusters of geometric patterns, possibly with the iteration and reiteration of a prayer, letters could sprout petals to become flowers, or wings to counterfeit the tumbling flight of hawks. Scribes reformed and beautified writing so as to make it worthy of divine revelation, and indeed the Quran has the status of divine speech. At the same time non-Muslim artists incorporated these messages in written, incised, carved, beaten, or molded forms into decor, and it has been noted by scholars that even in Islamic life itself the script lost its main function of expressing thoughts or communicating facts and became "primarily decorative."[26] The

primacy of the word in Islam is reflected precisely in the virtu-
ally universal application of its forms. The cursive, sliding
letters wrapping each other about in floating motions[27] may be
simultaneously viewed in their design and in terms of the mes-
sage they convey, or in either way.

Repetition was one of the distinctive aspects of Arabic
script, and a traditional test of the scribe's ability and steadi-
ness of hand was the repetition in close succession of individ-
ual letters, words, or lines.[28] Manipulated to form geometric
or mazelike patterns the script could form arches and mirror
images, as of an epigraph faced with its reversed image. The
vital connection between script and ornament means that al-
most all Islamic art is writerly, but also ideological, and suscep-
tible of "reading." There are letters in cornices, clothing,
plates, and chairs, as well as letters writhing into words in
books. A textile that at first glance seems bordered by a design
of alternating knots repeats over and over the word *happiness;*
a marble tombstone looks like a geometricized labyrinth,
whereas it also spells out the words of the Basmallah: "There is
no God but Allah, and Mohammed is his prophet." The specta-
tor who cannot read the script derives from it an intense aes-
thetic sensation, and in those who can, the omnipresence of
Arabic script and its plenitude are complemented or subverted
by the act of reading.

Writing, "Islam's response to the icons of opposing reli-
gions,"[29] chose the word to convey its core convictions,
where other faiths made use of figural images. Architectural
inscriptions in particular, often "more admired than read,"[30]
served the symbolic function of asserting the power of Islam
by their presence. Calligraphers became adept at designing
inscriptions for buildings, a task that conferred upon them
the mark of singular distinction. Verses from the Quran or
from the sayings of Mohammed (*Hadith*) displayed a per-
fected technique that exemplified personal achievement in
skill and spirit. These could in turn be "read" as attributes of
power, just as the epigraphs showed the faithful the sources
of their faith. The sameness of these inscriptions placed a
premium on calligraphic inventiveness, implying sometimes

that interest lay "not in unique personal statement but rather in the replication of accepted formulas with splendid artistry."[31] Secular buildings as well as mosques could carry such epigraphs, again chosen from a limited repertory of standard texts.

The curvilinear patterns (especially in Kufic script, the most sacrosanct of Arabic writing) repeated orthodox words of faith on innumerable surfaces in a masterful play of repetition. This entwinement of aesthetic and symbolic concerns characterizes the writerly mode of expression in art, as well as the musical property accruing to forms of the written word as a "sacred symbol."[32] The script and its calligraphic renderings on objects, in texts, and on walls became the vital symbol of Islamic belief and the formal expression of its aspirations.

The letters could also be viewed metaphorically. To those filled with admiration of the script the letters could come to resemble the names they composed. The similarity between the form of Mohammed's name and a worshipper bowing in prayer was often noted; and the letter *mim* looked like a mouth, the letter *ayn* an eye, the *alif* a youth, and so on.[33] An immense lore is based upon the properties of letters. According to occult treatments of the alphabet the twenty-eight letters were divided into four equal categories, corresponding to the alchemical elements of fire, air, earth, and water. Some combinations were therefore judged to be effective talismans against particular afflictions: for instance, "fire" letters could increase the intensity of a war or conflict, and letters of the "water" group could reduce or eliminate fever. Cabalistic researchers analyzed words for their numerical value, and magical procedures used the divine quantities derived from them. That letters occupied so prominent a place in mystical aspects of Islam was further reason that they should be used as metaphors in poetry imbued with mystical feeling. Scholars sought in letters hidden knowledge and special powers, and the idea of the ninety-nine most beautiful names of God fused the visual as well as the acoustical signifiers.[34] These, together with the signified names and the script as a whole, bore an implicit affirmation of authority and a dominant manifestation of power. For the written form of the Quran is the visual equivalent of the eternal Quran and is humanity's "perceptual glimpse of the divine," chosen from manifold possibilities for the words of Allah, transmitted to humanity through the prophet.[35]

The pictorial interlace of Arabic writing is what Orlando contemplates on the walls of an edifice not built explicitly for the numinous purpose of amorous consummation with Angelica (but certainly convenient enough for this purpose). The writing takes shape in his mind through a process of gradual accretion and imaginative exercise culminating in translation and rearrangement. The first thing Orlando sees is the brimming fullness of an artistic vision, embedded in the traditional but treacherous scene of quiet waters, wildflowers, sheep-filled meadows, and silence broken only by birdsong. Every step he then takes validates itself by orientation among public symbols. The pause at the trees and the entry to the cave, both familiar, belie the approaching disorder. Orlando then retraces the endlessly flowing lines—pictorial representations of the whole knightly journey, circuitous but easy to follow.

Elaborate and decorative, at the same time revelatory and numinous, the writing on the cave wall, the intertwined names drive home the truth of the words that Orlando repeats to himself without cease. As the writing floods Orlando's imagination it abolishes all possibility of differentiation between himself and that other who was "sì saggio" (so wise), or believed so. He incorporates them as well as the Islamic and feminine Others. The ensuing wildman charades comprise a dialogue for one driven mad (as all madmen are in Ariosto) by despair.

More than anything it is the sheer excess of the writing that represents the cause of the chaos. This irreducible nucleus of the forbidden names and the epigraph of Medoro constitutes a center and a model for the whole labyrinthine plenitude of folly in Ariosto's work. It is the repository of a vast mimetic memory and the inscription for all the fictions that Ariosto demystifies. Beyond the decipherment of the writing lies a barren, undifferentiated, and empty geography that is finally unrepresentable, a chaos. *Orlando Furioso* can largely be defined in terms of hyperbolic amplification, whose ultimate condensation is found in Medoro's poem.

It is perhaps in response to the sheer excess of personnel, adventure, and vicissitude in his poem that Ariosto's style resounds with the figure of understatement (*litotes*). Understatement or demure periphrase exhibits a false naïveté. The Hippogryph appears to the Narrator a "grande e strano augello" (great and strange bird; VI.18.1). Astolfo returns to human form saved from his metamorphosis into a plant: " 'l parentado in questo e li cortesi / Prieghi del bon Ruggiero gli giovar molto" (For much his kindred and the courteous prayer / Of good Rogero with Melissa weighed) comments the Narrator (VIII.16.5–6). Orlando arrives at a wide tumultuous river, and a long euphemistic periphrase poorly conceals the urgency of his plight:

> Con gli occhi cerca or questo lato or quello,
> Lungo le ripe il paladin, se vede
> (Quando né pesce egli non è né augello
> Come abbia a por ne l'altra ripa e'l piede. . . .)
>
> (IX.9.1–4)

> (The paladin this bank and the other eyed,
> Along the river's channel, to explore,
> Since neither fish nor fowl, if from his side
> He could gain footing on the adverse shore.)

A shipwrecked Ruggiero flailing his way through the waves encounters its "importuno flutto" (importunate flux; XLI.22.4). Orlando's attack in his madness on a little fountain makes it "da contata ira poco sicura" (little safe from such wrath; XXIII.130.8).

The reader's compensatory interpretation of this condensed and litotic style tends to obscure its presence. Another obviously competing factor is the abundance of amplification in the narrative. As Ariosto condenses feeling into the significant gesture or implies with a courtly epithet the presence of unbearable degrees of suffering, the amplitude of the story compensates for reduction in obvious, discursive analysis and in the naming of names. The linguist Alexander Žolkovskij points out how narrative amplification derives directly from the events themselves:

> The writer succeeds in colligating the elements of an event in such a way that certain of its significant aspects are amplified. In this way the course of events itself comes to constitute an amplifier of their understanding by the reader, and consequently the so-called objective representation of reality expresses at the same time the attitude of the author toward that same reality.[36]

Understatement and amplification thus prove themselves compatible, and the latter subordinate to the former. They apply to the poet's fictions in harmony, whereas only amplification applies to the roles within the poem. The play of imagination is at issue for both, but the poet creates his "amplifications," in the words of Žolkovskij, with "a magic that consists precisely in obtaining a miraculous effect with an (apparently) minimal, *purely symbolic* effort."[37] For the relay runners in the poem the illusion of a possible end, otherwise termed the fulfillment of their desires, is a reality that is led by the poet into new and unexpected turns of events. Each feeds on illusions and fosters them in his ambition to ascend above and beyond others. *Orlando Furioso* represents the culmination of Ariosto's experience of such blindness, such singleness of desire. And where the gods are domesticated, and humanity the measure of its own actions, man's aspiration to be more than a man—in love or in arms—can be achieved only by dehumanization or madness.

As much as the traditional blueprint of insanity still current in his time, Ariosto's depiction of Orlando in his fury may be attributed to this assessment of madness as the nonhuman. It is an endpoint for the dominance of human personality: the very element that precludes all possibility of amplification, hence not condensed into a few words or stanzas, not implied by the lack of commentary, nor echoed in substance by other (even mad) characters. It is perhaps the only nonredundant event in the poem.

Amplification, decorative interlace, and ceaseless entwinement, the salient traits of the Arabic writing on the cave, are ushered into Ariosto's poem under the sign of Fortune, herself a sign of blindness. It is Fortune that first favors Angelica's escape (I.10.6) and then Fortune again that disperses her pursuers, Ferraù and Rinaldo, at the first bifurcation of the poem (I.23.5). It is more than apposite that amplification represents everywhere the dialectic of response and retaliation vis-à-vis blind Fortune, in terms of the ceaseless quest for self-aggrandizement and self-satisfaction. Thus the narrative plenitude and complexity both ensure the continuity of the narrative—which subsists on its own bid for survival and renegotiates a new contract with the reader at every turn— while they undermine the fictitious presuppositions of the action. The world is reduced to the common denominator of man's excess.

Ariosto's poem hurries slowly, pushing ahead of itself the resolutions to various conflicts and delaying the final confrontations (as of Ruggiero and Rodomonte) with still more displacements, more embellishments. At nearly every point in the braided chains of events a confrontation is hidden, immanent. Ariosto's world does not point vertically beyond itself, only horizontally at ours. It does not contain the possibility of self-knowledge. The poet opposes to the excesses of the world those of his own imagination, simultaneously condensed in potential import and amplified by contact with matter in its infinite variety. Medoro's little poem, inviting every passerby to read its message, finds analogous "contact with matter" in the writing that can envelop everything in its fold: the only signs capable of denoting all others. It is not his translation of words that made Orlando go mad, and there is nothing *in* the writing that must produce this effect. It is simply the event of reading that makes it possible for Orlando to stop pursuing Angelica and the poet to arrive at the endpoint of amplification. In that excess of beautiful curves lies only a lack of both reason *and* folly, a superabundance that—for poor Orlando—abolishes all possibility of differentiation between reason and unreason. This is the all-pervasive flooding of the unprepared imagination that Erasmus calls (in the *Moriae Encomium*) "infinity doubled."

# Chapter 5

## Ariosto's Multiple Vision

My previous chapter referred to the "binary form of accurate understanding" as it concerned the maddened Orlando, who could not be saved by the anaesthetic of self-irony from obsession and its concomitant rigidity. We will test this assumption now, exploring and delineating the perfectly contrary movement of Ariosto's writing as it affects plot construction. I hope to reveal in this chapter the ubiquity of doubling and muliplication as the very replication of the poet's vision.

The conflict of love and honor that governs the adventures of Ruggiero and (in lesser measure) of Bradamante forms the spine of Ariosto's epic poem. Even the madness of Orlando, its second subject, can be inserted into this overarching scheme. Orlando hyperbolizes a basic polarity: he has deserted the Christian army to devote himself to Angelica, his supposed beloved. The same clash of duty and pleasure is also answerable for those events that can be experienced as constants: the allurements of a lady persuade a knight away from the army; present charms outflank memory and principle; a new horse, even, causes the rider to abandon his trusted steed. Just as two kinds of knighthood confront one another through the juxtaposed Carolingian and Breton strains—Christian soldier against courtly wanderer, for one—and often within one and the same "character," so do two codes, two goals, two endings: those of epic and of romance.

In another sense *Orlando Furioso* constitutes the second part of a diptych. To Boiardo's "prewar" poem it offers a wartime conclusion. It is of major significance that Ariosto takes up his pen after the devastating social disruption occasioned by concerted foreign invasions of Italy. He undertakes to complete Boiardo's unfinished work under the mature conditions of a knowledge Boiardo could only experience as prediction. Ariosto's work, like that of his admired Castiglione, constitutes a memorial to a world holding its own (in literary terms) against adverse fortune and death. Indeed the very force of repetition itself serves to hold at bay the forces of destruction, all the more so insofar as it functions as a dynamic narrative element. The formally unrestricted text, capable of being prolonged infinitely, implements a sense of repetition that is independent of the static reenunciations of epic in general. Whereas epic accustoms the reader to a given set of epithets and combinatory possibilities, presenting them as permanent, Ariosto's repetitions do not subserve any static tautology, nor do his psychological parallelisms boil down to ritualized messages. The systems of opposition on which the large-scale conflicts repose attest to a *permanence of change,* the recurrence of an event enabling its reinterpretation according to its immediate context.

Ruggiero and Astolfo both ride the Hippogryph, but Astolfo's ride represents no shirking of his duty or delinquency from his primary journey, whereas Ruggiero in his leisurely tour of the world notably forgets Bradamante and his army. Rodomonte shows the inconstancy of madness as he veers from extreme misogyny to the consuming love for Doralice, thus drawing closer to the insanity of Orlando. As Rodomonte goes on to pursue Isabella to the point of tragedy, the two reveal themselves to be at variance in important respects. Orlando's madness proceeds directly from his consistency, Rodomonte's from his inconsistency. Similar actions are each accompanied by singular causes or by their own time and space. It is as if Ariosto had substituted for spiritual progress, for the upward journey of any given character, a scheme in which the event itself usurps any one character's role, as an element mapped on a flat terrain that could be compared with a painting lacking in perspective.

Ariosto has his princely Ruggiero and Bradamante learn much of their destiny from artistic displays by means of tapestry or sculpture as well as conjured visions.[1] But there is only one stable mirror in *Orlando Furioso,* the mirror image of the world as perceived on the Moon.[2] Astolfo sees revealed there the detritus of vain earthly hopes and efforts, their emblems in the written signs of broken treaties, ignored love letters, and rejected poems. The Moon is the double of the world, and the repetitious *altri* that describes its geography easily misleads the reader into believing that he is experiencing something other than yet another instance of the duplicated resemblances forming the realms of Nature.[3] This "mirror" approaches the type of the medieval *speculum,* parodying the didactic work composed for the benefit of the knight or prince or courtier during the late Middle Ages and Renaissance; the mirror that enabled the reader to confront his own image, compare it to his previous experience of self, and see in the comparison achievements yet to be attained, perfection to be striven for.[4] Astolfo views among the vials of "sanity" the inversion of earthly images and their deceptions. But the effects of the mirror are ephemeral; Astolfo's failure of mind will also be repeated beyond the limits of this text.

For the rest Ariosto's repetitions of plot elements or functions do not seem to reflect each other. They fall at irregular intervals on what seems to be a flat picture-plane. But like forgotten perspective itself, the perception of single-plane chaos is only another perception, enduring only if the reader continues unwilling to supply perspective for himself. The repetitions of the poem's construction tend to occur at the (provisional) crossroads in a bifurcating path. In a painting such a path could be perceived as a foreshortened V. But as the eye enters, positing another picture plane, interpretation ensues. For example, the first encounters of Angelica with Rinaldo and Ferraù find them fighting over her, "clicking into place like the last term of a syllogism,"[5] and as they disappear after her, the mathematics of the poem takes the following course:

> Da quattro sproni il destrier punto arriva
> ove una strada in due si dipartiva.
>
> (I.22.7–8)

> (Them, while four spurs infest his foaming sides,
> Their courser brings to where the way divides.)

What is important is that opposition, dualism, and repetition are conveyed narratively in dynamic terms, the immense romance geography of the poem opening out into the seemingly fortuitous duplications of the labyrinth. The contradictions that grip characters in the vicissitudes of love and war are exclusively plot-functions.

The narrative ballet comprising the exchange of male and female roles for certain characters provides an overarching case in point. Whereas the search for completeness in the blending of male and female natures to be found in the Platonic and Renaissance conception of sexual love receives its most frequent expression in the static, discursive terms of treatises and (later) in the chiastic, fundamentally immobile conflicts of such epics as *Gerusalemme Liberata* (Jerusalem Delivered), Ariosto allows it to be understood through the ambiguity or interchange of identities and other narrative adaptations of the strivings and quests of romance. The "maleness" that distinguishes Bradamante from all but one of the poem's other heroines completes the search and makes her, paradoxically, a fit companion for Ruggiero, the best response to a fundamental, "existential lack,"[6] and a new exemplar of the desired union between the beauty of Venus and the bravery of Mars. Beyond this combinatory achievement, however, a host of nuances remain to be discovered. When Ruggiero, wounded by Mandricardo, is nursed by Marfisa, Bradamante's jealousy shows her, however fleetingly and iridescently, a female Orlando. Her anxiety threatens to drive her to suicide (XXXII.44). Her actions include those of a hyperbolized Petrarchistic lover, a docile daughter (XLI–XLII), and a heroic defender of (alternately) men's and women's rights.

Again purely in narrative terms, Bradamante is "doubled" by Marfisa, the only other heroine possessing notable masculine traits. She, too, falls in love with Ruggiero, and his fascination with her merely redoubles his original and fated attachment to Bradamante. Whereas Bradamante is a sufficient counterpart of Ruggiero to be considered nearly his sibling, Marfisa is indeed revealed to be his sister (XXXVI.59). And the confrontation of Ruggiero and Bradamante as warriors is both a continuation of the Bradamante-Marfisa opposition and a hyperbolizing of the fundamental love-war dichotomy played out to the hilt. Ariosto's Narrator announces and specifies it in the first line ("le donne, i cavallier, l'arme, gli amori"). To weave his varied tapestry Ariosto fully exploits the linearity of narrative, taking the reader through sequences of actions so disposed that successive canti recall, echo, parallel, or contrast with each other, shaping the reader's response by the relation of elements to each other over a vast expanse. Like plot elements, generic features often appear in complementary distribution. The conventions of a degenerated courtly code still serve as points of departure; these in their turn clash with the rigorous ethic of epic poetry. The embrace of the poem captures every manner, plebeian or noble, to which the Matter of France had been subjected in the course of centuries. It confronts them finally with the ungovernable recollections of a Carolingian "Turpino."

The winding narrative subdivides the theme of love into a potential infinity of refractions. We begin with the pandemonic love of Orlando for Angelica, set against the comedy of the successful (though sorely tried) love of Ruggiero and Bradamante. The counterplay of *humanitas* and *ferinitas* (brutishness) occurs on two planes that incline, however, toward one another. Alternations of overwhelming rages with the measured progress of the future royal couple counterbalance the vicissitudes of the war taken as a whole. It is of course the enduring hostility between the two lovers' countries and faiths that impedes their marriage. Only as a direct result of his experience in battle, and in conjunction with the ending of the war, can Ruggiero win Bradamante's hand. Since the war provides the focusing point for the widespread conflicts among various pagans and Christians (who are repeatedly returned to the field of mass warfare), its completion is delayed far into the poem (XLII). The final pagan resistance, that of Rodomonte, is defeated only in the very last lines.

But this dualism is constantly undermined by competing dualisms or neutralized by a bifurcation of circumstances. When the poem shifts to the climactic battles of Biserta and Lipadusa, religious feeling on both sides is presented with no indication that the "Saracens" are deluded or that their gods do not heed them. Absent is the kind of traditional "Muslim" chaos that signifies dissolution in either *chansons de geste* or Tasso's Christian epic. One is tempted to compare Macone's indifference ("nulla sente" [XL.13.4]) with that of Athena rejecting the offerings of the Trojan women in the *Aeneid* (I.482).[7] Religion simply becomes a sign for doubling and opposition. For example, just before the battle of Lipadusa, Brandimarte, himself once a pagan, offers Agramante the possibility of conversion to Christianity, which the latter rejects. Meanwhile the shipwrecked Ruggiero undergoes a "true" conversion (XL.47) and is baptized as soon as he reaches land. Again, there exists a similar symmetry between Orlando's affection for the same Brandimarte and Bradamante's for Ruggiero, another converted pagan.

In accordance with the lack of religious constraints, supernatural realms lose their mysterious or dark aspects. As the Moon is the double of the world, the vertical geography of "Inferno" and "Terrestrial Paradise" (XXXIV–XXXV) is dependent on the recognition of a contrast of a literary and epistemological nature between Ariosto and Dante. When the world of romance is at issue, its multiple tributaries of river and wood seem governed by no law of combination or succession. The exception is that of the geographical tours provided for Astolfo and Ruggiero on the Hippogryph. They ride no longer in the labyrinth of romance but above a geographically charted terrain that the poet has perceived to be a small world. The horizons of transcendental experience merge with the quotidian and take on a recognizable shape. The reader is given to understand that the experience of triumph, or pleasure, or foolishness, or waste can no longer be invested permanently or definitively in any human agent or located at any focal point. Ariosto's momentary vision of a realm of supernatural activity superimposed on that real world does not outlive the contradiction—historical, ideological, or narrative—that it was invented to resolve.

This seemingly fortuitous result derives from a patterning made incongruous or invisible by the mediated narrator's skills. One aspect of this patterning resides in conceptual doubling: that of poetry and history, of love and war in their infinite subdivisions. The very linkage of the dynasty of Ferrara with the empire of Charlemagne and the Breton knights generates a stream full of crosscurrents, the most powerful of these bearing the narratives of Ruggiero, Bradamante, and Orlando. Ariosto also distinguishes various kinds of warfare and treats their oppositions. The relative conduct and import of battles and duels in *Orlando Furioso* appear as a point of debate whenever warlike conflict is prolonged. The advent of firearms as a modern means against the other, older magic of enchanted weapons; the diverse personal qualities called for in the duellist and soldier; and the entire gamut of juxtapositions of single combat and mass warfare are dealt with in their crucial connection with the chivalric code. When the outcome of a war is made dependent on a series of duels between individual knights—a single combat between Ruggiero and Rinaldo, then a triple contest between Orlando,

Brandimarte, and Oliviero on one side, and Gradasso, Agramante, and Sobrino on the other—the conflict is revealed as a structural generator of subdividing oppositions. The fictions of poetry are juxtaposed with those of history.

Ariosto comments in tranquil but trenchant fashion on the calamities of his own age. His account of the war between Carlomagno and Agramante is accompanied by remarks on the contemporary Italian military scene. For example, he compares the situation of the Saracens in France, who had suffered heavy losses despite their successes, to the recent battle of Ravenna in which so many French captains were killed (XV.2). Some similar allusions are acts of deference to Alfonso d'Este and recent Ferrarese triumphs. In describing the defeat of Agramante's fleet by the forces of Astolfo and Orlando, Ariosto refers to the battle of Polesella (1509) in which a Venetian fleet in the Po was routed by a numerically inferior Ferrarese force. He himself was not present, the Narrator informs us, but anyone who was there will understand the situation of the Saracens (XL.5.5–8).

The conduct of legendary warfare contrasts, again, with the horrors of modern war. In turn, the nostalgia for a Golden Age of chivalry is overlaid by an awareness of the complexity of all human nature, on one side, and on the other by the advent of modern military techniques. At the same time the Narrator's protest against brutality is not a complete digression from his tone of romance. It is worked into the poem so that the arquebus, which comes to symbolize the new warfare, is used for treacherous purposes only. First the evil Cimosco destroys Olimpia's forces with it, then ambushes the gallant Orlando. Orlando captures it and throws it into the sea, moving the Narrator to lament its rediscovery in recent times, when it has destroyed the chivalrous conduct of warfare (XI.26). This meditation is easily revealed as a confrontation of the idealized past with the demystified present, and the fact that chivalrous ideals and practices loom large in the poem allows them to be opposed (as a refined but antiquated code) to prevailing ethical decay, their seeming permanence to present entropy. But again, even within the confines of the chivalrous world, the generous, courteous, high-souled knights have to live in a society penetrated by cunning, hypocritical, and treacherous rogues, and their rigid ideals are not suited to meet them.

The problem is no less acute in duels than in battle. From the wealth of incongruities resulting from the incompatibility of the chivalric code and the necessities of existence there emerges Ariosto's parody of courtly love involving Zerbino, Isabella, and the hideous Gabrina. Having lost a duel in which it was agreed that the loser would take Gabrina as his lady, Zerbino accompanies and defends her, although he would like to cut her throat (XXI.68). He remains tied to his chivalrous oath when he unhorses Ermonide, the brother of the man Gabrina had once betrayed. At last he is able to pass Gabrina on to his false friend, Odorico, who breaks his promise within a day and hangs her from an elm tree (XXIV.45). Whereas before the reunion with Isabella Zerbino is bound to defend the loathsome Gabrina, the parody of chivalric practice passes to Isabella after his death. She, in turn, has to be accompanied by an ineffectual and physically disgusting hermit as if by her knightly protector (XXIV.90–92).

Another dialectical plot motif derives from the dichotomy between inconsistency (abutting sometimes in madness) and perfect constancy. The Narrator punishes Rodomonte for his fickle infatuation with Isabella and for his inconsistency in falling in love just after delivering a tirade against women (XXXIX.3). Isabella, ever faithful to Zerbino, is rewarded with immortality when Rodomonte unwittingly kills her (XXXIX.26–27). But the Narrator's subsequent indictment of women like Angelica in the last strophe of the same canto acts out Rodomonte's previous condemnation of women's inconstancy (XXX.74.1–4). What finally emerges is the structural and dynamic opposition between the self-renewing terms of the dialectic.

As if to reflect the play of identity and otherness within the self and vis-à-vis the other that characterizes love stories, the language of warfare often doubles that of love. Ariosto's descriptions of single combat, such as the final duel between

Rodomonte and Ruggiero, flow into a fierce embrace of the combatants. War and love potentially pit everyone against everyone and come mutually to signify each other. Virgil's narrator is a conquering warrior. Having announced in the third of his *Georgics*[8] that he would prepare to compose an epic on Rome, in the exordium to the *Aeneid* he supersedes the muse of love, poetry, Erato, with "a more noble order of things." But Ariosto's Narrator is himself a generally mad lover composing at lucid intervals.

The enduring connection between the two exordia also derives in part from Ariosto's imitation of Virgil's *style noble,* but from there on the difference takes precedence, definable, however, only in relation to that abiding bond. Where such obvious divergences of form, language, and intent exist, recourse to a stock of reliable topoi affirms that the older poem has been reread and revised. Since Plato's *Republic* (IX) at least, wrath and desire could be understood as interchangeable within the single passionate being. There scarcely exists a love in the poem without its coefficient in the realm of duelling. And when the combat between two knights fighting for a lady takes place before her very eyes, her presence subdivides the conflict so that war and love can be viewed at work simultaneously. In accordance with the effect of this topos, the separate medieval traditions of romance and epic that contend for pride of place in *Orlando Furioso* are conflated by the adoption of a style that somewhat elevates the tone of romance while somewhat reducing that of epic.

Ariosto's narratives tend to convey a balanced view of love and, consequently, of woman. Ariosto's Narrator is indeed ready to espouse either side of the *querelle des femmes.* He raises questions about the injustice of laws regulating feminine sexual conduct, and his presentation of women in love has even been claimed to approach an "androgynous" ideal in the freedom it concedes to women.[9] But two points must be recalled in this connection. Ariosto's Narrator is a self-proclaimed mad lover, hence an inconsistent, unreliable speaker. His effect is a leveling not so much of roles or opinions as of linguistic and literary styles. Bradamante duels with

Rodomonte (XXXV.40). Her female identity is clear to him, as well as the fact that she is fighting to avenge another woman, Isabella. Rodomonte accompanies his advances with a sexual boast that comically takes the place of the epic self-glorification of a warrior before combat:

> Io son di tal valor, son di tal nerbo,
> ch'aver non dei d'ander di sotto a sdegno.
>
> (XXXV.47.1–2)

> (To fall by me thou needest not disdain,
> I with such strength, such nerve am fortified.)

Bradamante defeats Rodomonte on both counts and rides off, seeking a duel with Ruggiero. In the meantime she confronts Ferraù and vanquishes him by the beauty of her eyes before they come to blows (XXXV.78), just as Medoro had affected Zerbino. When he reports back to Ruggiero, Ferraù is not sure whether his opponent was actually Bradamante or one of her brothers (XXXVI.13). This situation is mirrored by Marfisa's rushing to accept Bradamante's challenge in her brother's place.

The stress on Bradamante's femininity in time of war, or on her warriorlike, masculine traits in moments of amorous reflection emphasizes chiefly the duality of her role as woman and warrior. Women's roles in *Orlando Furioso* emphasize the double nature of Ariosto's project and draw attention to the "romance" aspect of the poem. They furnish transitions away from epic modes. Even Bradamante appears so as to juxtapose (by her doubleness) the obdurate differences leading to the paradoxical confrontations of romance and epic. The misogynous tales that thread their way through much of the poem, such as that of the Rocca di Tristano, or of Marganorre, or of the homicidal women, subserve a counter-romance aggregate of elements set as obstacles to the integrated whole that the reader is invited to desire. The eventual marriage of the proto-Estensi is the nearest approximation to that whole, a graceful compliment inflated to hyperbolic power. Viewed at closer hand, Bradamante as the personified combination of these disparate elements that seek perfect union at rest allegorizes the impossibility of integrating them into one whole.

Analogous to the lack of balance between the two natures is that of the single triumphant hero. From the outset Orlando shares Ruggiero's distinction, one as the raison d'être, the other as the title hero of the work. The two are buttressed by a number of other hyperbolized figures: Brandimarte, Rodomonte, even Astolfo, involved in multiplying episodes, possessing overlapping virtues and vices. It is this doubling and multiplication that permits these "characters" to slide into the status of character-functions. A basic shift occurs from the charismatic hero to the possibility of a simple transfer of leadership, and the emphasis comes to fall on the infinite possibilities of change.

Morton Bloomfield has shown[10] that the technique of multiplying the hero, the better to diminish him, is already present in the late medieval romance. According to his analysis an "antiheroic force" came to the fore, manifesting itself in opposition to the concept of the single epic hero. The former focal point of an entire work—such as Roland in the *chanson de geste*—gave way to several possible forces: either a "self-destructive heroism"[11] epitomized by such passionate lovers as Lancelot, Troilus, and Tristan, or an overarching depiction of self-heroism of the author himself, or by destruction of the single charismatic figure, "creating various heroes in the same work so that no one would stand out by himself."[12] Ariosto may be said to have deployed all three of these forces. In the twelfth century as in the High Renaissance, the shift was probably accompanied by a parallel shift from the singlemindedness of the *miles christianus*. Bloomfield finds the response of splintering the hero "characteristic of most of the literature of the later Middle Ages in Western Europe."[13] Not only the figure of the hero itself but episodes and epithets became transferable, and the same poem could celebrate diverse, sometimes opposed qualities. "The decline of the hero in the later Middle Ages . . . reveals a sense that human power is finally powerless and human goals finally disappointing,"[14] writes Bloomfield, and the same might well have been written of Ariosto's era.

In his classical work on the double, Otto Rank terms repetition the temporal form of doubling.[15] "It is those inevitable repetitions inherent in cyclical time," he writes, "that seem to rob the individual of all potency"; even the recollection that an event has occurred before paralyzes the remembering will with "the awareness that the memory of what has occurred in the past is at the same time the foreknowledge of what will be repeated in the future, the debilitating sense that time is cyclical and that recollection is prophecy."[16] In accordance with this ontological negativity, the heroes of *Orlando Furioso* are protean (in the aggregate), and they travel light. Titanic proportions are not appreciated, as they are later in Tasso. An attribute such as a sword or horse may serve to link two users but also passes easily from hand to hand. Orlando's sword for the battle of Lipadusa is Balisarda, Ruggiero's weapon at the beginning of the poem. Eventually Orlando returns the sword to Ruggiero (XLIV.16), and it strikes for Ruggiero against the Saracens just as he is converted to Christianity.

Ariosto shows that loving couples tend to resemble each other. Brandimarte and Fiordiligi provide a continuation of the Zerbino-Isabella pair. Each couple is separated for a long time and scarcely comes together again when the male is killed in battle. As individuals, Brandimarte (of one pair) is linked with Isabella (of the other), for they are among the very few to whom Ariosto extends the promise of Paradise (XLI.100). Brandimarte has been killed by a pagan, Gradasso, but with a Christian sword, Orlando's Durindana. When he finds Brandimarte's body Orlando echoes the prayer that the Narrator has offered for Isabella (XXXIX.27;XLIII.162). Finally, the death of Brandimarte has left a shortage in the Christian ranks, so Ariosto spares Sobrino, a Saracen, recruiting him to the Christian side with a compensatory effect.

Two main variants of the reproduced situation predominate. Either two correlated stories with a similar situational base end differently, or two clearly opposed situations find the same resolution.[17] Sometimes Ariosto connects the two episodes linearly. Two narratives begin with a knight's discovery of a beautiful maiden chained to a rock: the episode of Ruggiero and Angelica and that of Orlando and Olimpia. But they end in opposite ways: the "libidinosa furia" of Ruggiero toward Angelica and the paternal protection Orlando offers to Olimpia. Another example of this kind of doubling is furnished by the adventures of Doralice and those of Isabella. Both are Spanish ladies, Doralice from the ill-famed "Moorish" Andalusia and Isabella from the royal house of Aragon, a territory ennobled by the Catholic dynasty of Spain (indeed, the very family of Eleonora d'Este!). Doralice is engaged to Rodomonte, but on the road the Tartar Mandricardo ravishes her. At first she despairs, but Mandricardo manages to console her, and their subsequent encounters are more enjoyable to her (XIV.34). Isabella is the fiancée of Zerbino, and she is ravished by Odorico, but she does not surrender herself easily (XIII.28). Both ladies lose their intended husbands, but when Zerbino is fatally wounded Isabella decides to withdraw from the world to a convent, ready to die rather than betray the memory of her beloved. Doralice, when Ruggiero kills Mandricardo, resigns herself to love Ruggiero rather than have no lover at all (XXX.72). While Mandricardo lived he had been useful to Doralice; dead he is of no use at all (XXX.73). The narratives are linked, finally, by Ruggiero's killing of Mandricardo, who had succeeded Rodomonte.

In the second kind of doubling—that which produces the same ending for opposed situations—characters initially presented in their opposition to each other begin to behave similarly as the narrative progresses. We encounter the same sort of jealousy in the noble Bradamante (XXXII.10–25;XXXII.37–43) as in the notably discourteous prince Clodione, who has been overcome despite the courtly tenet that love teaches politeness and measured behavior (XXXII.92–93). Brandimarte, a gentle, pious knight, produces Rodomontades similar to the most hyperbolic behavior of that titanic paladin. For instance, in canto XIV (117.7–8) Rodomonte appears as an infernal being, accompanied by an allusion to Dante's Lapaneus, who cursed God in *Inferno* (XIV.63). Rodomonte is a descendant of the giant Nimrod, who directed the building of the Tower of Babel (XIV.119), and his mass slayings also portend the madness of Orlando. The Narrator informs us that Rodomonte has left unfinished the tower with which he had marked Isabella's tomb (XXIX.35), a strange analogue of Nimrod's tower.

Rodomonte's bestial fury is similar to Orlando's as he is maddened by Doralice's preference for Mandricardo (XXVII.122.66). This insanity has however the distinctive feature of inconsistency, and the heartbroken Saracen (by contrast with Orlando) mends quickly as he consoles himself with the pursuit of Isabella (XXIX.1–10). Whereas Orlando's wrath turns chiefly against himself, Rodomonte's extends toward Isabella, whom he intends to rape as soon as she has given him the promised magic potion (XXIX.18). Orlando turns instead on Angelica only when he does not recognize her (XXIX.60). Again, by contrast to Orlando's unilateral and univocal love for Angelica, the story of Rodomonte's passion for Isabella bifurcates into the capillaries of the various subterfuges initiated by both parties.

It is when Rodomonte explicitly confronts Orlando on the bridge, their matched strength and insanity locked into combative embrace, that the parallel reaches its fullest extent. They fall together, two "fools from a bridge," as the proverb has it.[18] To fight Rodomonte is to fight the inner beast, so like the mad Orlando Ruggiero eventually pairs off with Rodomonte in the close embrace of combat: "gli cinge il collo col braccio possente" (whom by the neck he with strong arm has caught; XLVI.124.6); "gli stringe con Ruggier sì, che l'abbraccia" (He grips Rogero so, fast locked they stand; XLVI.131.6). Nowhere does Ariosto put more strain on the capacity of amorous language to express extreme opposition in combat. The duel is purgative, for any threat of "enragement" on Ruggiero's part is finally removed when he eliminates Rodomonte in the last lines of the poem. To extend the parallel to the extremity of conflict, when Orlando appears at Biserta to turn the course of battle, he wears as his insignia the Tower of Babel (XLI.30.3−4) pulverized by lightning. It is a sign that he has overcome Rodomontian madness.

Orlando, meanwhile, has subsided to a secondary level of the narrative. Having "lost" both Angelica and his friend Brandimarte, he gives over the banner of insanity to Ruggiero and to Fiordiligi, Brandimarte's lover (XLIII.164). Like Rodomonte, Orlando does not find his love; the embraces of war elbow out the poem's long-postponed nuptial embrace. Even the last note is not one of union and repose, although the doublings of the last three canti appear to have prepared it.

These canti form part of Ariosto's interspersions made explicitly for the final version. They find Bradamante temporarily divested of her warrior aspect; the oppositions exist only between males. Bradamante takes over the "angelic" function of the unapproachable beloved, and the prize of battle. She is now a disputed bride, her parents favoring a match with Leone, the heir to the throne of Constantinople, while she and her brothers insist that she is sworn to Ruggiero. A new meekness binds her, and she seems unable to resist conflicting claims (XLIV.74.6). A scrambling of these ensues. Ruggiero has set out to fight his rival, Leone, but through a string of unforeseeable complications becomes deeply obligated to him and agrees to fight for the bride *on his behalf.* The conflict of love and duty is thus hyperbolized to its utmost but remains able to bifurcate yet again. For Ruggiero at this point, honor consists in that owed to Bradamante both as his intended and as the cofounder of the Estense line, and that owed to his benefactor Leone for other chivalric reasons. In addition, Bradamante has extracted from Carlomagno a guarantee that she need not marry any man who can defeat her in combat. Therefore, Ruggiero must finally champion his friend Leone's cause by wielding his sword against his own lady. The oppositions of love and war come full circle, to the crash of the demolition of the chivalric code.

Ruggiero wishes to die by Bradamante's hand (XLIV.59), as earlier she had wished to die by his (XXXII.43). Honor compels him to strain toward victory in his friend and rival's

name. He has paired himself with the most unfortunate part-
ner possible: a Christian and another lover of Bradamante, but
also a friend and benefactor. Even this comical position has
already been prefigured in the poem: Ruggiero's duel with
Bradamante's brother, Rinaldo (XXXVIII.68–XXXIX.8).

Bradamante does not know Ruggiero's identity at this
moment. He is taken by all present for a Byzantine prince,
and the onlookers find him a perfect match for Bradamante
(XLIV.81). Like his beloved in so much of the poem, Rug-
giero is, for this moment, not what he seems. Declared the
winner, he despairs and retreats to the woods, leaving Brada-
mante to Leone. As will be seen in detail, his sister Marfisa
takes up Ruggiero's cause and his fighting stance with more
diligence than he himself shows (XLV.113). Only a stroke of
Fortune evidenced by the sudden abdication of the Byzantine
prince finally and belatedly gives sanction to the marriage of
Ruggiero and Bradamante. But Fortune still permits the final
intrusion of Rodomonte, who storms onto the scene seeking
revenge for his duel with Bradamante. To the end, then, it is
dissension, not union, that rules the plot; dualism, not unity,
that provides its ending. The search for repose in final truth
we know to be a major cause of madness in *Orlando Furioso*.
Both curiosity for the absolute and absolute curiosity are
severely punished.

That Ariosto chose to end his poem's definitive version
with a doubling section, that he added this and three other
major "echo" passages to what had gone before (the other
new episodes are those of Olimpia, Marganorre, and the
Rocca di Tristano) shows that he had amplification in mind,
but specifically by repetition and comparison. The new epi-
sodes furnish the bulk of the new material, and their cumula-
tive and collective effect is to topple the hierarchy of the
chivalric world represented in other, lesser works as a unity.
Ariosto's irony adds to the doubling, the later episode com-
menting and improving on the former. It is not the effect of a
balanced vision but of two warring contentions expressed on
the level of plot. Even the first of a pair of episodes contains
abundant clues to its own destruction; its replication con-

firms them. But Ariosto's irony is functionally partial. Never does he claim to abjure meaning utterly, a stance that would handicap irremediably the project of his encomiastic poem. In fact, the reference that anchors the poem to praise of the past—the heroic adventures of Ruggiero and Bradamante—simply points, courteously, to the conviction of the present by a better, fabled past. Whatever is a copy of that beginning must also surely be a diminution. The running on of time is a running downward; to come after is to be fated to repeat. Nowhere does Ariosto explicitly suggest that someone will repeat the lives of the Estense originals.

Within the poem, however, that postulate awakens questioning. The poem itself, a copy, must be a scaled-down imitation of the ever-elusive virgin truth, a double of Creation that cannot approximate its force. The divided characters and their subdivisions, the continually bifurcating conflicts and rapprochements of the plot lines reproduce the eternal inadequation endemic to the writer's profession itself. If there is an original to copy from, the search for it is an infinite regress, the issuing copies readable only in serial form.

Even the union of Ruggiero and Bradamante is bound by this consciousness of a permanence of change. For the predictions of the hermit who baptizes Ruggiero include those of his death, only seven years after his conversion to Christianity, at the hands of the traitorous Maganzesi (XLI.61). This is the same family of Gano who brought about the death of Roland, who is in no small measure an *auctoritas* for Ariosto's poem. And in fulfillment of the hermit's prophecy, Ruggiero and Bradamante will actually replicate the tragic pattern outlined by the pairs of Zerbino and Isabella and of Brandimarte and Fiordiligi: a lengthy separation and search for reunion followed—alas—by a brief reunion and the tragic death of the male.

Is this not, then, also a glorious inflation of the theory of *translatio imperii,* or the movement of imperial power? The bed canopy given to Ruggiero and Bradamante, worked with complicated tapestry designs depicting the future of the Estense line, had first been given by its maker, the prophetess

Cassandra, to Hector. It traveled to Greece after the capture of Troy and later to Ptolemaic Egypt, Rome, Constantinople, and now west again, to Paris. This movement of power from one realm to the next in the course of history outlines what will happen to the stability of the Ferrarese regime, undercutting any claim to permanence. As a dynastic symbol it suggests clearly that power and security may at any time be transported elsewhere on the steed of chance and "madness," anywhere, even if just beyond reach. Here in the sphere of encomium time is indeed cyclical and recollection prophecy. It is, however, in motion, not static. Accordingly, Ariosto's poetic recurrences tend to be paronomastic, not strictly repetitious. They include a plus or minus factor and occur in dialectical juxtaposition, not as refrains. The world reveals itself to be in flux, but not without superficial ordering.

The movement of the "Carolingian" plot is structured, therefore, in four parts that form two natural pairs. The first disperses the warriors from Paris; so does the third part. The second section concentrates them there for a great battle, and the fourth and last does the same, resolving the war in Paris. Again, the quadipartite structure of *ottava rima* remains the basis of Ariosto's prosodic method. This is, as Brand points out, the "standard pattern which conditions our ear to a certain cadence, any deviation from which we note consciously or subconsciously and which the poet can use for particular effects."[19] Brand also notes another means whereby the *ottava* can emphasize doubling: "the rhyming couplet at the end of the octave, by virtue of its rhyme and its position, has a special function in Ariosto's poem where it is used with much greater care and effect than in the poems of any of his predecessors. It frequently forms a genuine conclusion . . . it may sum up a lengthy description . . . or provide a sort of finishing touch, a witty comment or mythological adornment."[20] The way is thus open for the final two lines to split off from the body of the octave to form an epigram or commentary.

Otherwise the octave may split in half, the first four lines offering a statement, with embellishment or comment contained in the second and possible redoubling in the final two lines. The following example was chosen entirely at random. In the course of a battle Rinaldo's horse, Baiardo, meets with a huge birdlike monster, which the Narrator greets with his customary blend of wonder and disbelief:

> Forse era vero augel, ma non so dove
> O quando un altro ne sia stato tale;
> Non ho veduto mai, né letto altrove
> Fuor ch'in Turpin, d'un sì fatto animale;
> Questo rispetto a credere mi muove,
> Che l'augel fosse un diavolo infernale;
> Che Malagigi in quella forma trasse,
> Acciò che la battaglia disturbasse.
>
> (XXXIII.85)

> (Perhaps it was a bird; but when or where
> Another bird resembling this was seen
> I know not, I, nor have I any where,
> Except in Turpin, heard that such has been.
> Hence that it was a fiend, to upper air
> Evoked from depths of nether hell I ween;
> Which Malagigi raised by magic sleight,
> That so he might disturb the champions' fight.)

The first four lines describe the Narrator's puzzlement before so strange a creature, introducing the corollary that even his authority, Turpino, might not have attained such curious feats of storytelling. The final four lines move toward a distinctly separate thought, that perhaps the creature is a devil. But the second half of that group trivializes the notion of infernal origin by its reference to the mischievous and probably incapable Malagigi, as well as the use of the litotic "disturbasse" to put that personage's evil intent into action.

To undercut even further the deadness of final meaning Ariosto employs links of a chiefly or purely phonetic nature, which interconnect various characters (or character-functions) and episodes. One of these is the phonetic pairing of names: Agramante-Agricane (both Saracen kings, taken from *Orlando Innamorato*), Bradamante-Brandimarte, Fiordiligi-

Fiordispina, Orrilo-Orrigille, even the Orca and the Orco. These are sometimes "speaking names"[21] that point to some common trait of their sharers—obviously the case for the two flowerlike ladies, also for Bradamante and Brandimarte, who are both as brave as their names suggest. The two *orridi,* also continued from Boiardo's poem, are traitors, one an unfaithful lover, the other a sneak attacker. Their two stories are intertwined in canto XV through Grifone, who fights Orrilo and subsequently falls in love with Orrigille. A sexual opposition divides the Orco, who consumes only male victims, from his female counterpart, who devours women (VIII; X and XI). Ariosto takes the sexual doubling further: the escape from the Orco by means of disguising oneself in sheepskin recalls the stratagem of Ulysses (*Odyssey* IX) employed to elude the Cyclops. But in *Orlando Furioso* it is a woman, Lucina, who attempts it but (again unlike Ulysses) is caught in the act.

The character-functions and episodes directly related to the fused Carolingian and Breton material by no means contain all of the doubled and multiplied elements. Even the interstices of created pauses in the stories of knights and ladies make use of doubling and twinning by filling with new stories. Two *novelle,* for instance, fitted between sets of heroic episodes amplify the latter from within.[22] Both stories echo not only each other but the theme and purport of the main narrative at the places where they are inserted. They are based on the *querelle des femmes,* which was a staple of polite conversation in the High Renaissance. As in such representative instances as Castiglione's *Libro del cortegiano,* the attitudes toward women expressed in *Orlando Furioso* range from elaborate defense (usually by the Narrator) to confidential advice and veer sharply from encomium to absolute condemnation. These tales share a common subject: the sexual voracity of women and their ensuing lack of faithfulness to their husbands. They are linked by similar plots as well. In each one the chastity of a wife is subjected to trial until overcome. But the second story, in accordance with Ariosto's seeming preference for repetition with a difference, or *paronomasia,* is itself doubled. The pendant to it shows the reverse image, that of the sexual indiscrimination and complaisance of the husband!

By this turnabout ending the second story represents what has only been alleged by the teller of the first (as we shall see). This is narrated by an innkeeper to Rodomonte to justify and encourage his jealous anger at women, but it is followed by the remonstrances of a "giusto vecchio" who has heard all and speaks up for the women's side. Incontinent they may be, but incontinence is shared by both sexes, and men are never reproached for it. Women react to the pattern set by their men; it would be better to liberate all adulterers than to punish the female more severely, and so on.

The first story tells of an exceptionally handsome and desirable knight, Jocondo, who is summoned to court by King Astolfo (not at all related to the paladin) for his rare good looks, which exceed the unusual beauty of the king himself. Jocondo has to leave his devoted wife behind and does so with the parting gift of a little cross. A long way down the road (which he travels with his brother), he finds that he has left the gift behind. As he reenters his house to get it he finds his wife in the embrace of a manservant. Without betraying his presence he resumes his way and reaches Astolfo's court in distraught condition. Jocondo languishes there until one day he spies the beautiful queen (who doubles his own wife as an apparently faithful consort to an exceptionally handsome man) in the arms of a hunchbacked dwarf. This section of the story is most obviously self-doubling.

When Jocondo tells all to the king, they set out together, telling no one, to avenge themselves on all unchaste wives, and the second half of the story begins. At first, Jocondo and King Astolfo plan not to return to court until they have taken the "spoils" of a thousand wives, but they tire of the constant search for new women and decide to find one who can be shared by them both, in the same bed. In other words, the experiment with multiplication is channeled back into doubling, or halving.

In order that no jealousy may interfere with their friendship, the woman is to be faithful to them both equally. They turn up a young girl named Fiammetta (who bears no relation other than her name to any character in Boccaccio by that name). The arrangement works efficiently, but en route Fiammetta is reunited by chance with a former lover. She arranges that one night this man will lie with her, between her two regular lovers but unbeknown to them. As planned, Astolfo and Jocondo each hear some nocturnal going-on on that occasion, but each believes it to be the other making love to the girl. The next morning their altercation over property rights in Fiammetta yields the truth, and the two men laugh themselves to tears, leaving her with a handsome dowry to which each contributes equally.

Rodomonte hears the story out but silences the even-tempered old man who speaks in favor of women. Maddened by hatred of the female sex, Rodomonte storms out of the inn and shortly afterward discovers Isabella. A new episode of fury begins.

By contrast, Rinaldo receives the companion piece to this story, some fifteen canti later, with equanimity and readiness to derive useful meaning from it. Throughout the poem Rinaldo has not deviated from his advocacy of equal sexual freedom for men and women. He now ponders the possibility that his own wife may be unfaithful to him during his long absence from her. He is presented by his host, another inn-keeper, with examples that justify his decision not to inquire into his wife's doings.

This innkeeper, once young and handsome, had married a wife parallel to himself in beauty and loyalty, but the sorceress Melissa fell in love with him. Failing in all other allurements to win him from his wife, Melissa offered him the chance to test his wife's fidelity. Let him drink once from a magic chalice, and if the wife has not remained chaste the wine will spill upon him; if she has, it will flow neatly down his throat. He drinks once and all goes well, but Melissa then suggests an interval of separation and a means of en-trapment involving—again—a feigned departure by the inn-keeper. Upon this leavetaking Melissa appears to the wife in the guise of a former suitor, promising her rich gifts in exchange for her love. The innkeeper witnesses his betrayal, and the sole comfort remaining to his declining years is the chalice and the opportunity to offer it to his guests, who may now test their wives' chastity with a drink.

Pleased by his own forbearance in refusing to accept this challenge, Rinaldo continues his journey of the moment. A boatman tells him a tale that furnishes a near-double and corollary to that of the chalice. This time a jealous husband, like his wife before him, falls prey to a new lover. Just as in the previous story, a sorceress proves indispensable to the outcome. Judge Anselmo of Mantua has a beautiful wife, Argia, who is bored with their sedate conjugal life. Soon she has an admirer, Adonio, whose name suggests his extreme beauty. He is a descendant of the founders of Mantua. Having spent all of his money in trying to win the lady, he sets out on the road, a ruined man. There he sees a peasant beating a serpent, and because of his fabled origin from a line beginning from a serpent's tooth, he intervenes for the snake and frees it. Meanwhile Anselmo has been named ambassador from Mantua to the Papal court. As he leaves he begs his wife to remain faithful to him, the more anxiously in that he has consulted an astrologer who warned him that his wife would betray him for money.

But Manto, the founding ancestor of Mantua, is on Adonio's side, for he has rescued a serpent, one of her own. This same serpent returns to him as Manto herself. She subsequently takes the form of a miraculous talking dog that produces unlimited wealth just by shaking itself. Together the lover and the dog persuade Argia to acquiesce in his design. Upon return and discovery of the intrigue, Judge Anselmo tries to murder his wife, but the magic dog saves her by rendering her invisible.

Without pausing to exploit the resonances between this tale and the larger narrative of *Orlando Furioso* Ariosto turns to the pendant that redoubles it. Anselmo, searching furiously for his wife, arrives at a rich and splendid palace and immediately covets it. The price is announced to him by its owner as "that which would cost him least." But this powerful personage, although his desire for Anselmo parallels that of his wife for her handsome cavalier, is a hideous "Ethiopian." Indeed, when the turnabout ending has the wife discover Anselmo, she makes it clear that his transgression exceeds hers. Summarizing, the boatman and Rinaldo praise Argia and blush for her husband in the new double context of the homosexuality and the repulsiveness of his lover.

The ebb and flow of certainties in these tales—the one heard by Rodomonte and the other, with its corollary and double, heard by Rinaldo—refer immediately to the *question des femmes* but far more generally to the rejection of absolute truth. The host with his chalice is punished for his aspiration to certain knowledge; Rinaldo renounces his chance for it. No topic could be better adapted to double truth than the matter of sexuality, and the inconsistency commonly acribed to woman alone is revealed in the stories as the single constant factor that groups survivors together. The Narrator's dialectical ruminations on the topic of woman are to be understood as governed by the context of a permanence of change. Canto XX, for instance, begins with the eulogy of deserving women, asserting that they have been deprived of their due by the envy and ignorance of writers. This is one of many passages in which the Narrator addresses the ladies themselves. Indeed, ladies in general are thought of as being an important part of the poem's audience, and the Narrator is concomitantly anxious to dispel the idea that he is not their true friend. Accordingly he will neutralize and discredit some of the misogynous views he himself may have expressed to this audience, offering to praise a hundred for every one blamed. In other words, having stated that the praiseworthy are rare, he offers obligingly to falsify this "truth." So when canto XXVIII opens with a statement on women's infamy, the Narrator claims to include it only because "Turpino" does.

We could hardly be offered a clearer signal of the poet's obvious choice to produce the misogynous artillery, nor does he denigrate the more immediate "authority" of the innkeeper through whom a misogynous story is relayed. And when the first story at last finds correspondences in the very last—such as the parallel between the hideous dwarf beloved of King Astolfo's queen and the vile, homosexual "Ethiopian"—the symmetries simply stand as examples, mere deixis contrasted with pointed moralization, of the parallel sexual venality of male and female. The unreliable Narrator has availed himself of the binary system on all the levels of Memory, Invention, Disposition, and Elocution. The stratagem of the story within a story even facilitates our final understanding of the entire male-female controversy as represented in turn within the very idea that furnished the means of representation in the first place. This is to say that the signifying idea finds within itself the outcome of its role *as representation* pure and simple. The signifier has no function outside what it represents; it is entirely transparent to it. But this represented conclusion, the possibility that everything will find its justification on another scale, does not seem near or benign.

Perhaps the chief means whereby Ariosto illustrates the impossibility of complete identity is that of twinning. This *forma mentis* extends inward to the core of the poem, which celebrates the nuptials of two nearly like beings. Even Ruggiero and Bradamante, like many of the others, are capable of standing for each other. Their myth thereby participates in the universal myth of the Divine Twins[23] through which the origins of many a reign are explained. But they in turn have other, *real* siblings: Ruggiero's twin Marfisa and Bradamante's, Ricciardetto. Moreover, they depart from the canonical Divine Twins in respect of the cross-sexual aspect of all of the pairings. The lack of polarized sexual roles in *Orlando Furioso* ensues from a pattern of continual binary fission, both within the poem and anterior to it. Twinned characters are opposed along the lines of religion and, as importantly, of sex.

Even the smaller units of plot and diction participate in the crossings that are suggested by the alternations of its very first lines. No sooner are the events of the poem under way than a kind of transvestitism seems to take hold of the character roles. King Sacripante (I.53) greets his beloved, Angelica of Cathay, with the joy of a mother receiving a long-lost son.

Pinabello (II.39.1–2) contemplates the abduction of his lady with the sorrow of a mother bird for her male offspring, or a mother fox losing her child to an eagle (II.44.3–4). This time he is actually addressing a woman whom he takes for a man, thereby effectuating a second-level exchange of identity. It is Bradamante, not Ruggiero, who follows the encomiastic thread of the pattern followed by Aeneas in Virgil. After a mock-descent into Hell imaged by her fall from a precipice (II.75–76), Bradamante receives a vision of the future Estensi (III.14–20) analogous to that vouchsafed Aeneas in the sixth book. Not until the final canto will Ruggiero have a similar vision (XLI.61).

Cross-sexual twinning in the first half of the poem, prior to Orlando's mad scenes, most frequently takes a form distinct from that in the second half: direct sex reversal expressed in outward appearance. A character, most frequently Bradamante, is placed in a situation traditionally associated with the opposite sex. The second half of *Orlando Furioso* intensifies the doubling of Christian by Saracen characters, a development that completes the progressive order of all the doublings inherent in the Ruggiero-Bradamante couple. Thus the ground rules prove subject to change as distinctions previously validated in some context become obsolete as they run counter to a different set of expectations.

When Atlante explains his motives for sequestering Ruggiero in his enchanted castle, these are revealed as the same motives that drove Thetis to hide Achilles from war (IV.31). But Bradamante undoes this enchantment by taking on the role of the knight-errant rescuing the ad hoc damsel from the sorcerer. Ruggiero continues as the object of desire (IV.47) when his impromptu flight on the Hippogryph leaves Bradamante with the fear that the same fate will befall her beloved as once befell Ganymede. That comparison is reinforced by frequent reference to his soft beauty. Whether ravished from his lady's embrace or struggling in combat, Ruggiero is a general object of aesthetic admiration (for example, XXXVI.31.4–6: "le spalle e'l petto, / le leggiadre fattezze, e'l movimento / pieno di grazia" are terms that would suit Bradamante equally, or less).

Astolfo, Ruggiero's kinsman, at times occupies a similar quasi-feminine status. When Alcina makes off with him it is by luring him onto the back of a whale, a masculine Europa (VI.41). The banquet Alcina serves him is compared to that at which Ganymede serves (VII.20.7–8), recalling the anterior image of Ruggiero. The implied feminization achieves more explicit motivation when Alcina's transforming realm is called "effeminato e molle" (VII.48); for the submission of both men to women categorizes them as adherents to a feminine way of life (VII.53–55) by contamination. Against the generally Virgilian patterns of this part of the poem, a reference to Hercules illuminates a comparison between Ruggiero's enslavement and that of Hercules by Omphale; like that hero Ruggiero too had been a "fanciullo avezzo a strangolar serpenti" (VII.57.4). Again Melissa taunts him for becoming Alcina's "Attis" (VII.57.8), implying that the force of his attraction to Alcina has castrated him. For a moment the "Herculean" characterization that attaches more generally to Orlando in the poem has gravitated to Ruggiero, by way of an exchange of masculine for feminine traits that Orlando is never forced to undergo.

But Ariosto's diction can play tricks with the externals of situations, causing a fleeting, seemingly misbegotten, incongruous association by means of word placement or connotation alone, as when Orlando seeking Angelica is compared to Ceres searching for Proserpina (XII.1). To describe the pain of a slighted lover, Grifone, Ariosto revives the image of the suffering Dido:

> Vorria il miser fuggire; e come cervo
> ferito, ovunque va, porta la freccia.
>
> (XVI.3.5–6)[24]

> (The wretch would fly; but bears in him a dart,
> Like wounded stag, whichever way he flees.)

Angelica's lover, Medoro, is also described in feminizing terms, with his delicate coloring and curling golden hair (XVIII.166.7–8). Even the motive for his entry into the plot is reminiscent of a famous heroine: like Antigone determined to bury her father's body Medoro feels compelled to bury his dead. And he defends the body of Dardinello like a she-bear defending her cubs (XIX.7). His tender beauty disarms even the valor of Zerbino, who spares him for love alone: "d'amor tutto e di pietade ardea" (he burned entirely with love and pity [my translation];XIX.12.8).

Sexual role reversal and neutralization overshadow even Orlando. Mandricardo picks up the sword Orlando has dropped and claims to have frightened Orlando into leaving it behind:

> E dicea ch'imitato avea il castore,
> il qual si strappa i genitali sui,
> vedendosi alle spalle il cacciatore,
> che sa che non ricerca altro da lui.
>
> (XXVII.57.1–4)

> (Saying the Count, in yielding to his foe
> That sword, the Beavers' known device had tried;
> Who, followed closely by the hunter, know
> Their fell pursuer covets nought beside.)

The comparison to the self-castrated beaver explicitly equates the sword with the phallus and neutralizes Orlando's sheer heroism without the need for doubling or for the actions of the formidable young women like Bradamante and Marfisa who bestride the pages of the poem.

The island of the homicidal women (XIX.57–118) hyperbolizes the same theme. On this island all men are relentlessly exploited by the institutionalized lust and domination of women, but the latter are cast down by Marfisa, herself a warrior endowed with some awesome phallic attributes. Marfisa believes that the strength of her sword will compensate for the deficiencies of nature when she is called upon, in the place of a man, to satisfy ten women in one night ("ma dove non l'aitasse la natura / con la spada supplir stava sicura" [Secure, where nature had her aid denied, / The want should with the falchion be supplied.]; XIX.69.7–8). She fights an extended duel with the unwilling champion of the women's customs, and when neither can gain the advantage, persuades him to join her. This warrior proves to be Guidon Selvaggio (XX.6), the illegitimate half-brother of Rinaldo and Bradamante. Here the binary oppositions dramatized by combat are joined to cross-sexual doubling. Each of the two major figures, Ruggiero and Bradamante, has been represented by a sibling of the opposite sex, Marfisa being Ruggiero's twin. The confrontation of the two sides is itself neutralized, however, as Marfisa and Guidon Selvaggio decide together to destroy the misanthropic institutions of the island.

Whereas Bradamante continually demonstrates the practical equivalence in the field of the sexes, her brother, Rinaldo, and half-brother, Guidon, together champion this equality in word and deed. Rinaldo decries the harsh law of Scotland that decreed the punishment of Ginevra for unchastity although men go unaccused of the same (IV.66.5–8). Guidon represents an extreme position, for the female supremacy on the island displays an unnatural imbalance demanding correction by a corresponding extreme. But in the process of righting the balance the Narrator first informs his reader that the history of the man-hating regime began with an injustice against women: they were abandoned en masse by their lovers after leaving their home in Crete to follow them (XX.21 ff). Again Ariosto presents the male-female controversy in dialectical form, extending it past the confines of the narrative in both directions.

Like Bradamante and Rinaldo, Marfisa and Ruggiero also prove to have a third sibling. This is Ricciardetto, introduced in canto XXV, who is saved from execution by Ruggiero because of his perfect resemblance to Bradamante. This similarity, amounting nearly to twinship, occasions the play of appearance and reality in numerous passages. Noting the captive Ricciardetto, Ruggiero declares:

O questa è Bradamante
O chi'io non son Ruggier com'era inante.

(XXV.9.7–8)


(Or this is Bradamant, or I no more
Am the Rogero which I was before.)


Ricciardetto's imprisonment was caused by a similar con-
fusion: Bradamante had once again been taken for a man by a
princess, Fiordispina, who fell in love with the man she took
her to be. When Fiordispina discovered the truth she contin-
ued, nevertheless, to love Bradamante hopelessly. Hearing of
this, Ricciardetto decided to take this opportunity to win
Fiordispina, whom he, in turn, has loved a long time, by
impersonating his sister. He tells her that he is Bradamante
transformed into a man and amid imagined fanfares takes
possession of her (XXV.68). The language of war returns to
the description of love:


Non rumor di tamburi, o suon di trombe
Furon principio all'amoroso assalto,
Ma baci ch'imitavan le colombe,
Davan segno or di gire, or di fare alto:
Usammo altr'arme che saette o frombe,
Io senza scale in su la rocca salto,
E lo stendardo piantovi di botto,
E la nimica mia mi cacciò sotto.

(XXV.68)


(Neither the rattling drum nor trumpet's ring
Initiate the amorous assault,
But kisses like the dove's to war we bring,
And these give signal to advance or halt.
Our arms are neither arrows nor the sling.
Without a ladder, then, the wall I vault,
And plant my banner quickly, with a blow,
And thrust my helpless enemy below.)

The episode, which had opened with the man, Ricciar-detto, resembling a woman, flows directly into the opposite, as Bradamante herself is taken for a man. Her brother's tender appearance contrasts with the sexual prowess evoked by martial imagery. In other ways Ricciardetto has not figured much as a warrior, but Bradamante can in fact perform all the feats of warfare that are assigned only metaphorically to her brother. The incident understandably confuses Ruggiero, though it does allow him to repay a certain debt to Brada-mante: early on she had rescued him from Atlante; now he has saved her brother.

The tension between the contending roles of sibling and lover comes to a head as Ruggiero and Marfisa are paired in combat against the treacherous Maganzesi. Their deeds in arms are exactly equal (XXVI.16), but they are opposed in the comparison of their constancy. Ruggiero is delaying the conversion he had promised to his Christian beloved (XXII.35), but Marfisa adheres steadfastly to the Saracen cause as she understands it, deferring an eagerly awaited duel with Ro-domonte in favor of the larger war against Carlomagno (XXVI.87). Ruggiero makes an apparently equivalent decision to defer a duel over the ownership of the steed Frontino, in order to march against Paris. Viewed in the context of his slowness to keep faith with Bradamante, even his seeming adherence to duty emerges as culpable, and for one reason only: Ruggiero's duty has subdivided itself yet again. Marfisa faces no similar dilemma. She will convert swiftly to Christianity as soon as she realizes that she is Ruggiero's sister and that they are of Christian descent (XXXVI.78).

Prior to this epiphanic moment Ariosto allows the hyperbolic opposition of twinship and lovers to reach its breaking point. Marfisa is allowed to fall in love with Ruggiero and cure his wounds, generating the dramatization of the erotic pattern woven into their relationship. She is in fact doing for Ruggiero what Angelica had done for Medoro before the consummation of their love, and at last the two warrior women confront one another as rivals. At first, the Narrator stresses their equivalence by awarding a provisional victory to Bradamante, attributable only to her magic lance (XXXVI.23). And parallel to Marfisa's triumph over the homicidal women was Bradamante's overthrow of the misogynous customs of the Rocca di Tristano (XXXII). But Bradamante destroys that law both as warrior and as woman: first her valor unhorses the knights who come to duel with her, earning her admission to the castle; then as a beautiful maiden she surpasses the lady whose cause she had embraced. Now she joins in the duel with Marfisa bearing that extra advantage, but the conflict has reached its terminal point. Atlante's sepulchral voice (XXXVI.27) intervenes magically to reveal the twinship of Ruggiero and Marfisa, thereby skirting the impieties of fraternal combat (war) and incest (love).

Emerging from this maximally stressful opposition is a gentler Bradamante. In accordance with that development, the Narrator's stirring account of women's military courage that opens canto XXXVII quickly becomes a prolonged encomium of Vittoria Colonna (XXXVII.16–18), a notably peaceful heroine whose military connections reside only in the careful emphasis of warlike qualities in her husband (XXXVII.20). Bradamante will take up arms twice again: first, in the episode of Marganorre that patiently lengthens the theme of misogyny, and then against Ruggiero.

The Marganorre tale is to be closely compared with that of the homicidal women in canto XX. As a result of their indecent attacks on married women, the sons of King Marganorre had been put to death. In revenge Marganorre separated the women from their men as if they had been the Lemnian women; thus the victims of misogyny were misinterpreted as active man-haters. The story encloses an exemplum of constancy akin to that of Isabella. Drusilla, because one of King Marganorre's sons has murdered her husband and taken possession of her, must appear to accept him, but like Isabella against Rodomonte, she resorts to deceit. Again Ariosto singles out a lady for her constancy, and when her plan fails, the Narrator (as in Isabella's case) prays that she may rejoin her husband in Paradise (XXXVII.74). So does Ariosto remove from from the sphere of Nature the most convincing examples of consistency, leaving change and flux to rule on earth.

Just as Marfisa, Astolfo, and Guidon Selvaggio had overthrown the persecution of males by females on the "homicidal" island, the trio formed now by Marfisa, Ruggiero, and Bradamante overthrows the system of persecution instituted by Marganorre. But the new episode serves as a paronomastic commentary on the first. No balance is righted, although Marfisa participates in both successful raids. For the matriarchal system they set up to replace Marganorre's regime quite resembles the social patterns they had destroyed on the island! However they may have tended toward the construction of a balance, the human coefficients of that plan do not achieve it; they have been, it might be said, reassigned.

At the close of canto XXXVIII Rinaldo and Ruggiero, still a pagan, are made the symbols (as champions) of their respective armies and decide to settle the larger conflict by its microcosm, single combat. Ruggiero regrets having to fight the brother of his lady and tries to parry rather than thrust (XXXVIII.89.5). The unhappy situation emphasizes the wrongness of his fighting on the Saracen side regardless of his promise to convert to Christianity. Two kinds of delay are involved: that implicit in the desultory fighting and, of course, the "religious" motif, which here begins obviously to build toward the point at which the two lovers will actually fight each other. Rinaldo serves as the final substitute for Bradamante before she herself must raise her sword against Ruggiero, raising the conflict of love and duty to its utmost narrative paradox.

Their submissiveness to the process of binary subdivision characterizes all the heroes of *Orlando Furioso* who do *not* go mad: the fallible, sensual Ruggiero contending with his own courageous aspect and his manifest destiny; the warrior and maiden Bradamante; Astolfo, at once the explorer on the Hippogryph and the foolish slave of Alcina. The narratives that enfold them show how characters and events can reform into their own polar opposites, how the effort by anyone to dominate chance merely flows into a subsequent phase. Thus the relation between two elements in the chain may be one of contradiction, but also of intimate kinship. The oppositions are never static but subject to all kinds of spatial and temporal movement. Repetition keeps the series open. Any plot element may have its answering one, and any seemingly unique event or personality may have its double. The conception of the hero and of heroism emerges as irremediably trivialized, reduced to absurdity vis-à-vis this radical version of the Renaissance practice of imitation.

The entire structure of *Orlando Furioso,* permeated with doubling, twinning, inversion, and bifurcation, dynamically transports Petrarchan man onto the narrative plane. More properly speaking, Ariosto attacks identity and wholeness by opposing to them the continuous process of binary fission. Just as in the inverted view of the earth proposed by the trip to the Moon, just as in the reversal of recorded history and poetry proposed to Astolfo by San Giovanni, the poem offers knowledge in the form of the play of opposition and affinity. The situations Ariosto spins out are double or multiple in their specific external structure, but even on the level of their interrelation to interpret them at all is to come up with double meaning. Astolfo on the Moon is able to interpret what he sees by turning it upside down so as to maximize difference and thus understand it more clearly. Reversal and transposition are the tools: the hierarchical inversion of the relations between terms.

It is illuminating to think of the situation in *Orlando Furioso* as a kind of ideogram having two different meanings for two interpreters, or subdividing into two divergent situations, or eliciting two contrasting reactions depending on the interpreter. They may be called punning situations—just as some juxtapose the distinct universe of discourse of love and war, others those of the practical world and the earth viewed as sublunary planet, and yet others force characters to double or splinter against themselves. Like a pun, such a situation jocosely replicates an ideogrammatic middle ground; it is the point of departure for the comparison and contrast of two things. And like a pun, its ground is fortuitous, arbitrary, fully dependent on the vagaries of a sign system whose origin and final sense remain tantalizingly within vision and beyond grasp.

A pun also serves to reactivate the cultural apparatus that produced it, since both of its meanings come from that reserve and are themselves affected by it. An obvious example is the eroticizing of one of the meanings by usage. In fact double meanings are obviously favored in environments that seek to eroticize previously nonerotic meanings and by users who derive pleasure from the simple recognition of an erotic sense. This kind of meaning is neatly distinct from that sought by the discarded epistemologies preceding Ariosto's High Renaissance. Among the latter are that of morally based allegory and its correlate, the *hidden* meaning. That kernel of ultimate sense that would reward either exegetical research or imitative striving is now rendered null and void. The metaphorized languages of chivalry in its decline provide superlative vehicles for the momentary encounter and recognition of halves by their other halves, and of self-love by its own aggrandized image.

A hero in *Orlando Furioso* may declare and even partially implement his choice to move from the physical to the spiritual, from word to idea, to turn upward or move inward, but the materialism that undermines him is little less inexorable than that aspect of words themselves. Similarly the pun does not define words but establishes their power relations while playing with a specious equivalence relation. The clash between separate series of associations when they are brought into contact by linguistic factors mocks the referential function of language itself. From such a situation, as from a pun, a virtual, intrusive meaning rises to the fore while previous meaning is relegated to virtual status. This juxtaposition and reversal make latent patterns manifest, but again only within a general context of imitation or self-love.

It is precisely within such a context that *Orlando Furioso* emerges as the most apt, the most nearly perfect expression of its historical moment. The poem has to stand as its creator's answer to the call for a myth of origins, and the founders of the Estense dynasty, Ruggiero and Bradamante, serve as its link between mythology and history. They straddle a gulf between literary tradition and contemporary politics; they turn a less fabled present into an idealized past; they sum up, as one perceptive reader of *Orlando Furioso* has remarked, the end of an idyll.[25] But the most graceful compliments of the court poet inveigle and persuade to their own questioning: what more than the sameness of sound connects Hercules and Hippolytus to Ercole and Ippolito d'Este?

The Ferrara of Ariosto's time, though a sheltered principality governed by an entrenched line of long-standing rule, found itself undergoing the reality of encroachment by powerful nation-states. Resting on the possession of an acquired and stagnant capital that had to be guarded by limited warfare, Ferrara turned nostalgically to the configurations of literary feudalism for its poetic representation.[26] Itself neither quite a feudal nor a national entity, Ferrara came to be artistically portrayed as a cross between a fairy tale walled city and a pastoral seat of good government, from Boiardo to Tasso's *Aminta*. Beyond doubt it lay closer to the pole of feudalism than to that of the nation-state, and perhaps something of the laxity of late feudal rule penetrates the organization of both of its Orlando epics. But it was partially in order to counter the extensive disruption of his society by invasion and war that Ariosto responded to the demand for the creation of literary selves for the Estensi with hyperbolic excess. The systematic doubling and multiplication are accompanied by a critique whose trenchancy renders *Orlando Furioso* an independently self-consuming text.

It is surprising to a reader perusing the poem as an encomiastic and mythologized history that there is no important father figure anywhere in it. Carlomagno, conventionally the father of his army, reappears in his latter-day disguise as a comic figure; Ruggiero's and Bradamante's parents are mentioned but never emphasized despite the poem's stress on dynastic expectations. It is as if there were no one prince to posit as the focus of praise. Like the absent, invalided Duke Guidubaldo di Montefeltro of Urbino in Castiglione's *Libro del Cortegiano,* the "father" of Ferrara provides no implicit point of comparison for heroism in *Orlando Furioso.* Whatever ambiguous material can be amassed to mask this lack, it subsists in Italian sixteenth-century literature and fairly protrudes from a work that purports to celebrate origins.

Apart from the "endorsement by dignification" of Ruggiero and Bradamante,[27] the multiplication and doubling undercut the possibility of domination by any hero or heroine. This relation could be analogized by a sibling relation beyond the literary boundary: that of a number of brothers and sisters of one family scrambling for pride of place. In their resemblance to one another Ruggiero and Bradamante represent a balanced moment of unified tranquility that justifies the creation of an epic based on their love. But this coupling of lovers depicted as near doubles of each other, or "sibling," also represents a narcissistic act of self-begetting and self-possession. The political directives that could issue from such a union bid the interpreter to regard the political aspect of the union as divinely fated, cutting off any temptation to view the despotism of Ferrara as the domination of some negative or inadequate "father" over his progeny.

Among the conceptual implications of doubling in *Orlando Furioso* is the observation, by Otto Rank, that the brother is one of the most common forms assumed by the figure of the double in the products of human imagination. Rank identifies doubling with narcissism, self-regard, and aggression. According to his examination of pathological doubles, these represent elements of morbid self-love that actually impede the formation of a balanced personality. Rank's studies participate in and further motivate the transposition of the Freudian theory of narcissism to the analysis of societies as wholes. He locates the very origin of doubling in narcissism, and (with specific import for the study of the High Renaissance in Italy) as part of the guilt that the narcissistic ego feels at "the distance between the ego-ideal and the attained reality."[28] According to this view, the ego's superabundant self-love and consequent overestimation of its own worth cause it to construct another near-self or mirror image.

It is through the sibling relation that doubling most frequently takes place in literature. And the case of an individual "unable to free himself from a certain phase of his narcissistically loved ego development"[29] can be fruitfully compared, I believe, with that of a proud, despotically ruled, and externally menaced society such as that of Ariosto's Ferrara. The poet's ruling hand that creates in multiples may move to diminish each and every thing it touches, but his procedure is also an integrative one.

A variant of the Narcissus myth retold by Otto Rank has it that Narcissus became inconsolable after the death of his twin sister, who resembled him in everything, until he viewed his own reflection. Though he knew he was gazing only at his reflected image he still felt a certain assuagement of his grief. "Sometimes he thought he could see his beloved twin in the water, and thereby, however fleetingly, entrap death."[30] The less cheerful and more widely diffused version tells that Narcissus, entranced by his reflection, took his own life and even in the nether world continued to see himself in the Styx.[31] According to either version the narcissism of the culture of Ferrara found its most apt expression in a myth whose content consists in its own process of perpetual motion through a garden of forking paths with provisional repose in mirroring and twinship.

In accordance with the generally rhetorical emphasis of High Renaissance literature in Italy we may therefore search more profitably for the sense of the repetition and doubling that are characteristic of *Orlando Furioso* with its goals rather than its origins in mind. The poem assumes a double duty: that of giving pleasure in its particular social and political environment, or purveying the past to the future, so to speak, without abdicating its responsibility to the Narrator, a man of superior experience. It can do both so long as it adheres to a conception of literature that is transitive rather than static, a string of actions rather than a collection of objects. The doubling and multiplying within and without the confines of the text argue processually that writing consists mainly in the new disposition of elements of an existing, hence stable, body of expression. *Orlando Furioso* emerges as evidence of a moment in which the author was able to keep in tenuous balance the unaccountability of his poem to its screen-texts and its full accountability to historical circumstance.

# Chapter 6

## Ecphrasis and Encomium

The purpose of the final chapter of this study is to demonstrate the importance, in Ariosto's scheme, of writing by means of pictures—not "images," but pictures in the sense of arranged montages that summarize the poem's representative intent and stipulate what its historical import will be. The "writing on the wall" led to our consideration of entwinement and interlace, both as expressed in the structure of *Orlando Furioso* as a whole and in the idea of Arabic writing that Ariosto playfully brings to life. The fifth chapter proceeded from that conclusion to reveal a world of doubling and multiplication that comprises Ariosto's plot structure. Now if we have begun to comprehend these procedures as ways of seeing, it follows that in a fundamental degree *Orlando Furioso* provides a literary analogy to a work of visual art. To examine the means in this case is more clearly to assess the ends. With such an aim in mind it is appropriate at this juncture to inquire into the uses of "artistic" description, or learning as if from art works, in Ariosto's vast poem.

The use of ecphrasis as a means of transcending the boundaries between the arts came into its full promise in the Renaissance. This kind of description was exemplified by the *Imagines* of Philostratus the Elder, who had furnished its definition as a verbal description of art objects and exemplified it by Homer's verbal painting of Achilles' shield.[1] Through imitation of characters, history, psychological effect, and natural scenes, Homer was said to have exceeded the bounds of visual art by creating the illusion of life. The role of ecphrastic verse in evoking visual phenomena is emphasized in the statement of Simonides of Chios, made as early as the fifth or sixth century, that "painting is mute poetry and poetry is a speaking picture."[2] The praiseful context of ecphrasis often applies in secondary degree to the vividness of the painter's work, and ultimately to that of the describing poet himself, thereby constituting a hierarchy of objects to be praised in the poem. Ariosto's bravura assertions of his ordering powers are often delivered with the aid of comparison to works in the plastic arts: at various times he is a painter, a sculptor (III.3–4), and (like any creator of texts) a weaver spinning out a yarn for his many-colored tapestry (II.30.5).

The increasingly secularized and rational world (all that is opposed to Orlando's madness) that emerged from the collapse of feudalism had imposed upon itself a preference for spatial and aesthetic rather than temporal modes of awareness.[3] The value that reposed in verbal evocations of art and paintings in the Renaissance was an offshoot, also, of value placed in imitative skills generally. To be sure, Ferrarese society reflected itself in the pool of eloquence, but did so as gladly in the more transparent one of visual art. It was at least as likely to perceive its image in paintings, statues, and frescoes with a figurative nostalgia that unsurprisingly found its way from visual art into poetry. Visual art occupied a paramount rank among the arts of the Renaissance, and the narrative poetry inspired by pictorial ardor emerged as mirror, portrait, and copy.

A coalescence of Platonism and pragmatism helps to explain the fundamental shift in the purpose and function of the artist in the Renaissance. It is to be compared to the explicitly persuasive function of the poet as Ariosto defines it in his seventh *Satira:*

> Ma tu, del quale il studio e tutto umano
> e son li tuoi soggetti i boschi e i colli,
> il mormorar d'un rio che righi il piano,
>
> cantar antiqui gesti, e render molli
> con prieghi animi duri, e far sovente
> de false lode i principi satolli.
>
> (49–54)

> (But you, whose studies are all 'human,' and whose subjects are woods and hills, the murmur of a stream that outlines a plain— you sing of ancient great deeds, and with prayers soften hard minds, and often satiate princes with false praises.)

Aside from his reference to the murmuring stream, Ariosto is defining the poet as an entity including both the courtier and the painter. Each is set forth in stock terms doubtless intended for easy recognition. A large body of theoretical material and poetic reflection in the fifteenth and sixteenth centuries had identified poetry and painting as sister arts concerned fundamentally with the imitation of concrete things and with actions of more than common status or significance.[4] Poetry could be conceived of figuratively as a kind of painting, each applying its terms to the other, providing that the theorist chose not to reflect too carefully or profoundly upon their manifest differences.

The practice of both painters and poets seemed based upon such prescriptive texts as Alberti's, or later, Lodovico Dolce's treatises on art. Painters could derive inspiration from literary themes for their compositions as poets could try to conjure up before the reader's eye such images as only the visual arts might adequately convey. The need to stress and exploit the mimetic potential of literature underlay the persistence of critical comparisons of poetry and visual art. To destroy the barrier between each art, with its limited modes of signification, and human beings, whose speech and physical presence combine in semiosis appealing to all the senses, is the primary motivation of the desire for a "speaking picture." It is no wonder therefore that longing for such a picture surpasses the appreciation of visual art as mute poetry. "A speaking picture would be almost a person."[5] It would betoken external reality both insofar as it would have the "reality" of its maker and at the same time "signify him, or reality in general."[6]

Indeed, the apocryphal stories that support the speaking-picture figure—such as that of Zeuxis's painted grapes so real that birds try to eat them—are symptomatic of this boundary breaking between art and life. Next to the "speaking picture," the mute poem appears a lesser thing; painting is poetry minus voice. Simonides' statement suggests that a poem has everything to gain by the analogy with painting—all of its own symbolic properties and the seeming "presentness" of a visible medium as well. Painting in its turn, however, acquires not a voice but some ineffable property termed poetic. The main thrust of the interartistic comparison is that poetry requires the supplement of physical presence, whereas painting has presence and is also poetic (that is, aesthetic) without using language.[7]

This kind of interpretation depends upon taking Simonides' metaphors as prescriptive, not descriptive. Leonardo's critique of Simonides summarily reverses the hierarchy implied in his parallel: "If you call painting mute poetry, poetry can also be called blind painting. Now think, which is the more damaging affliction, that of the blind man or that of the mute? . . . If the poet serves the senses by way of the ear, the painter does so by way of the eye, a worthier sense."

Other influential comparisons of painting to literature from antiquity to the Renaissance have always recognized that poetry is like painting because both have as their subjects existent reality and both are limited in their mimetic adequacy to that reality. The shared ground of the arts in the *ut pictura poesis* conception is their assumed iconicity—the argument of mimesis.

Although the traditional answer in Ariosto's time to the question of what constituted innately poetic subject matter generally conformed to Aristotle's maxim that poems should imitate noble human actions, the symbolic nature of literature—which realizes limitations on its efficacy in the realm of direct sensory appeal—was also recognized. The symbol lacks the feeling of "presence"; by contrast with visual art, verbal art achieves whatever likeness or presence it can claim through relational means. The claim that painting and poetry approximate the being of actual things underlay the effort to confer upon language a pictorial vividness of representation. According to the *ut pictura poesis* argument, the function of an art was to evoke images, appealing to the intellect through the senses. The transference from one art to another of symbolic content could result in a profoundly iconographic painting—as in the case of reinterpreted mythological subjects. Or pictorial representations could give rise to certain kinds of poetic description. The contribution of each would begin in the imagination of the recipient—that is, in his capacity to re-form images and draw ethical and intellectual norms from them.

It is with this spurious alliance between the notion of poetry as painting and its status as a means of public edification that the present chapter is concerned. Ariosto's use of description mediated by *reported* art consists of more than just a masterfully disposed (and disputed) array of panegyrical topoi. Nor does he reel off the praise of his benefactors, the Estensi, through the transparent rhetorical device of tapestry, shield, sculptured fountain, or the rest, merely as a bow to the aesthetic influence of similar things at court on his own work. Certainly his use of ecphrasis (εκφρασις, *descriptio*), definable chiefly as the "verbal evocation of art"[8] and of its content as imaged by art, owes much of its importance to traditional means (and ends) as well as to the exhilarating presence of works of art at the Ferrarese court. But we must go beyond such evidence to uncover the effect of the intrinsic and internally motivated alliance between encomium and ecphrasis, or poetry as painting and poetry of praise.

Praise, like any other imaginable topic, involves both "narrative" and "descriptive" language, and both kinds of discourse obviously appear in varying proportion in all texts. The representation of processes (events, actions) constituting narrative "proper" and the representation of static elements (objects, persons) constituting description are inextricably entwined despite the efforts of rhetoricians to separate them. This kind of distinction owes its existence, perhaps, to classical rhetoricians and their descendants down to the Russian formalists and French structuralists who constitute their natural heirs.[9] Two more viable kinds of distinction make it possible, however, to categorize (for descriptive purposes) a narrative discourse, which corresponds temporarily to its object, and a descriptive discourse, which while pressing forward in time refers to matters conceptualized as simultaneous. One distinction is of course that of the temporality of content. The second is more flexible and consists in the delegation of "story time" or narrative duration to a given topic. Whereas the narrative of action can be made to correspond not only in terms of succession but of duration to the succession of recounted events, literary description necessarily changes to a linear direction the simultaneity and immediate juxtaposition of static elements. For the purposes of narrative analysis, theorists such as Shklovskij have distinguished between "dynamic" and "nondynamic" elements in a narrative—those that transform a situation and those that provoke no change in the action. The two categories can be justly compared to the two posited extremes of "narrative" and "descriptive" discourse, the one concerned with movement and the other with stasis.

Descriptive writing is still often linked to painting in words. But obviously even such writing is the expression in sequential terms of what "occurs" instantaneously and simultaneously outside the text. Aristotle's *Poetics* succinctly distinguishes, therefore, between the rhythmical arts (dancing, poetry, music) and the arts of rest (painting and sculpture), saying nothing further about the difference between poetry and painting.[10]

The Renaissance, however, proved docile to the notion still labeled *ut pictura poesis*. Aware of the classical definition of sculpture as a mute poetry, admirers of Ariosto found ways to enlarge the poet's comments on painters of his time into a coupling of the two arts. One of the most striking features of this general effort is the adduction of poetry as a major influence on the lives of painters, for example by Vasari:

> Benche il Cielo desse forma alla pittura nelle linee e la facesse conoscere per poesia muta, non restò egli per tempo alcuno di congiugnere insieme la pittura e la poesia: a ciò che, se l'una stesse muta, l'altra ragionasse, et il pennello con l'artifizio e co' gesti maravigliosi mostrasse quello che gli dettasse la penna e formasse nella pittura le invenzioni che se le convengono.[11]

> (Although God gave form to painting as lineament and made it known as mute poetry, He did not long delay in conjoining painting and poetry: so that if one is mute the other speaks, and the brush with artifice and marvelous gestures shows what the pen dictates to it, and forms in painting the inventions that are proper to it.)

It may well be because of the supposed inspiration that caused the painter to imitate the poet that Ariosto was frequently cited as an example of a poet whose praise could help make the painter's fortune. The two themes of inspiration and of profitable praise are so entwined in Renaissance views on art that the writers scarcely distinguish between them. This Renaissance precedent continued into the seventeenth century. The Venetian biographer Carlo Ridolfi relates the frequent visits of Ariosto to Titian as he painted:

> il quale conferiva con esso lui le composizioni che andava tessendo del divino suo poema, traendo da' suoi ricordi molte degne osservazioni per le descrizzioni de' siti e per le bizzarrie

delle livree e per descrivere le bellezze di Alcina, di Angelica e di Bradamante in quello introdotte, perche la pittura fa l'officio di muta poesia e la poesia di loquace pittura. . . . Potevasi ben dire che fossero accoppiati insieme l'Omero e l'Appelle della moderna età, onde ebbe material quel gran poeta di commendare la virtù di Tiziano, rassignandolo nel suo Furioso tra celebri pittori di quel secolo.[12]

([Ariosto] discussed with him the inventions he was weaving into his divine poem, drawing from his recollections many worthy observations and descriptions of places and the peculiarities of dress, and for describing the beauties of Alcina, Angelica and Bradamante that were to be introduced into it; for painting performs the office of mute poetry and poetry, of speaking painting. . . . It might well have been said that the Homer and the Apelles of the modern age had been paired, so that this great poet had material reasons to commend the virtues of Titian, placing him, within the *Furioso,* among the celebrated painters of that century.)

This writer follows Lodovico Dolce, who had proposed Alcina as the perfect example of feminine beauty, worthy of Titian's brush and of "quanto i buoni poeti siano ancora essi pittori" (how good poets are also painters).[13] In a host of writings *Orlando Furioso* appears as a comprehensive interpretative code of colors, motifs, gestures, emblems, typical postures, and emotional stances. For instance, in Giovanni Paolo Lomazzo's *Trattato dell'arte della pittura, della scoltura e dell'architettura,*[14] "melancolia" (melancholy) could be exemplified by Sacripante at various points in Ariosto's text; "ferocità" (ferocity) by Rodomonte; and "meraviglia" (wonder) by the movement of raised eyebrow and tightened lips described by Ariosto in his evocation of a reader's surprise:

Io vi vo' dir, e far di meraviglia
stringer le labbra e inarcar le ciglia.

( I will tell you things that will make you
tighten your lips and raise your brow [my translation].)

The poetic example comes to this theorist of painting far more easily and often than the example from nature. This is more surprising in the case of the astronomer and physicist Galileo, who in taking up the old dispute on the relative merits of Ariosto and Tasso chooses to liken Tasso's historical certitudes to the work of intarsia in wood and Ariosto's dynamism to painting in oils, for:

> nel colorito a olio, sfumandosi dolcemente i confini, si passa senza crudezza dall'una all'altra tinta, onde la pittura riesce morbida, tonda, con forza e con rilievo. Sfuma e tondeggia l'Ariosto, come quelli che è abbondantissimo di parole, frasi, locuzioni e concetti.[15]

> (in oil painting, gently shading the borders, one passes without crudeness from one tint to another, and the painting emerges soft, round, with clarity and in relief. Thus Ariosto shades and rounds his work, as one abundant in words, phrases, locutions and conceits.)

Galileo joins those writers who find in Ariosto paragons that recommend themselves to the aspiring painter, and for whom *Orlando Furioso* suggests a catalogue of figurative comparisons.[16] According to these theorists both arts concern themselves fundamentally with the imitation of human beings and with actions of more than common significance and should be viewed as sharing some of the same techniques and methods as well as the same fundamentally rhetorical aims: to please and to move. Terms applicable to one kind of work can be readily applied to the other so long as the discourse remains essentially limited to the vague ambience of their projected effect. Although painters indeed normally called their depictions of historical and monumental scenes *istorie*, historians sometimes received praise as painters for their fine descriptive passages.

The gradual reversal of emphasis in evaluating the influence of one art upon the other in the course of the Renaissance would form a fascinating subject of study in itself. According to the civic humanism of the fifteenth century exemplified for painting by Alberti's *Trattato della pittura*,[17] humanists would naturally turn to rhetoric to provide the form and the means of treating the new and still heterogeneous art of painting. Writing as a painter, Alberti produced a book that has been justly characterized as essentially oratorical and specifically Ciceronian in both its form and its conceptual foundation, as well as being imbued with oratorically derived content. Instead of turning to the observation of nature for models of movement and gesture, Alberti turns to Roman oratorical practice and its preoccupation with propriety and effective gesture.

It is also from Cicero[18] that Alberti draws the passage that urges the orator to take his proofs from every available source, selecting the best from each in order to create a more perfect unified whole. He illustrates this concept with the already overworked tale of the painter Zeuxis and the Venus of Croton—later adopted as a matter of course by Castiglione into the context of a *linguistic* syncretism.[19] Both the orator in Cicero and the painter in Alberti are discouraged from slavishly drawing their "inventions" from predecessors in their own art. Alberti counsels the painter of an *istoria* to think the parts out well from the beginning so he will know how each element ought to be executed and where located. In the public work "we will take from our drawings just as we draw maxims and citations from our private commentaries."[20]

These prescriptions delineate an *ars ratio* not far removed from Cicero's advice to the orator, who must choose and organize those parts of his case that will most effectively achieve his aims. With the addition of some ten major points from Quintilian, "the means of Ciceronian rhetoric and Albertian painting . . . are basically the same."[21] "Affective gesture is at the core of Alberti's theory of painting as it is in Cicero's theory of rhetoric."[22] To make the emotive link between observer and painting stronger, Alberti urged the inclusion of a "commentator" who looks out from the painting and sums up its emotive content by his own visible emotion while transmitting this state to the observer.[23] This insistence on gesture and emotive symbolism supersedes the discussions of such technicalities as one-point perspective and color—for more than these, bodily movement reflects and projects emotion and is akin to "rhetorical colors."

In effect Alberti proposed the insertion of a silent "orator" into the frame and among the contents of a picture. Furthermore, his discussion of color constitutes the first writing in art theory to indicate the relationship between colors and the emotions to be elicited from the observer. Alberti derives the discussion chiefly from Cicero, who states that the voice is like a lyre with its tones like colors: for the orator they are aural, expressing the emotions of the soul by means of the body; for the painter they are visual and exploited in the same way.[24]

The Quattrocento Florentine could still subordinate concern with parallelism of painting and oratory to an overarching passion for language, and it is well known that Alberti, drawing from Latin tradition, was equally engaged in the potentialities of the vernacular as a means of literary expression.[25] So wide a gulf stretches between his time and place and that of the Ferrarese poet of the High Renaissance that it may seem useless to allude to them both in the same limited context. But the comparison of these widely divergent humanists serves to elicit the quality of change that produced, in the course of time and in a society oriented to visual art, the advocacy of a "painterly" writing and the assumption that the manifestation and sign of truth are to be found not in reading or hearing but in evident and distinct perception.

It is from this notion of "seeing is believing" that Ariosto derives his comic exordium to canto VII, where he makes the paradoxical distinction between the naïveté of the skeptical reader and the sophistication of the credulous one:

> Che 'l sciocco vulgo non gli vuol dar fede,
> Se non le vede e tocca chiare e piane;
> Per questo io so che l'inesperienza
> Fara al mio canto dar poca credenza.

Poca o molta ch'io ci abbia, non bisogna
Ch'io ponga mente al vulgo sciocco e ignaro;
A voi so ben che non parrà menzogna,
Che 'l lume del discorso avete chiaro.

(VII.1.5–8;2.1–4)

(Rejecting whatsoever is a wonder,
Unless 'tis palpable and plain to view:
Hence inexperience, as I know full well,
Will yield small credence to the tale I tell.

But this be great or small, I know not why
The rabble's silly judgment I should fear,
Convinced *you* will not think the tale a lie,
In whom the light of reason shines so clear.)

The hierarchical reversal of the values of seeing and hearing actually affirms, for nonfools, the primacy of seeing. Since *il lume del discorso* (the light of discourse) has displaced the old scholastic *lume dell'intelletto* (light of intellect or understanding) in Ariosto's flattery of his believers, it is the specific emphasis on speech (contrasted with visual representation) upon which this implicit critique falls. Even the Narrator, who is probably lying, has to base his argument on things he has "seen" (VII.1.1).

The affirmation of seeing, or having seen, things that are necessary to the encomiastic purpose of *Orlando Furioso* is not confined to the Narrator but extends in numerous instances to the various "characters." Such occasions crystallize into the ecphrases of the poem and include "visions" as well as visualized works of art of various kinds: statues, tapestries, frescoes. The continuance of the ecphrastic tradition (from the shield of Achilles onward) must of course be viewed as one of Ariosto's means of reinstating the pagan gods to their ancient splendor. But the narrative function of these described art works (and of living beings described in terms befitting art works) is to document or mark a way of seeing. The language that pertains to artistic description in the narrowest sense is allowed to think for characters, without bringing the manipulation of notions of "nature" and "art" to the surface of consciousness.

It could be argued, of course, that the former hierarchization of oratory over visual art, which had characterized earlier discourse on art itself, always contained a potentially powerful visual element: that is, the concomitants of oratory in gesture and expression could be understood as visual factors enjoying considerable independence from the spoken message they were intended to enhance. But nowhere, even in Alberti's book whose subject is painting, is there any divorce of visual representation from the *istoria,* nor is there any satisfaction afforded those who would believe the visual image a sufficient means of summarizing thought.

Ariosto often approaches the topical division between "nature" and "art" as a linguistic transparency to which he enjoys adding cloudy liquids. For example, the beauty of the Alcina rivals *both* nature and art (X.11), in a bit of play that merely privileges a neutral "poetry." Conversely, the works of art he describes as such often seem to move and breathe in a Utopian concord, once again, of animation and nonanimation. At the palace of Rinaldo's mysterious host the bronze door figures "sembrano spirar, muovere il volto" (seem to breathe, to turn their faces; XLII.74), and in the same ecphrasis one of the fountains captures eight noble ladies in motion as they support a ceiling with one hand and hold an overflowing cornucopia in the other (XLII.79–80). The description strains at the limits of expressive ecphrasis, as if to capture in words an organic entity no less communicative in itself than the one hypothesized in the fiction.

If such digressions, as post-Ariostean *litteraturs* often believed, serve the purpose of relieving the monotony of the *gesta* that comprise the basic material of epic, as well as that of enlisting the dignity of the arts to rebuke vice and praise virtue, the essential anthropomorphic trait of the described images of painting and sculpture still remains *movement, not discourse.* The observer cannot pierce the veil of gesture to the intuited vision underneath as he can in the prototype of such panoramas, Homer's shield of Achilles. There the figures actually speak, transcending the imposed limitations of "graphic" art. The *visibile parlare* of the sculptured reliefs in Dante's *Purgatorio* (X.95) supplements the postures and groupings of figures to speak with an inner voice to the inner man. But the ecphrases of Ariosto follow Virgil's lead in their silence and the stress on their pictorial perfections. Like the painted scenes Aeneas admires at Dido's palace his creations preserve all of the ambiguity accorded to a mute representation.

The fact that logic of discourse among the figures does not explain their behavior gives the representations in Ariosto's poem a particular aptness for the task of courtly flattery. Their ambiguity allows many things to be "read" into them. Since the images—prophecies of the glories of the Estensi, recollections of their fabulous origins, justifications of their past exploits—are constructed as a kind of living mythology, they not only testify in the long run to the wealth, prestige, taste, and learning of the patrons but (as mutely) to a number of mythological analogies that offer to be inferred from them. The patrons are the new gods, celebrated in Ferrarese pictorial art and in the reportage of art.

Seznec describes in his seminal work, *The Survival of the Pagan Gods*,[26] the frescoes of the Ferrarese painter Francesco Cossa at the Palazzo Schifanoia, works painted about 1470. These brilliant paintings of classical scenes eulogize court life. Their execution epitomizes a medievalizing, international protomannerism. A *Triumph of Venus* conforms to

> the prescriptions of medieval mythography. Venus is crowned [as in a medieval manuscript previously discussed] with a wreath of white and red roses. . . . She has not even lost her escort: Amor, her son, . . . is painted on her girdle, and at a little distance appear her attendants, the three Graces, standing on a rocky plateau. . . . These details betray the continuity of the literary tradition; others, still more striking, attest the persistence of influence from the North. At Venus' feet kneels a warrior, attached to her chariot by a chain. Who would

recognize Mars, the terrible, in this gallant knight who, as the code of courtly love prescribes, kneels before his lady, at the mercy of her glance? He might be a Lancelot, or even a Lohengrin.[27]

That "the gods do not appear ill at ease in the midst of this little Italian court"[28] attests to the phenomenon already familiar to earlier centuries, wherein a whole people claimed as ancestor a mythological hero, choosing him for their progenitor and patron. This myth of origin serves to justify princely pretensions while creating a new identity for those newly arrived. Whereas mythological descent is indeed hardly ever absent from the learned writings of the Middle Ages on illustrious rulers, the shifting political circumstances of the Italian principalities and republics confer varied forms upon it. For example, the origins of Florence and Fiesole were celebrated as a pastoral myth by Boccaccio's *Ninfale fiesolano,* but with an unmistakable note of popular speech and in the then popularizing meter of *ottava rima.* The role of the myth in the gradual elaboration of a civic model of communication fulfilled the republican premises according to which this early Utopia was imagined.

On the other hand Ferrarese humanism, which brought the gods to the Estense court, "humanized" their immortality while bestowing inverse benefits upon the courtly patrons. This humanistic school also made its peace with the refeudalization of this part of Italy during the struggle between the Medici and the popes and celebrated the relative safety of Ferrarese despotism.[29] The literary and artistic vogues that encouraged late Gothic and Gallicizing expressive means emerge with renewed vigor from the ambience of Ferrarese political alliance: that between Ercole I and the French king, Charles VIII, against Venice in 1494. But they draw strength from traditional close ties between the Ferrarese and the French going back over centuries, which seemed to give the Ferrarese less to fear from the French than from the Venetians.[30]

Nowhere as in the Ferrarese sphere of influence does the Carolingian cycle of *gesta* constitute so continued a fashion.[31] The Gallic influence was itself symptomatic of the archaic, feudalizing trend that coexisted alongside advances in classical scholarship in Renaissance Ferrara.[32] Caught in tension between a neofeudalistic political structure and the advancing nationalism of surrounding powerful states, Ferrara's arts retreated to the graceful international protomannerism that has been so well characterized, so far as Franco-Flemish culture was concerned, by Huizinga in *The Waning of the Middle Ages*. It hardly requires reiteration, however, that in a line of poems celebrating the "cycle" it is precisely the classical element integrated into Ariosto's critique of his own time that conceptually distinguishes *Orlando Furioso* from any previous enterprise based on similar *matière* and secures for it an Olympian stance vis-à-vis all the others. Anachronism thus becomes another source of fun in the poem and a fact of Ferrarese cultural life that facilitates the reevaluation of feudalistic mores.

The adoption of a cluster of standards such as those of chivalry, viewed through a literature of honor and virtue as well as the more proximate mirror of visual art, is so fascinating a phenomenon precisely because it escapes the confines of localized nostalgia and idyllism. It is not only that, as Huizinga remarked, "every opinion or delusion of an epoch has the status of a fact,"[33] or that a structural relation may have existed between the chivalric ideals of honor and virtue and their expression in war, in politics, and in ceremony. Nor does the interest of this persistent epistemic model consist in its political backing in class tension, namely, that hereditary nobles came increasingly to compete for advancement at court with nonnobles or that knights had to be recycled (in accordance with changing military mores) into courtiers.[34] Ariosto's juxtaposition of incidents of mock-combat with incidents of real warfare, which can be understood as seriocomic reaction to the anachronism of single combat in an age of artillery and handguns, addresses larger issues regarding "honor" and "fame" as much as the fluctuating circumstances of sixteenth-century warfare.[35]

Chivalry has nearly always been deemed decadent. In the twelfth century it had already seemed contaminated by adulterous courtly love, and a number of lyric poets (composing already in forms reduced from epic) inveighed against its demise. Dante's lines lamenting the knights and ladies of the past find new life, as is well known, in Ariosto's exordium, "Le donne, i cavallier, l'arme, gli amori." By the time our poem opens chivalric decay is a topic to itself, canonized in a number of nostalgic literary references. Indeed, it may be taken in its whole as an influential example of infinite regression toward a Golden Age.[36] Its triumph is impossible to situate in any historical moment. The discrepancy between its exalted aspirations and the aristocratic frivolity or gross carnality of knighthood applies to all the centuries of its existence. In turn, chivalry is sufficiently hospitable to the contrasts of *ira* and *concupiscentia,* love and duty, arms and letters, to constitute a convenient measuring device for any dualistic situation, however removed in time.

Of the rhetorical categories that pertain to the topic of chivalry, the category termed *epideictic* is most appropriate. The praise of the past finds in chivalry the topics and formal appeal that are required for an effective restatement of the myth of origins. On this pivot of chivalry, the ecphrases of *Orlando Furioso* effectuate an implicit domestication and rapprochement of gods and men.

It is well known that *Orlando Furioso* juxtaposes conflicting attitudes toward Ariosto's patrons. The ambivalence between protectiveness and destructiveness of the Estense reputation is revealed in nearly every reference to them as well as to the couple Ruggiero and Bradamante. He purchases his liberties at the price of personal restraint and litotic tropes, often drawing attention away from the person praised and toward the act of praise itself so that its form usurps its content. The brilliant tableaux to which public interest is diverted offer a view of history that will not impinge acutely on the reader's moral life. Meanwhile this ambivalent context actually permits Ariosto to establish a historical frame for his work, seeming to give it a base outside fiction. The celebratory pseudoprophecies may be mostly magic, painted under the supervision of Merlin—but they are interlaced with allusions to recent or contemporary history, or directives of Ferrarese politics. Ariosto's denigration of firearms and mass warfare, or his admiring evocation and justification of Ferrara's French policy, thus finds its place on a spectrum from fact to fiction.

In accordance with the prevalent drift of Renaissance epic to historicize its heroes, Ariosto addresses himself to the "group" sense of history. He adds Merlin's prophecies of the Estense future not to foresee change but to reaffirm continuity, choosing for this message a time-honored means. Indeed, from the medieval *Vita Merlini* by Geoffrey of Monmouth there extended a literature of political prophecy based on privileged seeing.[37] In the midst of an iridescent canvas (*tela*) of entwined fact and falsehood, the sculptured reliefs on the fountains of Merlin clearly differentiate themselves from the shifting illusions offered to the delectation of the credulous.

Especially in the final edition of 1532 we find a panoramic treatment of the sequence of French invasions of Italy, for instance, as depicted on the walls of the Rocca di Tristano (XXXIII.1–58). Ariosto continues as before to attribute the major portion of Italy's troubles to the French alliance. What counts in the praiseful assessment of Alfonso and Ippolito d'Este is their successful preservation of Ferrara, partly by means of this alliance. In the Rocca di Tristano section the battle of Ravenna (1512) recurs thematically for the triumph as well as the suffering caused by the sack of Ravenna. But this dispassionate judgment does not leap from the page; it has to be sought out and deduced.

The function of eulogizing princes was the basis of the economic situation of the Renaissance artist. Analogously Orlando's fame could be won only with the aid of Ruggiero. This fact is clearer in the light of comparison to the last great work on chivalry. Don Quixote was to succeed Orlando, and eclipse him, as a figure catalyzing and embodying a critical, illusionistic art. And like Ariosto, Cervantes advances a devastating critique of books and bookish culture. But Don Quixote acquires his immortality exclusively at the hands of Cervantes, through the speech of the pseudochronicler's pen, the most discreet and the most powerful self-glorification of the artist. In the deliverance from encomiastic necessity lay the unity behind the perspectivism that is attributed to Cervantes (but is ultimately more true of Ariosto), a unity by which the illusion and disenchantment of Don Quixote are finally separated. But the subtle, antagonistic parallelism subtending the double progress of Orlando and Ruggiero follows these characters even into the final reaches of Ariosto's poem. If Boiardo's tale of Ruggiero and Bradamante had been intended to counteract the story propounded by humanists hostile to the Estensi, that they descended from Gano di Maganza (the Ganelon who betrayed Roland to the Saracens), in the *Innamorato* and the *Furioso* they are imbued with virtue (at least in potentia).

The descent of Ruggiero from Hector of Troy (III.17), as well as the "medieval" intermediary, "Buovo d'Antona" (XXVI.72), is affirmed. Melissa's harangue to Ruggiero (VII.56–64), which contains a restatement of praise for Ippolito and Alfonso d'Este, is surprisingly suffused with a courtly Platonism:

> Deh non vietar che le più nobil alme
> Che sian formate ne l'eterne idee,
> Di tempo in tempo abbian corporee salme
> Dal ceppo che radice in te aver dee.
>
> (VII.61.1–4)

> (Forbid not of the noblest souls the birth,
> Formed in the ideas of the ETERNAL MIND,
> Destined, from age to age, to visit earth,
> Sprung from thy stock, and clothed in corporal rind.)

The "eternal ideas" refer to neo-Platonism intimately bound with courtship in the form of praise.

On the Moon, it is true, Astolfo sees services rendered in courts appear as a heap of broken bottles (XXXIV.79). The other detritus includes verses composed in the praise of lords, in the image of cicadas who have burst themselves with song (XXIV.77). These lie near the heaps of gold and silver formerly offered to the same princes in the hope of reciprocal favors. They emblematize a contractual relation gone awry: for classical culture had upheld the notion of lordly "benefices" rewarded by the gratitude of their subjects. The benefice was understood as a gift determined by a rational and just choice. In *De beneficiis*[38] Seneca presupposes a corresponding gratitude and goes on to state that such gratitude should extend to any giver of benefice. Subjects, too, could render services.[39] The measure of a favor was not in its intrinsic value but in the potential ability of the giver.[40]

It is in this kind of context that Ariosto presents the gift of his poem to Cardinal Ippolito as an act of gratitude, recapitulating the motifs of classical humanistic tradition. As Cicero had said, some kinds of gifts are offered through services, according to obligation (*ministerium*); others are given as that which the giver is fully free to dispose of as he wishes. For Ariosto the poem would not identify him in the *ministerium* (from which the word *minstrel* happens to be derived) of a courtier but constitutes a material over which he has free control:

> Quel ch'io vi debbo, posso di parole
> pagare in parte e d'opra d'inchiostro.
>
> (I.3.5–6)

> (Then, with no jealous eye my offering scan.
> My pen and page may pay the debt in part.)

The poem is all the "umil servo" has to give, Ariosto declares, but conversely only the same humble servant is capable of giving it. The ambiguity of Ariosto's expressive syntax derives ultimately from his awareness of the deep division between the standard by which he measures his own poetry and the one his powerful addressee will probably employ. This ambiguity characterizes in turn the relation of giver and recipient outlined in the exordium: the great lord may not even condescend to interest himself in these verses!

Doubtless the promise to achieve high praise of the Estensi is to enhance the value of the gift. It will also raise the poem to the status of a historic epic in the wake of the *Aeneid*. For the corollary to the image of the poet as the custodian of fame is the idea that the truest poetry is the poetry of praise.[41] Since the grammarian Donatus had formulated in the fourth century a theory of praise that inserted the *Aeneid* into the genre of epideictic,[42] it was often concluded that the *Aeneid* had indeed been written according to the prescriptions of the encomium. Subsequently Petrarch traced poetry to the praise of the gods.[43] In turn, the encomium was supposed to inculcate virtue and implicitly castigate vice. At the core of epic tradition reposed an idea of Aeneas's journey that was conceived of as an internal voyage (of self-discovery and learning). His adventures figured the stages of his moral growth. The aspect of *Orlando Furioso* that deceptively encourages a comparative reading of Ruggiero also represents a critique not only of this allegorizing tradition[44] but of the encomiastic framework that embraces it. Ariosto's well-known subversion of Ruggiero's *Bildungsroman* of progress and conquest emerges ultimately from a dehierarchization of a formerly prevalent relation of fiction and fact. By the sheer force of juxtaposition presumed fact can be "removed to an overtly imaginary stage."[45]

Ariosto has justly been evaluated as outside the trend of "great claims" made for human self-formability.[46] The resulting ambiguity in the encomium of the Estense founder (and his descendants) increases through the very surfeit of hyperbolic cliché. Ariosto overmythicizes his princely patrons, thereby effecting a corresponding demystification. His means vary from juxtaposing ascending and descending symbolism to deforming the classical gods and sequences for satirical purposes, to equalizing fact and fantasy on a single narrative plane, to shading the sequential progression from "absolute invention to objective reality" so that each level is affected by the slippage of ontological value attached to the others. The effect serves to "derealize history" so that the obstacles to the marriage of Ruggiero and Bradamante—their different faiths, their duties in the war, his conflicts of chivalric loyalty, his infatuations with other women, the jealousies of Marfisa and Bradamante—not only end in the paradox of Ruggiero's having to duel Leone, who saved his life, and abjure his intended but appear no less urgent than the obstacles confronting Alfonso d'Este's French policy on the encroachment of barbarians in Italy. The parting eulogy of Zerbino's lover, Isabella, blends with the repeated praise of Isabella d'Este (XXIV; XXVIII) but especially where it is God who speaks:

> Per l'avvenir, co che ciascuna ch'aggia
> Il nome tuo, si' di sublime ingegno,
> E sia bella, gentil, cortese e saggia,
> E di vera onestade arrivi al segno:
> Onde materia agli scrittori caggia
> Di celebrare el nome inclito e degno;
> Tal che Parnasso, Pindo et Elicone
> Sempre Issabella, Issabella risuone.
>
> (XXIX.29)

> (I will that all, in every future age,
> Who bear thy name, be blest with genius high;
> Be courteous, gentle, beautiful, and sage,
> And to the real pitch of honour fly.
> That to their glory the historic page
> They may with worthy argument supply;
> So that for aye Parnassus' hill and well
> Shall ring with Isabel and Isabel.)

The contractual reciprocity established by encomium between the poet and the princely reader did not sustain itself in Ariosto's case. Ippolito d'Este never rewarded him in the here-and-now world of courtly functionaries. But the effort to legitimize the poem as an independent creation continues to operate, rising even to the Empyrean (XXXIV–XXXV).

Accordingly, whereas the concrete referent—the hero or battle or lady—ultimately bears only a verbally denoted relation to the poem, the latter obtains its "historical" and mythographic validation by skillfully utilizing the topoi of praise.

Given that chivalry contains an essentially regressive ingredient one might well ask how Ariosto's practice of poetic homage could possibly enhance the historical or future-oriented aspect of his poem. It would not be sufficient to answer that Ariosto's complicated praise-mockery of the first Estensi does so in itself, because of the studied critique the reader may gather from the mass of allusion and contemporary reference. A partial answer would be that he brings the epic hero down to earth as a being with capacities for error and doubt—no longer a paragon and therefore subject to alteration in time. Another partial explanation would assert that Ariosto patently attempts to assimilate and incorporate the lessons of recent history. His complex effects often depend on the reader's taking stock of the difference between some reconstructed fiction in the plot—such as the role of the Harpies in Astolfo's sojourn in Ethiopia—and the same phenomenon in the surrounding world, including previous fictions. His country's "Harpies" (XXXIV.1) are real and deeply rooted, and the symbolic use Ariosto makes of them makes present a personified, beleaguered Italy that nevertheless finds its metaphorical way into the celebrative orbit. At the same time, of course, Astolfo's persecution of Senapò's Harpies is treated as a historical event.

The act of equalizing fiction with history and reducing history to fiction, which obtains throughout the poem by means of interweaving and comparison, can be said to favor the perpetuation of history even as it questions the singleness of any one interpretation. Not only the occasional justification of Estense foreign policy or the accentuation of encomiastic intent (as in the crescendo of canti following St. John's problematic exposé) but the encompassing goal of fashioning his patrons into an artifact furthers their anticipated immortality. When Perseus boasted that in turning Phineus to stone he would make of him "monimenta per aevum" (a perpetual monument),[47] it is the same claim that Ovid makes for his whole poem at its end:[48] the preservation beyond life for eternity. If such a promise is first a tribute to his own art, its fulfillment endows the object with the superhuman permanence that belongs to stone. History thus moves from the fluidity of life to the hard purity of art.

*Orlando Furioso* includes within its inventory of subordinate genres the wedding poem, analogous to the nuptial aspect of the *Aeneid*. However momentous an event the celebrated marriage might be, epithalamia permit or even encourage mockery within the general context of gaiety. Not all is praise and elevation: readers have long noted the ability of Sappho, in her wedding poems, to change from a singing to a prosaic style in lines mocking the bridegroom as well as the various doorkeepers of the wedding chamber.[49] Although the epithalamium obviously adapted itself to numerous purposes of panegyric, Ariosto engages it in a far wider sphere of literary action. It becomes part of a principle of courtship that he implements in order to keep alive the topos of reciprocity and to transcend his estrangement from the society of the Cardinal.

It would be easy to read *Orlando Furioso* as a courtly masque.[50] Each of the character-functions could pass to some member of a court, taken in its essence. If we briefly pillage the most basic work on the Renaissance court, Castiglione's *Book of the Courtier*, we find in the unreasoning ferocity of Rodomonte or Sacripante (personified by Gasparo Pallavicino) the absurd superpoet of Petrarchistic love (the "Unico" Aretino) who evokes the mannerisms of Orlando's longing for Angelica; the loyal, graceful nature of Zerbino or the rationalized bravery of Rinaldo (Ludovico Canossa); and the caprices and joking of Astolfo (Bernardo da Bibbiena). Beyond these superficial outlines of types, the analogies between the two works penetrate as far as Medoro's winning of Angelica. Castiglione's first book suggests a useful device for a courtier wearing a mask that may distinguish him from the mass in the memory of his lord: Let him disguise himself as someone of inferior rank, such as an uncouth shepherd. Then if he performs superbly on horseback the show will be doubly effective, since the horseman so greatly outstrips the expectations of the onlooker. Medoro is a shepherd, no courtier: but the semiotic properties of this character obviously include the "noble shepherd." By expressions of finesse and chivalric probity such as his insistence on burying his dead king, Dardanello, Medoro shows his adherence to the knightly class, at least in spirit.

The comparison of motives between Castiglione and Ariosto is revealed most of all in the links forged by each author between the work of praise and that of an expressly Platonistic courtship. Each is imbued with Bembo's particular brand of Ficinian Platonism as exemplified in his dialogues, the *Asolani* (1505), which hierarchize the three natures of love. There is a love full of torment, another mixed with joy and pain, and finally a third that liberates the senses and is raised to the vision of God. These loves aid in Ariosto's depiction of a panoply of amorous attitudes either wrathful or rational, the first chiefly characterized by the pair Orlando-Angelica, the second by the Ruggiero-Bradamante pair. Angelica and Medoro attain the midpoint between these loves. Even if the Medoro-Angelica coupling is to be taken at face value as that of a princess and a rustic, this aspect nevertheless accommodates both a courtly ethic and the mythological precedent of Venus and the satyr. On a Correggio canvas commissioned for Isabella d'Este for her Studiolo, Venus sports with a satyr in a representation of animal love whose monitory quotient would exist only in the eye of the beholder. Other subjects for the companions to this painting lend themselves easily to encomium: Andrea Mantegna's "Minerva Triumphing over Venus" (Logistilla over Alcina?), Perugino's "The Conflict of Love and Chastity," Costa's allegories of virtues and vices. The variety of loves constitutes a particularly apt corollary for the poetry of praise, each an ascending hierarchy of value.

The system of courtship easily embraces the aspirations of a Platonizing education. Relations between patron and courtier take on the lineaments of those between the ephebe and his admiring teacher. In Castiglione's fourth book it is stated that the goal of a courtier is to become the educator of his prince. This aim can be achieved only through winning the game of courtship and doing so less in order to triumph obviously over opponents than to display a "winning" degree of individual excellence.[51] The situation that ultimately encourages a state of anarchical individualism disguises itself in a cloak of stylistic magic, masking the reverence directed to those at the pinnacle. Broadly conceived, the Ladder of Love reproduces the stages of courtship. Together they attest to a *forma mentis* that not only governs but validates the next "move." At the lowest mimetic degree much Renaissance Platonizing camouflages the practical need to show striving and reverence. The Ladder may also serve as a diagram for a system of rigid social classifications.

Ariosto effortlessly intertwines the topoi of chivalry with the hereditary rights of rulers. When Ruggiero comes to sword blows with Mandricardo because the latter has been sporting the Trojan eagle insignia that has belonged to Ruggiero's line since antiquity, Mandricardo offers the rival claim that he has conquered by right of arms the shield with its eagle together with all of the fabled weapons of Hector of Troy. Mandricardo defends himself with reference to this pre-Ariosto incident.[52] But Ruggiero's right to the eagle is truly hereditary: "Tu te l'usurpi, io 'l porto giustamente" (You usurp it; I wear it justly; XXVI.104.8). As if to underline this argument, Mandricardo is also carrying Orlando's "usurped" sword, and Ruggiero upon seeing it is seized with indignation. There is no telling how the duel would have ended if Ariosto had not made the claims of general warfare interrupt it. The two "Saracens" declare a provisional truce in the interests of their common work for Agramante, just as two courtiers in Castiglione's book would indefinitely defer arguments whose violent solution is forbidden in a system of courtship.

A recent critic of Estense Ferrara has alleged that it is due to the suppression of its bourgeois elements and their conversion into components of aristocratic life that the category "borghesi-cortigiani" (bourgeois-courtiers) more than any other class expresses "incertezze, contraddizioni, incapacità di vedere gli elementi essenziali della vita altro che come elementi generici" (uncertainties, contradictions, incapacity to see the essential elements of life as other than generic).[53] He postulates a camouflage or mystification of the social structure and relations in the Ferrarese despotism that involve a conspiracy of the arts in an idyllic moment of evasion, "cullandosi nell'armonia di musiche e di colori i rapporti umani si svigoriscono in sensazioni estetizzanti a cui sono subordinati e subalterni i rapporti sociali" (lulling oneself with musical harmonies and colors, human relations weaken into aestheticizing sensations, to which social relationships become subordinate and subservient). The "vague elements" could include the realities of turbulent political chronicle translated into the nobility, antiquity, and legitimacy of the Estense dynasty, particularly insofar as all these elements are associated with Ippolito, a single, synecdochic representative.[54] The link with the present invites many kinds of connection between the generic model and the presentness of contemporary cultural and artistic concerns. Although Ferrara still bore a closer resemblance to a feudal organization than to a contemporary nation-state, it found its own way to emphasize a Franco-Italian rather than a Latinate culture, but this ambience accommodated a qualified neo-Platonism that dwelt by definition on the vague or general.

The paradox revealed by the comparison of what poetry and painting are capable of "stating" helps to explain how painting (or sculpture) can be understood as more vague or general than writing. If Renaissance civilization "[ha] mirato sopratutto all'esperienza figurativa"(has aimed above all at figurative experiment)[55] this desire for concrete representation invited its own reproduction in linguistic terms. Ecphrasis is the reproduction, or imitation, of that wish. We might go further: on this trajectory of desire are to be found those writers who insist upon the relations between Ariosto's poetry and the figurative arts of his time.[56] It tempted many a writer to dwell on Ariosto's passage of "painterly" language, such as his description of Alcina. Even the poet seems to declare his rivalry with the painters:

Di persona era tanto ben formata
quanto me' finger san pittori industri.

(VII.11.1–2)

(Her shape is of such perfect symmetry,
As best to feign the industrious painter knows.)

The generic imagery seems to evoke the colors. Nouns assume adjectival duties, as in *neve, avorio, rose, giglio* (snow, ivory, roses, lilies) used as modifiers. So strong is the dream of a total representation that it is appropriately allied with the Renaissance concomitant, the striving for the perfect work of praise.

Ecphrasis normally depicts its object (of painting, sculpture, or other visual art) with admiration and praise. In fact Hermogenes expressly says that many people do not distinguish ecphrasis as a separate exercise because its true place is in close connection with a fable, a narration, a commonplace, or an encomium.[57] Accordingly, the crescendo of the Ruggiero and Bradamante (Estense) story in the second half of Ariosto's poem is accompanied by a considerable increase in the number of ecphrastic passages.[58] From the beginning to the center of the poem we find a total of only four passages of extended description. Two of these deal with artifacts (Merlin's tomb, III, and Alcina's realm, VI), and two with persons (Alcina herself, VII, and Olimpia, XI.65–75). But Orlando's mad scene sums up the nonencomiastic aspects of the poem. Its second half becomes increasingly devoted to the dynastic and political theme. The hyperbolic increase in the frequency of ecphrastic passages seems to prompt internally San Giovanni Evangelista's long speech that reviews the entanglement of poetry and history.

What is new in that speech is precisely the saint's reversal of the canonical hierarchy obtaining between those two subjects in poetry. Whereas history traditionally dominated poetry in the alliance that made poetry a branch of history, San Giovanni subsumes both under the rubric of poetry, or fiction. In this rehierarchized scheme even the angels become like courtiers, whose business it is to make poetry out of raw matter, or the contrary: the Arcangelo Michele sowing Discord among the pagans hastens to correct a tactical error that has produced chaos in the Christian camp instead:

> Come servo fedel, che più d'amore
> Che di memoria abondi, e che s'avveggia
> Aver messo in oblio cosa ch'a core
> Quanto la vita e l'anima aver deggia,
> Studia con fretta d'emendar l'errore,
> Ne vuol che prima el suo signor lo veggia;
> Così l'Angelo a Dio salir non volse,
> Se da l'obbligo prima non si sciolse.
>
> (XXVII.36)

> (As servant faithful to his lord, and more
> In love than memory strong, who finds that he
> Has that forgotten which at his heart-core,
> As precious as his life and soul should be,
> Hastes to repair his error, nor before
> He mend that fault, again his lord will see,
> So not to God St. Michael will ascend
> Until he has achieved his holy end.)

The Archangel's efforts are directed chiefly to making his changes unobtrusively and out of the sight of God! A useful way of reading this stanza is in the light of Castiglione's book, which dictates that graceless actions should be committed only in secret.

From the Fountain of Merlin (XXVI.29–53) and the encomium of "Isabella" in both guises of fictional character and Estense duchess in XXIX.28 and 29 the text proceeds to a proliferation of encomiastic passages. These emerge from cantos XXXII through XXXIII (the Rocca di Tristano), XXXV (the allegory of the swans), XXVI (spoken by Ruggiero himself about his origins), XXXVII.5 through 24 (on the Ladies), XLI.63 through 67 (spoken to Ruggiero by a knowledgeable hermit, about his descendants), XLII (the Host's palace with a stone fountain composed of figures of great ladies and their poets), and XLVI (Melissa's tapestry).

Merlin's Fountain displays verbal inscription as part of its sculptures. Each female figure of gold and white is supported on the shoulders of two carvings of stalwart males who open their mouths to speak the words of praise spelled out in *scritture* (writings). Two of the laudatory poems are reproduced in full. The first, for Diana d'Este, admonishes the onlooker to overlook Diana's haughty pose:

> Non guardar (dice il marmo scritto) ch'ella
> Sia altera in vista; che nel core umana
> Non sarà però men ch'in viso bella.
>
> (XLII.90.2–4)

> (Regard not [said the marble] if she wear
> A haughty port; for in her heart, humane
> The matron is, as in her visage, fair.)

But the verse is visually broken by the incision of narrative discourse. It reads "Don't look," as if speaking of the goddess and a spying Acteon. The second "inscribed" verse by Ariosto is interrupted in the same way. It is about an unknown lady who may be taken to represent Alessandra Benucci Strozzi, Ariosto's own beloved. The verse reads:

> Chi vorrà di costei (dicea l'inciso)
> Marmo parlar, quanto parlar n'accade,
> Ben torrà impresa piu d'ogn'altra degna;
> Ma non però ch'a fin mai se ne vegna.
>
> (XLII.94.5–8)

> (He that would speak—would speak her praises true—
> [Declares in fine the sculptured marble's lore]
> The fairest of emprizes would intend,
> But never bring his noble task to end.)

Here the actual term *inciso* (which also means "interruption" and is itself broken by enjambment) helps to break the line just before the word *parlar*. The two laudatory poems, then, refer to "looking" and "speaking" in marked places: each condenses a set of terms for one of the two aspects of ecphrasis, which may be defined as "speaking about seeing." Each also instantiates the interplay of visual and verbal cues that analogize those in the artwork described.

It is just such a clue that leads us to the usefulness of this mediated account of seeing to the encomiastic poet. This passage deals with the interaction between word and visual image in elliptical ways so that the verbal "image" of the lady can remain vague while the inscriptions point toward the absent "core umano" in one case, and in the second case toward the impossible challenge of portraying the lady's spiritual reality. The subject as deity, mythological figure, or personal acquaintance stands outside the flux of history, unencumbered by any concrete detail that would limit her to some vocation or background. Communication is represented as a mystery to which only the initiate is admitted. The verbally represented work of art interposes another level of enigma between subject and reader. It implies that nature recognizes the lady herself as a realization of an otherwise disembodied idea.[59]

It is no accident that both Merlin's tomb near the beginning of the poem and Melissa's great tapestry that is to adorn the nutpial bed in the last canto present scenes that can only be viewed by the initiate—in both cases, Bradamante. These two "prophetic" works of art endowed with prophetic powers promise insight into the unknown (the full destiny of the Estensi). Of course as these insights are narrated indirectly to the readers they lose their occult properties, but it is important that within the rest of the poem the designs are so hermetic that only those addressed can understand the image:

> Sol Bradamante da Melissa instrutta
> Gode tra sè; che sa l'istoria tutta.
>
> (XLVI.98.7–8)

> (But Bradamant, to whom the whole was known,
> By wise Melissa taught, rejoiced alone.)

The human, social, and political corollary of such mystical camouflage is the rhetorical imperative of marking the subject of encomium as uniquely initiated and thus uniquely worthy of receiving the work of art. Under the circumstances it is not surprising that Ariosto devotes much descriptive acumen to the work of art as a received event in which various persons delight while making it clear that the general reader will not enjoy a mystical insight comparable to that presumably enjoyed by a character. It is a communion from which miscellaneous readers are perpetually excluded. By singling out Bradamante the poet converts the need to honor the first Estensi into a means of excluding from the innermost circle even their own descendants, together with the rest of his public. Like all devices that tend toward extended allegory, ecphrasis may serve as the means of its own unmasking.

The same double-face applies to various secondary features of ecphrasis, for example the topos of the great age of the described works of art. The identifications of artists or poets with archeologists dates at least as far back as Petrarch,[60] and the Narrator assumes it partially for himself. He takes for granted the poet's function of preserving the fame of painters. (We have seen how sympathetically Ariosto was understood by painters and writers on painting.)

The suggestion of movement that the artist elicits from inert matter often constitutes another secondary trait of art works described in literature. Details of endless movement or gesture produce an effect of permanence. The fusion of a chiefly descriptive language with its accompanying narrative content superimposes upon the notion of movement a predominance of attitude and posturing, "a series of poses which are a poetic equivalent to arrested motion."[61] Where the mimesis strives to assert itself as the reality of that which it is only supposed to imitate it can temporarily deny the whole external narrative process. This momentary substitution exceeds the simple function of prolonging anticipation and the reader's desire, like any other retarding "device." It is a separate pastoral element within the already idyllic context of encomium. The descriptions beamed through the characters who experience the vision directly resemble the dreams of a wakeful Narrator.

This oneiric aspect may account for the persistence in ecphrastic poems of the connection between the ecphrasis and an ethically superior realm suggested by the description. In Poliziano's unfinished *Stanze per la giostra di Giuliano de' Medici* (Stanzas for the Tournament of Giuliano de' Medici), the basic movement of the hero, Iulio, from a bestial to a supremely "human" condition takes place as he is guided from the meeting with a beautiful woman, Simonetta, in the first section of the poem to edification in the palace of Venus.[62] But Simonetta actually represents the earthly Venus and thereby foreshadows the celestial Venus who subsumes the other in Poliziano's scheme. Although the corporal Venus is realizable in the world, her celestial counterpart is imaged only on the *intagli,* or bas-reliefs, of the palace. The beauty of Simonetta is the lure and goad that at once prepares Iulio and prompts him to seek the beauty of the goddess, the "real" or divine goal of human desire. In this way the verbally represented creation emerges as the more concrete and the paradox of ecphrasis actually emphasizes the goddess's remoteness from the world and her membership in the realm of ideas. Independent of these stipulations is the "naturalness" of the pictured representations themselves.

The psychology of pictorial representation in the Renaissance promoted the venerable claim that art aspires to the ever more faithful rendering of nature, or more accurately, what the art historian Ernst Gombrich terms "recognizable images."[63] The assumption of mimesis as the single most important attribute of a work of art conditions the evaluation of its expressive qualities.[64] Since ecphrasis is concerned with communicating what the painting itself expresses, it draws into itself whatever expressiveness the figures in the painting may be alleged to possess.[65] In the course of the Cinquecento the psychologically based narrative that could be drawn from descriptions of painting came gradually to exceed in significance the presence of naturalistic detail as reported from the visual "model." Numerous painters were thought to have benefited directly from the influence of Ariosto's poetic "painting." The type of sign to which paintings belong, however, is to be understood as distinct from the discursive element of language. Whereas language, as a "passkey" system,[66] encompasses all other types of sign, the necessarily restricted field of visual art (even as reported in language) can be represented only by a certain linguistic means.

Description breaks the pattern of narrative by placing the describing subject, the Narrator, in a position of inaction. Often this includes watching something or someone. That is perhaps one of the reasons why Ariosto's Narrator appropriates ecphrases nearly all to himself directly. A prolonged moment of self-consciousness of a character would interrupt the crossing and intercrossing of follies. By producing coherent descriptions of himself, or of a narrated event, or of a painting, the Narrator clears himself of folly. The fact that several of the ecphrases are presented as visions experienced in magical or trancelike circumstances underscores the disjunction between the self-conscious descriptive language and the narrated, oblivious characters. That disjunction, in turn, facilitates the frequent reflections on contemporary political, military, and artistic reality embedded in the descriptions by the clear-sighted Narrator (who is not limited to the single moment of viewing).

That the Narrator must plunge on afterward with the next event in his sequence makes it clear that he can at best share only vicariously in the mindless pleasure occasioned by the viewing of the painting or sculpture or tapestry. The descriptions lack independently constituted narrative meaning although they are often presented in the guise of instruction to characters who require it. They purposely *delay* the production of meaning and in that function are to be grouped with Ariosto's other numerous retarding devices. Seeing and reading are of course two distinct operations, but in the end whatever is seen can only be communicated in "readable" terms. The ecphrases that prophesy the Estense future articulate their message to Bradamante by automatically summoning up the human presence of her ancestors and descendants and by suggesting the narratives in which they could subsequently be involved.[67] For her to understand their import is to organize the painted and shaped elements into narrative structures.

The sort of pleasure the viewing subject derives from the contemplative enjoyment of representation is influenced by the impossibility in visual art of actually recounting a progressive action. This constraint upon art is at once the main source of its idyllism. The pleasure is all taken in the mimesis of events at a safe remove. It would have been possible to manipulate temporality without speaking of paintings and statues. Indeed, some of the ecphrases merely catalogue illustrious forebears of the Estensi:

> Vedete un altro Carlo, che a conforti
> Del buon Pastor fuoco in Italia ha messo;
> E in due fiere battaglie ha duo Re morti.
>
> (XXXIII.20.1–3)

> (You see, her goodly pastor to sustain,
> Another Charles set fire to Italy;
> Who has two kings in two fierce battles slain.)

The passage from the description of the "Rocca di Tristano" alludes to Charles d'Anjou, whose killing of the two German kings, Manfred, then Conrad, gained him the reign of Naples. The actual cruelty of this is epitomized in Dante's *Purgatorio*, where Manfred recounts it (III.112–45). In *Orlando Furioso* the moment appears as one of a very long chain of consequentially narrated military events led by the French in Italy. It might have been embedded in a contemplative passage comparing these exploits with other deeds in arms. It might have been recounted from the memory of a character imagined in the future. But Ariosto chose to reinforce this manipulation of historical time by making the narrative highlight Bradamante's pleased *reception* of the whole. The retention of that pleasurable (narrated) reality is experienced by the reader in secondary degree. That same reality might otherwise have turned painful or simply nonpleasurable had it been inserted into yet another turbulent series of events. The moments frozen into art constitute a pastoral element of art, a release (although they provide concrete instruction for Bradamante) from the continuing sequence without. To the noble patron the entire panoply of French enterprises in Italy, in which pictorial fascination blends with chivalrous admiration, subtly justifies the Ferrarese policy of alliance with the French over and above any implicit accusation.

To those Quattrocento theorists of art who, artists themselves, were occupied with proving the moral worth of painting, ecphrasis could be important even in cases that included the loss or deprivation of the original visual work. For Alberti Lucian's description of the "Calumny" of Apelles was valuable even without the painting.[68] Leonardo used it to show that painting could have a moral tone analogous to the moral of a poet's fiction. Some endorsements of the power of ecphrasis recognize it, however, as a substitute for visual art containing a discursive power forever denied to such art though lacking its communicative immediacy. It was accordingly a central concern of Renaissance art theory from Alberti onward that emotion could only be expressed by and through action. The ability of art to record gesture was an important factor, therefore, in the crucial change of emphasis from the fifteenth to the sixteenth century that consisted in the supersession of action by expression.[69]

Alberti discusses ecphrasis in the context of his characterization of the *istoria*: "The *istoria* will move the soul of the beholder when each man painted there clearly shows the movement of his own soul."[70] These movements of the soul "si conoscono dai movimenti del corpo" (are known from the movements of the body).[71] Leonardo continues this line of thought when he connects expression in painting with rhetorical expression. He recommends that a man represented speaking be depicted according to the subject of his speech.[72] These statements apparently rely on the predominant need of the painter to engage his representation in verisimilar action that will "speak for itself." Technical accomplishment in depicting nature demands a concentration on the *actions* that are to be expressive, even those of "nature" alone. For example, Leonardo describes in great detail the way things look in a storm or flood as if rocks and water possessed expressive powers.[73]

For Alberti a new subject, or *invenzione,* could easily owe its provenience to a poem. This dependence helps to explain how the *bella invenzione* could be attributed less to the talent of a painter than to his erudition.[74] It may therefore be argued that the oratorical element in painting was preeminent from the beginnings of Renaissance theorizing about it. But the psychological aspects of painting, already observed in Alberti's and Leonardo's treatises, supersede the imitation of objects in Cinquecento prose such as Vasari's.[75] The reversal of the order of precedence that gave priority to mimed reality made it "the taking-off point for the analysis of emotions." This means that the connection between rhetorical means and ends emphasizes the emotion expressed by the painting rather than the represented action. But where Alberti equates *representation* and *narrative,* making *action* transparent to them both, in Cinquecento theory the triad gradually becomes subordinated to the goal of persuasion. The description in poetry of works of art is subordinated to their desired emotional result. The trajectory from subject to painted or sculptured intermediary representation, to the "idea" of its glory and permanence, reveals itself as bidirectional. It is in the mediating artwork that the aim of courtship encounters its essential expression through compromise. A rhetorical resolution, or truce, of the competing claims of representation and idea is facilitated by a simple change of position on the ladder, hence of perspective. If the reified world—as epitomized by an art object—can never realize ideas, it may at least seek to align itself with the emanations of ideas so as to concretize the best possible replica of them. Ideas, or the Platonic concept of Ideas, can thus be made to subserve rhetorical motives.[76]

For even a provisional and conditional reconciliation of art and idea in the Renaissance to take place, the Platonic revival of the time had to accommodate the gradual intrusion of a new premise: the imitation of nature as an aspect of the idea.[77] As might seem obvious, the concept of the *artistic* idea presupposes a relaxing of the principle that Ideas are metaphysical substances in themselves, existing outside the world of sensory appearances and outside the human intellect.[78] The very notion that Ideas could reveal themselves within, or by means of, artistic activity runs directly counter to Plato's generalized contempt for imitative representation (as in the *Sophist* and in book X of the *Republic*). Although it would be excessive to say that Plato simply opposed art as such, he blamed it for producing either copies of things that only mimic the world of ideas or for creating illusions utterly lacking in truth value, therefore inferior even to the world of appearances.

That Ideas could reside in the mind of man opened the avenue of entry for such burgeoning fields as art theory to avail themselves of the Platonic concept of Idea, thereby paradoxically transforming it "into a weapon against the Platonic view of art."[79] The medieval assumption that the generation of ideas amounted to a privilege of the Divinity and was to be regarded not as a stimulus to imitation but as an object of mystical longing ceded to an increasing awareness of a relation between an inner conception and an external object in various fields of artistic activity. Although the parallel of artistic production with divine cognition survived the late Middle Ages well into the era of *Orlando Furioso*, the Renaissance "differed fundamentally from the Middle Ages in that it removed the object from the inner world of the artist's imagination and placed it firmly in the 'outer world.' "[80] It was possible, in fact, "to connect the theory of Ideas with art theory only by sacrificing certain aspects of either one or the other, and in most cases of both."[81] The normative validity and metaphysical origin of the Idea are fundamentally challenged. No longer, as Ficino had believed, are the ideas "true substances" and earthly things only images of them; nor are they "innate," or inherent to the human soul from its otherworldly preexistence. Rather, ideas can come into the mind of the artist as derived from reality, even as formed and sculpted. As conceived in the mind of a Vasari, "idea meant any image conceived in the artist's mind."[82] Concomitantly the artist's privilege and obligation is to acquire by his own efforts an understanding of the intelligible external object.

A new freedom for the artist is implicit in all of these tendencies and alterations in the direction of an earthly accommodation of the doctrine of Ideas. At the same time he could not aspire to invoke the claims of objective reality for his work. The creator's mind "no longer needed . . . regulations, valid *a priori* or empirically confirmed, as mathematical laws, the concurrence of public opinion, and the testimonials of ancient writers."[83] Formerly regarded chiefly as a symbol, art became regarded as chiefly iconic. The new external objectification of the work and of what it represented also individualized or personalized the artist as "subject." Gradually and in accordance with increasing attention to external accuracy and authenticity, philology and archeology were born in the Renaissance, with the dominance of classical poetics and rhetoric to follow upon their maturity.

The linked conceptions of personal artistic independence and of objective, external accuracy form a hospitable background to an understanding of this reversed hierarchy of subject and object. Artists did not abandon the search for the recognizable image but worked in the awareness that however standardized an isolated image might be it is invariably "colored" by paint or by rhetoric in the colors of necessity. Both pictorial and verbal art were viewed in terms of the persuasive power of display, which is more proper to the alogical picture than to the process of reasoned "demonstration."

Note that the uncommittedness and ethical opacity of Castiglione's *Courtier* are actually explained (or excused) by the author's claim that it is a portrait (*ritratto*) of the court of Urbino (not a book of precepts).[84] In painting, a complementary oratorical art is also possible. The concept of "surpassing Nature" came to stress, above the ability of art to create new and unimitated things, the power of the intellect that could translate into visible form a degree of beauty that is *unrealized* in Nature. That transforming power could be paralleled by oratory. Castiglione shows in the course of his book how a little court set into a rather unremarkable landscape could be permuted into a transcendentally beautiful place.[85] Together with the artistic aim of transforming natural objects, a second means of outdoing nature could thus be implemented by the creative fantasy. Man could freely alter reality beyond the known possibilities of variation and even bring forth such novel creatures as centaurs, chimeras, and hippogryphs.[86] The Renaissance conception of imagination did not yet differentiate between imagination and the creative fantasy. But it continued in the medieval notion of fantasy as the supplier of images to the soul and as a power capable of producing forms out of itself.

This conception is advanced in the treatise *De imaginatione* of Giovanfrancesco Pico della Mirandola, which can serve here as a paragon for imagination-theory in the Renaissance.[87] Its basic presumptions are the legacy of the High Middle Ages: that the imagination subserves the intellect while building images out of brute experience; that cognition originates from sensory experience, with the soul's utilizing the imaginative faculty for conceiving "likenesses of sensible objects only, and for placing them before the intellect."[88] These and similar statements emanate from a tradition of Aristotelian commentary, particularly the Aristotle of the treatise *De anima*. But although Giovanni Pico's nephew continues the line of commentators on *De anima* from Averroes, Avicenna, Aquinas, and Jean Gerson, he also shows his direct debt to Platonic and neo-Platonic belief in the reality of ideas (although he does not consider them innate). In his treatise the acceptance of Ideas continues chiefly to motivate his distrust of the imagination, for the reason that it deals with the inferior world of sense and experience. It is, however, the aspect most conveniently termed *Aristotelian* that concerns us with regard to the importance of "images" for the intellect. This primacy of the image, I believe, helps explain the usefulness of ecphrasis during those centuries as a means of transmitting and receiving "epic" messages.

Pico follows the lead of medieval interpreters of imagination in considering it as a term belonging to the realm of psychology, not aesthetics or rhetoric. In fact, he openly objects to an early distinction made by Avicenna between the phantastic and the imaginative. For Pico the dualism of the corporeal and incorporeal demands the mediation of the imagination. Such is the relationship between this faculty and the higher faculties that they cannot do without it (here the neo-Platonic side appears). In Aristotelian terms, again, whereas sensation requires the actual presence of the thing sensed, imagination does not require the presence of the thing imagined: "Inasmuch as cognition originates from sense . . . and inasmuch as sense itself, when informed with the likeness of a sensible object, immediately has recourse to fantasy . . . we must infer that the behavior of all animate beings arises from the nature of phantasy, the imagination."[89] Indeed, "the affections [of a man] are known from the phantasy which a man especially produces and on which he dwells, when he is moved by nothing from without."[90]

Something of the eventual turn toward rhetorical concerns that will be taken by thought about imagination can be discerned in Pico's attribution of human behavior to the results produced by the imaginative faculty. But his emphasis is on the primacy of sensory experience as a precondition of subsequent and independent image-building. Although it "produces forms out of itself"[91] and like the intellect is "free, unfixed, and devoted to no special object," its supersensory meanings, if any, remain uncharted.

Another tendency that could be said to lead potentially to an enhanced conception of imagination in an *aesthetic* direction is displayed in Pico's frequent reference to the relationship between imagination and memory, which he says are sometimes identified with one another.[92] Here the specific role of works of art comes into focus. We may read in this early treatise the foreshadowing of a conception of aesthetic memory such as the following remarks exemplify in our time:

What are the characteristics of aesthetic memory in art? Its incapacity to be realized on the level of the senses. The concomitant sensations which offer themselves to memory through the perception of a work of art cannot but remain memory and can never be lived other than in memory. . . . The greatness of a work of art always consists in the faculty left to memory of establishing—starting from the sensorial data offered by a given art—a certain margin of indetermination for all the rest.[93]

In the contemplation of a work of art, as in the dreams discussed by Pico, no actual sensations substitute for those that aesthetic memory offers to consciousness. Nevertheless the notion of images as a product essentially of aesthetic memory is at best only implied. "Phantasy," Pico writes, "has sometimes been called 'picture' by Plato, and for the reason, I should suppose, that in its sensorium are painted the impressions of things, and the various appearances receive form and are fashioned at will, in a manner not unlike that in which painters depict the various and dissimilar forms of things."[94] Even when the sensible object is removed, "visions present themselves even if we shut our eyes."[95] On the strength of such visions man's behavior is formed. Both good and bad come from the imagination, though Pico is more likely to dwell on its negative aspect. It can corrupt the reason and deceive the intellect, sway the passions, and afflict man with defects of judgment. If its instigation to wrongdoing is curbed the beneficial effects of the imagination can be turned to good action. Only let the higher faculties guide it, therefore, and it may act as the lens through which the intellect beholds the truth. On it, as on wings, the mind may rise to the contemplation of the divine.

The fluctuating evaluation of the ethical results of imagination has a crucial parallel in the assessment of the ethical value of art, as interpreted from Platonic texts in the Renaissance. Both of these are directly to be related to the increasing awareness of what Kenneth Burke calls "imagination as a suasive device": the very outcome of Ariosto's use of ecphrasis in *Orlando Furioso*.[96] Understanding of the conjunction of psychology, rhetoric, and aesthetic memory in the evolving conception of Imagination facilitates a comprehension of the exemplary value of talking about artworks.

Man is moved to action, Pico wrote, for the sake of either real or apparent good; but desire depends upon perception and the ensuing formation of images. Our actions thus depend on the nature of this power. Both imagination and reason can originate movement. The movements originated by imagination are dangerous except insofar as they are controlled by reason. Because of the persuasive effect that an image may have upon an audience's acts and attitudes, the reproductive capacity of imagination (as distinct from the "productive" one that characterizes artistic creativity) retained its status as the definition of imagination.

In dreams and in willed imaginings, imagination renders the objects of sense, often in new combinations that may not themselves derive from sensory experience. And because of the forceful effect that a speaker's images may produce in his listener's acts and attitudes, the doctrine of imagination came to be applied to the results obtained by oratory. For Plato had it that like the painter the poet "will make a likeness of a cobbler though he understands nothing of cobbling [and] lay on the colors of the several arts, himself understanding their nature only enough to imitate them."[97] Each procedure involves the generation of images in the eye of the observer's mind.

The recombination of variegated elements of sensory experience, generally taken to be synonymous with imagination, may be fruitfully compared to Ariosto's own poetic procedure. Just as the imagination creates hybrid beings out of elements of many, such as centaurs or hippogryphs, Ariosto weaves his huge canvas out of the greatly varied fragments of reported reality through other "texts." For *Orlando Furioso* these pretexts were no less necessary than the sensory data that prompt memory, reflection, and recombination. Returning to the specific question of ecphrasis, for Bradamante to "see" her future in art, for the representation of this princess's own image of self not only to readers but to herself as a model of her own understanding, the rhetorical presence of a pictorial self-representation was necessary. The same holds true for every instance of ecphrasis in the poem. Just as the pictorial or sculptural representation also "implies" a viewer (and interpreter) who is a character in the poem and who will derive a specific content from the ecphrasis, that character in turn serves in an exemplary capacity to show the reader how he is to understand the composite image of an ecphrastic description and a viewer. The passage is about someone's learning something, and the awareness that this learning is taking place through the mediate, sensory object of an artwork appeals rhetorically to the reader's imagination, thereby inducing his correspondent reaction. To persuade the reader or listener of its significant reality, the presence of a "picture" has to be stipulated. Although the pictorial image is merely stipulated, its effect resides chiefly in the literary, even cognitive, legitimation whereby it is given the status of knowledge.

This status as a cognitive means at the same time enhances the stipulated truth value of the image. All the things depicted—Bradamante's ancestors and descendants in war panoply, caryatids in Renaissance dress supporting the magnified contours of great ladies, the apotheosis of Ippolito d'Este—thus attain the power of conveying, inaugurating, and justifying social realities and norms. They not only are recognizable images in the sense of being mimetically persuasive but also "re-cognizable" because they are images. It is the dignity of imitative art that is being reasserted in the ecphrases, even as the pictorial aspect is being temporally demoted as subordinate to its expression in language. Pictorial art comes to locate itself between the realms of sensory experience and theoretical contemplation. It can therefore act as the link between the imagination conceived of as a psychological entity and an increasingly rhetorical concept that moves, in the Cinquecento, steadily toward the aesthetic pole.

Although not fully poetized or even thematized until the advent of philosophical and literary theories that flourished in the nineteenth century, the aesthetic meaning of imagination may be understood as struggling against the barrier that would relegate it to a reproductive, image-forming capacity. When Alberti affirmed the effectiveness of the subject of a work of art independently of the artifact, he seemed to range himself still among those theorists who would attribute cognitive value to the "invention" alone. The affirmation that even the unpainted "invention" is delightful points back to a conception of essential value (represented within the "invenzione") in which the idea surpasses the image. The concept still contains, or at least does not contradict, Aquinas's determination that even the truth value of the work of art existed not in proportion to its agreement with the natural subject of the work but according to its agreement with the idea fixed in the mind.[98] The dignity of mimetic art gains slowly in tandem with the "slow vindication of sensory cognition vis-à-vis the priority accorded cognition through concepts." Alberti's statement is biaspectual: it also "emphasizes the *aesthetic* importance . . . of content."[99] Renaissance art, legitimized as the genuine heir of Greco-Roman antiquity, strengthened its position among the liberal arts by accumulating the respect due art as a means of cognition via second-order imitation. Art theory contributed to this result although it was primarily practical, only secondarily historical and apologetic, and in no way speculative.

In time the neo-Platonic doctrine of ideas came into service as a way of extolling representational art itself. In the *Trattato,* Alberti had cautioned the painter not to depend excessively on his inner promptings but to consult nature by constant observation. Just where he advanced the concept of Ideas he cautions the painter, "This idea of beauty, which the well trained barely discern, flees from the intellect of the inexpert."[100] An effect of such an endorsement of practical observation is to alter the concept of Idea to such an extent that it could be reconciled with that realistic creed and could even be used to support it. Turning now to the sixteenth century, we may note in Melanchthon an explicit analogy between Platonic ideas and the images immanent in the mind of a painter: "Certum est, Platonem ubique vocare Ideas perfectam et illustrem notitiam, ut Apelles habet in animo inclusam pulcherrimam imaginem humani corporis" (It is certain that Plato everywhere calls Ideas a perfect and lucid notion, as Apelles carries in his mind the most beautiful image of the human body).[101] Not only are the Ideas located in the mind of a mere man but, most importantly to our topic, they now "preferably reveal themselves in artistic activity. The painter, and no longer the dialectician, is now adduced as an example when the concept 'idea' is discussed."[102]

The value of ecphrasis in Ariosto's poem still depends upon the medieval emphasis on inner (if not innate) Ideas. Nevertheless the externalization of what Bradamante "sees" in herself, or what Ruggiero *inwardly* perceives to be his future duty, validates the concomitant externalization of the inner image. These instances in which the beautiful is put to the use of learning demonstrate that the messages are instilled by "showing," not telling. Thus the potential objections of the dialectician are short-circuited as is any potential objection to what "is." The literalization of the inner image runs parallel to Ariosto's total defiguralization of medieval narrative. The future becomes a work of art, a series of artifacts made by a self-legitimizing process. If the imagination must be limited by implicit definition to the imaging of what the memory reproduces and the incipient fantasy combines, then ecphrasis cuts short by means of words exactly what it is that words can do about everything: qualify, interpret, predict, warn. The lives of the Estensi are finally revealed, so far as Ariosto is concerned, as works of art, with all the immediacy and all the opacity of discourse that are proper to visual art alone. Such use of reported imagery emerges, like its stipulated visual original, as fundamentally lyrical, not dramatic. Of course this shifting evaluation of aesthetic experience as a means of knowing comes under the all-possessive appropriation of the poet, who thereby still accomplishes a subordination of other arts to the words that describe them.

It is known to all students of the *Ut pictura poesis* topos that one of Lessing's most convincing passages in *Laocoön* rejects Ariosto's description of Alcina as something resembling a picture.[103] The passage exposes the "pictorial" inadequacy of verbal expression: "Lucian too knew of no other way to convey the beauty of Panthea than to refer to the loveliest female statues of ancient artists. Yet what is this but an admission that language in itself is powerless here; that poetry falters and eloquence grows mute unless art serves as an interpreter in some degree?"[104] Alcina herself is "a painting with no picture."[105] The static (or lyric) and the dynamic (or dramatic) are each governed by its own art. "That which the eye takes in at a single glance (the poet) counts out to us with perceptible slowness. [Conversely] progressive actions [which I have characterized as 'dramatic'] cannot be considered to belong among [the subjects of painting]."[106] Rereading Dolce's praise of Ariosto's word-painting, Lessing judges from the effect of the prescriptive verses on Alcina "that what is best expressed by the painter in lines and colors is least expressible in words."[107]

Lessing's pioneering distinction is convincing so far as pre-Romantic art is concerned.[108] But for Ariosto the limitations on language could simply provide a pretext for language to appropriate visual art as grist for its mill. Horace's *Ut pictura poesis* had repeatedly been snatched out of context by art theorists and others, often to refer to Ariosto himself. Replaced in context, *Ut pictura poesis* might indeed refer to Ariosto, albeit in a very different sense:

> Ut pictura poesis; erit quae, si propius stes,
> Te capiat magis, et quaedam, si longuis abstes.[109]

> (Poetry is like painting; one work seizes your fancy if you stand close to it, another if you stand at a distance.)

So long as this precept is misunderstood and thus conceived of with reference to artistic media, it is easier to misconceive the nature of Ariosto's genuine relationship to it. If not, it could read as an admonishment to readers not to entangle themselves among the intricate paths and forests of *Orlando Furioso,* so as not to miss the way up—to a sane midpoint—to its panoramic vision of the world. From the meager, often illusory vantage points provided by a single, linear reading, this poem could deny its content of any cognitive value at all other than by way of snickering reference to prior texts. Like the huge painted or woven canvases to which Ariosto compares it, *Orlando Furioso* "shows" rather than "tells."

The praise of patrons, a form of verbal evidence of the decisive condition on the *Furioso*, also provides a helpful analogy to the need to express ideas through things. It was a time that found the aesthetic concept of imagination, as a *forma mentis*, in its infancy. The task of the poet was to reconcile "idealism" and "naturalism" in an encomiastic context—just as art theorists envisaged this rapprochement for painting and sculpture.[110] Since he had to do so in recognizable terms (such as "images"), Ariosto made the stipulated artwork act as mediator between psychological and aesthetic realms, and between idea and object. *Orlando Furioso* is the "Hippogryph" that bridges both "internal" and "external" realms of the imagination. Therefore its ecphrases epitomize it as a *summa* of what Renaissance fiction could offer—in terms of a *genuinely* "deconstructive" world-view and of the concomitant variety and wit—before painting did indeed appropriate first place among the arts of Italy, in theory as well as in practice.

# Conclusion

O*rlando Furioso* stands at the pinnacle of modern literary epic and at the crossroads from which the epic world is looked upon as discrete rather than continuous. Under the interpreter's gaze, thought and event crumble into a series of discontinuous states. The agglomeration of classical and medieval material unlocks the significance of many episodes that call into question our habits of reading and understanding. The traditional codes of the epic and romance reverse themselves or change places, so that the modes playing the decisive role in shaping Ariosto's masterpiece demand that everything be made ready to step out of character, play with narrative functions, and enter new combinatory frameworks. The latter, in turn, are as likely to dissolve upon prolonged scrutiny as is Atlante's castle of illusions. Myth, the hidden substratum, conserves its power only for those incapable of articulating it as story or fable. Ariosto leaves us without the proper names—Perseus, Bellerophon, Hercules, Circe, Jason—that would bare the "pre-texts," showing how the author is being "written through." The vibrancy of myth, a presence that has not been thoroughly articulated since the sixteenth century until now, collaborates in our reading with Ariostean world making to facilitate the celebration of randomness as seen through a magisterial, controlling mind.

This book has provided an impetus, I trust, to the demystification of Ariosto's epic antiepic and aromantic romance. The first three chapters dealing with literary satire and blended myths showed how the ancient materials turn up again not as direct heritage but as imports transformed. To say, however, that Ariosto merely ironizes on the individual story lines only occasions the smile of a temporary sophisticate and deprives the poem of wholeness and resonance at once. But to recognize that here the mythic journey and the poetic enterprise are one and the same unlocks the patterns of its movement and its cosmic perspective on the world.

The first chapter also showed that confronting his own poetic past in the satires helped Ariosto to return to his masterwork in the same spirit of laughter: no palinodes here, no recriminations. The limitations of Ariostean irony are marked by love, madness, and the ubiquitous, related condition of patronage.

Just as the poem elevates the mortal and fallible couple, Ruggiero and Bradamante, it sheds doubt on history as linear progress toward a point that would connect time and eternity. By making the Estense family originate in Troy, Ariosto problematizes Trojan origins, emphasizing that every great story has occurred somewhere before. My chapter on doubling and multiplication has dealt with this form of demystification by showing how every important event (and a great many others) repeats itself at least once, and how story lines tirelessly subdivide, in an endless process of binary fission.

Madness, too, emerges as a function of repetition and demythification. Ariosto invites us to be deceived by the content of the little "pastoral" poem composed in entwined Arabic script that is the immediate cause of Orlando's loss of self, but he finally reveals that effect as the result of a progressive,

relentless disintegration that is the lot of anyone hypnotized
by the mirage of textual order.

The truth content of pictures themselves ("seeing is believ-
ing") and their fitness to convey mythical status are finally
brought into question. Ariosto makes use of ecphrasis to ex-
pose the devices of verbal praise and the loopholes of images
and surveys the role of image making in the formation of
etiological myth. History is revealed as an artifact dependent
upon shifting and uncertain modes of transmission. The multi-
ple and ultimately incoherent sources of texts influence and
determine the path taken by the reader, establishing a plural-
ity of possibilities. Corresponding to their rise as objects of
appropriation in the course of the Renaissance, artistic im-
ages attest to the importance of their subjects to the point of
conferring upon them the very antiquity and authority arro-
gated to the images themselves. My sixth chapter has summa-
rized the value of visual art in this kind of representation.

The Narrator himself, interposed between author and
reader, splits again into two different figures: the "I" who is
writing and the "I" who is being written, so that we know the
author's "personality" only in and through the act of writing.
It emerges for us as the result of our reading. And although the
result tends to inform us that poems deal with repertoires of
elements and functions, still this poem strives to escape from
finite number, to say more than the words can speak, to say
what cannot yet be said. Its combinatorial games can be read,
also, as confirmations of values, even as they pursue the vari-
ous possibilities implicit in the material. The acceptance of
authority, indeed, survives in the adoption of so many well-
known schemes. But play triggers off a movement in the oppo-
site direction, away from authority. The refusal to see things in
the old way has been the motive force behind this study. It is up
to readers to confront Ariosto's labyrinth, to make way for
double perspectives and optical illusions, to exert the full mea-
sure of critical force, so as to live up to the demands of the
poem, merging old codes into one new reading. Captured
within the design, there lies the core of a universal joy and a
universal melancholy at the contradictions of life—a deep and

comprehensive joy and sadness that man can act only provisionally, that no perception is sure and no purpose surely rewarded, that the loveliest aspects of life are the most fragile and fleeting, that fame may be the path of wrongdoing, that everything must bear the imprint of a universally divided mind. Repeated contrasts only make the opposite of every single thing the more explicit, suspending final judgment.

Ariosto does limit the total proliferation of meaning, by comparison with a surrealistic or aleatory poem. As he measures betrayal by faith, love by cold indifference, bravery by cowardice, chivalry by mass warfare, friendship by enmity, and intellect by rank stupidity, a set of values is to be extrapolated from the poem. But the presentation of life as sets of terms has to be viewed as a diptych. The prerequisite to a sound reading, then, is the flexibility that allows an aerial view of both sides.

To that end—which in practice calls for us to demystify and demythicize—this book has been dedicated, not as an authority but as a corollary to the pleasure *Orlando Furioso* has afforded readers for over four hundred years. Each chapter has collaborated in the breakdown of the notion of one myth, one personality, one plotline, one image, and the replacement of these by comic recurrence. "Mountains stand firm," Ariosto reminds us, "but men tend to meet again" (XXIV.2). That happens at the very moment of Orlando's madness. May my work serve well enough that it, at least, may not have to be written again.

# Notes

## Preface

1. The most prominent exceptions should be noted at once. Most of them are chapters on Ariosto in works about Western epic or in the context of a wider topic. With regard to the material in this book the most influential criticism proved to be that found in such recent studies as the first chapter of Patricia A. Parker, *Inescapable Romance* (Princeton, N.J.: Princeton University Press, 1979), esp. pp. 40–44; Peter Marinelli, "Redemptive Laughter: Comedy in the Italian Romances," *Genre,* 9 (1976), 505–26; Cesare Segre, *Esperienze ariostesche* (Pisa: Nistri-Lischi, 1966); Robert M. Durling, *The Figure of the Poet in the Renaissance Epic* (Cambridge, Mass.: Harvard University Press, 1965), pp. 112–81; and A. Bartlett Giamatti, *The Earthly Paradise in the Renaissance Epic* (Princeton, N.J.: Princeton University Press, 1966). It is no accident that these represent mainly American scholarship. Of the numerous works in Italian cited in my bibliography the most helpful has been Daniela Delcorno Branca, *L'Orlando Furioso e il romanzo cavalleresco medievale* (Florence: Olschki, 1973), which deals mostly with the topos of enchanted weapons but carefully studies its subject in relation to late medieval works and in considerable depth; and Giorgio de Blasi, "L'Ariosto e le passioni (studio sul motivo poetico fondamentale dell'*Orlando Furioso*)," *GSLI,* 129 (1952), 318–62; 130 (1953), 178–203. William Nelson, *Fact and Fiction: The Problem of the Modern Storyteller* (Cambridge, Mass.: Harvard University Press, 1973), esp. p. 38, is an example of a generally useful though small book, which, like others that were of great help to me, does not concentrate on Ariosto. Rosamond Tuve, *Allegorical Imagery* (Princeton, N.J.: Princeton University Press, 1966), esp. pp. 360–85, contains a valuable comparison of Ariosto with Spenser. For the rest, the paucity of serious analysis of Ariosto's masterwork generally remains a matter, for me, at least, beyond understanding.

# Chapter 1

1. Peter Marinelli, "Redemptive Laughter: Comedy in the Italian Romances," *Genre,* 9 (1976), 526.

2. I cite the *Satire* from the edition of Cesare Segre, *Ariosto: Satire e Lettere* (Turin: Einaudi, 1976).

3. Georg Wilhelm Friedrich Hegel, *Aesthetics,* trans. T. M. Knox (Oxford: Clarendon Press, 1975), p. 31.

4. Edgar R. Wind, *Pagan Mysteries in the Renaissance* (New York: Norton, 1969), p. 97: "He foretold (in clear allusion to the cannon foundry of Alfonso) that the murderous engine would destroy the virtues of chivalry."

5. Giambattista Pigna's attribution of the title and his defense of *Orlando Furioso* are discussed in detail by Bernard Weinberg, *A History of Italian Literary Criticism in the Renaissance* (Chicago: University of Chicago Press, 1961), 2, 954–1072.

6. Eduardo Saccone, *Il soggetto del Furioso e altri saggi* (Naples: Liguori, 1974), p. 210, refers to the name of Hercules among the "repressed" aspects of the *Furioso.*

7. F. Gaeta, "L'avventura di Ercole," *Rinascimento,* 5 (1954), 227–60.

8. Among the sources for the rebirth of the classical Hercules mentioned by Gaeta are Petrarch, *De viris illustribus,* and Coluccio Salutati, *De laboribus Herculis.*

9. Pigna, *Romanzi* (Venice, 1554), cit. Saccone, p. 218. See also for Hercules, Erwin Panofsky, *Hercules am Scheidewege* (Leipzig: Teubner, 1930); Theodore Mommsen, "Petrarch and the Story of the Choice of Hercules," *Journal of the Warburg and Courtauld Institute,* 26 (1953), 178–92; and Erika Tietze-Conrat, "Notes on Hercules at the Crossroads," *Journal of the Warburg and Courtauld Institute,* 24 (1951), 305–9.

10. Seneca, *Hercules Furens,* 1096. I cite from the edition and translation of Frank Justus Miller (Cambridge, Mass.: Harvard University Press, 1979).

11. Seneca, *Hercules Furens,* 1278–81.

12. Ibid., 1285.

13. I cite from the edition and translation of Frank Justus Miller (Cambridge, Mass.: Harvard University Press, 1976), p. 16.

14. Unless otherwise noted, I cite *Orlando Furioso* from the edition of Nicola Zingarelli (Milan: Hoepli, 1959).

15. Patricia A. Parker, *Inescapable Romance* (Princeton, N.J.: Princeton University Press, 1979), p. 21 and passim. She refers (p. 9) to the "Furioso's revelation of the ubiquity of fictions and its subversion of hierarchies founded on stable centers of 'truth,' " such as the *Aeneid,* discussed esp. pp. 40–44 and notes.

16. See Philip Slater, *The Glory of Hera* (Boston: Beacon Press, 1968), p. 354, for a discussion of Athena in the aspect of a patriarchally minded goddess, with particular reference to Euripides' *Eumenides.*

17. Marinelli, "Redemptive Laughter," p. 519.

18. Note the resemblance of minor characters to parallels in the *Aeneid,* for example, Bradamante's mother Beatrice to Amata, Virgil's queen, who likewise would not have her daughter marry an unlanded husband.

19. Viktor Shklovskij, "On the Connection Between Devices of *Syuzhet* Construction and General Stylistic Devices," in *Russian Formalism: A Collection of Articles and Texts in Translation,* ed. Stephen Bann and John E. Bowlt (New York: Harper and Row, 1973), pp. 48–72, is a representative instance of the many works in which Shklovskij sets out this concept of plot construction.

20. The idea of function to which I refer is relayed by D'Arco Silvio Avalle from Ferdinand de Saussure, in Avalle's essay, "La sémiologie de la narrativité chez Saussure,"*Essais de la théorie du texte* (Paris: Galilee, 1973), pp. 20–56. The article consists mainly of Saussure manuscript notes with some analysis. Ariosto's "typiciza-

tion" of persons and situations is discussed in my Chapter 5. Blasucci (*Studi su Dante e Ariosto* [Milan: Ricciardi, 1969], p. 117) notes in passing that because of stylization and certain procedures of "evasion," "la realtà umana o naturale perde i suoi caratteri individuali e si risolve in una pura astrazione pitagorica, dove domina la legge del numero."

21. For the Dante inventories to date, see Cesare Segre, *Esperienze ariostesche* (Pisa: Nistri-Lischi, 1966); and Blasucci, *Studi su Dante e Ariosto;* also Carlo Ossola, "Dantismi metrici nel Furioso," in *Lodovico Ariosto: lingua, stile, e tradizione,* ed. Cesare Segre (Milan: Feltrinelli, 1974), pp. 65–95.

22. Elizabeth A. Chesney, *The Countervoyage of Rabelais and Ariosto* (Durham, N.C.: Duke University Press, 1981) pp. 66–67, contains a good discussion of Ariosto's leveling of mythological and nonfictional strata.

23. Cit. Hayden White, *Metahistory* (Baltimore: The Johns Hopkins University Press, 1973), p. 94.

24. For example, Dieter Kremers, *Der rasende Roland des Ludovico Ariosto: Aufbau und Weltbild* (Stuttgart: Kohlhemmer, 1973), which adopts this theory as its premise for further analysis.

25. Francesco Caburacci, *Trattato di M. F. C. da Immola, Dove si dimostra il vero, & novo modo di fare le Imprese, Con un breve discorso in difesa dell'Orlando Furioso di M. Ludovico Ariosto* (Bologna, 1580), p. 81, cit. Weinberg, *A History of Italian Literary Criticism,* pp. 980–83.

26. See Erich Auerbach, *Mimesis,* trans. Willard F. Trask (Princeton: Princeton University Press, 1953), p. 137; also Luigi Cesati, "Contatti e interferenze tra il ciclo brettone e carolingio prima del Bojardo," *Archivium Romanicum,* 11 (1927), 108–17, which shows that as early as the Franco-Venetian poems the character of Orlando shifts between the roles of Christian paladin and courtly knight.

27. François-Marie Arouet [Voltaire], "Epopée," *Questions sur l'Encyclopedie* (1771) (Paris: 1875–78), p. 573; also see the preface to his poem, *La pucelle d'Orleans,* in his *Oeuvres complètes,* 2d ed. (Paris: Baudouin, 1825–28).

28. Italo Calvino, *Il castello dei destini incrociati* (Turin: Einaudi, 1973), pp. 45–46. See the excellent analysis of this book in light of the *Furioso* by Marilyn Schneider, "Calvino's Erotic Metaphor and the Hermaphroditic Solution," *Stanford Italian Review,* 1 (1981), 93–118.

29. Sumary information on the Ariosto allegorizers is given in Don Cameron Allen, *Mysteriously Meant* (Baltimore-London: The Johns Hopkins University Press, 1970), p. 284. See William J. Kennedy, "Modes of Allegory in Ariosto, Tasso and Spenser" (Diss. Yale, 1969), which is more helpful in the matter of allegory than the subsequent version known as *Rhetorical Norms in Renaissance Literature* (New Haven, Conn.: Yale University Press, 1978), pp. 95–181. Although not cited in this chapter, the fundamental work on the Ariosto quarrel in the later Cinquecento is contained in Weinberg, *A History of Italian Literary Criticism,* 2, 954–1072. A. Bartlett Giamatti, *The Earthly Paradise in the Renaissance Epic* (Princeton, N.J.: Princeton University Press, 1966), discusses the Alcina "allegory" in the chapter on Ariosto; see also Thomas M. Greene, *The Descent from Heaven: A Study in Epic Continuity* (New Haven, Conn.: Yale University Press, 1963).

30. Daniela Delcorno Branca, *L'Orlando Furioso e il romanzo cavalleresco medievale* (Florence: Olschki, 1973), p. 45.

31. For example, XLI.85, in which Gradasso has taken possession of both the sword Durindana and the steed Baiardo at the battle of Lipadusa but knows in advance that he will lose his life there nevertheless.

32. Probably Lucian, whom Erasmus translated together with St. Thomas More for a 1506 edition, served as a precedent for both the *Encomium* and *Orlando Furioso.* Lucian's method of learned parody, cutting several ways at once, and his

agile irony at the expense of general credulity, specifically regarding poetic messages, prompted Ariosto's borrowings from several of his works. This matter has been well treated by Cesare Segre, "Nel mondo della luna ovvero L. S. Alberti e Ludovico Ariosto," in *Studi in onore di A. Schiaffini* (Citta di Castello: Nistri-Lischi, 1965), p. 1025. Lucian's *Vera historia* should be singled out here as possessing a particular influence, especially where Lucian claims he is at least being truthful enough to call himself a liar. The *Vera historia* together with Dante (*Paradiso*, XXII) and Cicero's "dream of Scipio" in *De republica* VI.16, constitutes a source of Astolfo's journey to the Moon.

33. For theory and exemplification as regards the basic tropes of metonymy and metaphor, see Michael and Marianne Shapiro, *Hierarchy and the Structure of Tropes* (Bloomington: Indiana University, 1976).

34. Samuel R. Levin, "Allegorical Language," in *Allegory, Myth and Symbol,* ed. Morton Bloomfield (Cambridge, Mass.: Harvard University Press, 1981), p. 13.

# Chapter 2

1. In this chapter references to Boiardo's *Orlando Innamorato* are to Giuseppe Anceschi's edition (Milan: Garganti, 1968) by canto, strophe, and line.

2. Commentators at least since Walter Bruni have recognized the Petrarchan elements embedded in *Orlando Furioso* (*OF*). See, for example, Nino Capellani, *La sintassi narrativa dell'Ariosto* (Florence: La Nuova Italia, 1952), p. 50: "nel Furioso c'è anche un altro petrarchismo: c'è la trascrizione in ritmo narrativo del più vero e grande mondo lirico del Petrarca...." See also the references in Roberto Fedi, "Petrarchismo prebembesco in alcuni testi lirici dell'Ariosto," in *Ludovico Ariosto: lingua, stile e tradizione,* ed. Cesare Segre (Milan: Feltrinelli, 1974), pp. 283–302; and the important essay by Emilio Bigi, "Petrarchismo ariostesco," in his *Dal Petrarca al Leopardi* (Milan: Ricciardi, 1954), pp. 63–66.

3. I have in mind the tradition of source study as a means toward developing epistemological information, established by such books as Erwin Panofsky, *Studies in Iconology* (1939; rpt. New York: Torchbooks, 1962).

4. The indispensable source study remains Pio Rajna, *Le fonti dell'Orlando Furioso* (Florence: Sansoni, 1900), which favors discussion of Ariosto's more recent antecedents. For those aspects of the poem that have been rehearsed in detail, see Eduardo Saccone, "Cloridano e Medoro," in his *Il soggetto del Furioso* (Naples: Liguori, 1973), pp. 161–200. In this essay Saccone shows *how* the two pagans are assimilated to parallels in *Aeneid* IX and Statius, *Thebaid* X, but without exploring their connections in depth. Saccone also examines the attribution by Pigna of the poem's title to the suggestion provided by Seneca's *Hercules Furens*, pp. 214–22, but does not deal in substance with mythology or with classical literature.

5. See, for example, David Quint, "Astolfo's Voyage to the Moon," *Yale Italian Studies,* 1 (1977), 398–408; and "The Figure of Atlante: Ariosto and Boiardo's Poem," *MLN,* 94 (1979), 77–91. The latter article argues that Atlante provides closure for the poem as epic. I would qualify in two ways the author's statement that "the impetus towards closure of the *Furioso* narrative reveals an authentic human temporality...." (84): first, that this closure is of a chiefly formal, as opposed to a semantic, nature; second, that it functions almost exclusively with respect to the Ruggiero-Bradamante couple, leaving untouched such open characters as Alcina and Angelica.

6. See Cesare Segre, *Esperienze ariostesche* (Pisa: Nistri-Lischi, 1966), and Luigi Blasucci, *Studi su Dante e Ariosto* (Milan-Naples: Ricciardi, 1969), for working inventories of Dante quotations.

7. See Daniel Javitch, "Rescuing Ovid from the Allegorizers," in *Ariosto in*

*America: Atti del Congresso ariostesco*, ed. Aldo Scaglione (Ravenna: Longo, 1976), pp. 85–100; and Robert Hanning, "Ariosto, Ovid and the Painters: Mythical Paragon in *Orlando Furioso*," ibid., pp. 100–116.

8. For the theory of tropes followed in this brief section, see Michael and Marianne Shapiro, *Hierarchy and the Structure of Tropes* (Bloomington: Indiana University, 1976).

9. C. P. Brand, *Ariosto: A Preface to Orlando Furioso* (Edinburgh: Edinburgh University Press, 1973), contains the most thoughtful discussion of the encomiastic theme in *OF* among contemporary critical works.

10. Erich Auerbach, *Mimesis: The Representation of Reality in Western Literature*, trans. Willard F. Trask (Princeton, N.J.: Princeton University Press, 1953), p. 117.

11. Lanfranco Caretti notes in his essay, "La poesia del Furioso," *Ariosto e Tasso* (Turin: Einaudi, 1961), p. 35, that the poem as a whole is uncentered: "Tutti i luoghi del Furioso . . . tutti i luoghi dell'inesauribile geografia ariostesca divengono infatti, di volta in volta, temporanei centri della vicenda, punti vitali di confluenza o di intersezione di alcune delle sue direttrici. Per tal modo l'Ariosto alla cosmogonia teocentrica medievale sostituiva definitivamente una cosmogonia antropomorfica nella quale il centro era, in ogni momento, liberamente variabile."

12. Quint, "The Figure of Atlante," pp. 78–79.

13. For example, by Simon Fornari, *Spositione sopra l'Orlando Furioso di M. Ludovico Ariosto* (Florence, 1549–50), p. 233, discussed by Bernard Weinberg, *A History of Italian Literary Criticism in the Renaissance* (Chicago: University of Chicago Press, 1961), 2, 954–57.

14. Frequent references to Ariosto's filiation with classical texts occur in Cesare Segre's edition of *OF* (Milan: Mondadori, 1964).

15. Virgil, *Aeneid* IV.246–51, trans. H. Rushton Fairclough (Cambridge, Mass.: Harvard University Press, 1928). Subsequent references to and translations of Virgil are from this edition.

16. Ovid, *Metamorphoses* IV.657–62.

17. Some commentators glossed Homer's lines to mean that the columns supported the earth also. An inventory of these lines is provided by the invaluable reference work of Wilhelm H. Roscher, *Ausführliches Lexikon der griechischen und römischen Mythologie* (Leipzig: Teubner, 1884–1919), p. 706.

18. Servius's commentary on the *Aeneid* contributes largely to the tradition of Atlas as polymath and singer. He writes that Atlas was Hercules' teacher in philosophy and, in one version, that of Mercury also: "Hic Atlas, Iapeti filius, in Africa natus dicitur. hic, quod annum in tempora diviserit et primus stellarum cursus vel circulorum vel siderum transitus naturasque descripserit, caelum dictus est sustinere, qui nepotem suum Mercurium et Herculem docuisse dicitur, unde et Hercules caelum ab Atlante susceptum sustinuisse narratur, propter caeli scientiam traditam." (It is said that Atlas, son of Iapetus, was born in Africa. He, who divided the year temporally and first described the course of the planets and the circuits of the stars and the nature of their travel, is said to uphold the heavens. He is said to have instructed his descendants Mercury and Hercules, wherefore it is told that Hercules assumed the support of the heavens from him—on account of the knowledge of the skies which was conveyed [translation my own].) See *Servianorum in Vergilii Carmina Commentariorum*, ed. E. K. Rand et al. (Lancaster, Pa.: Harvard University Press, 1946), 1, 303–4.

19. For Plato I have used the edition and translation of B. Jowett (New York: Random House, 1920), pp. 3–84. Further references will be cited in the text.

20. In a number of other accounts the mother of Atlas was Clymene or Ge; see Roscher, *Ausführliches Lexikon*, p. 707. These versions offer no explanation of the rise and fall of Atlantis.

21. The fundamental study and edition of the *Ovidius Moralizatus* is in Fausto Ghisalberti, "L'Ovidius Moralizatus di Pierre Bersuire," *Studj romanzi*, 23 (1933), 5–132. I cite from his edition of manuscript M. Translations into English are my own.

22. Ghisalberti, "L'Ovidius Moralizatus," p. 88. Note the appearance of Medusa as a king's daughter, which recurs to versions older than Ovid's in which Medusa is a rich and powerful queen. For these, see the masterful work by J. Fontenrose, *Python: A Study of Delphic Myth and Its Origins* (Berkeley: University of California Press, 1959).

23. Ghisalberti, "L'Ovidius Moralizatus," p. 119.

24. Leslie George Whitbread, ed. and trans., *Fulgentius the Mythographer* (Columbus: Ohio State University Press, 1971), pp. 61–62.

25. C. DeBoer, ed., *Ovide moralisé* (Amsterdam: Maatschappij, 1919–38), pp. 142–43, lines 6303–311. Subsequent references to this work will appear in the body of my text, by lines only.

26. Augustine, *De civitate Dei* XVIII.8.

27. Giovanni Boccaccio, *De genealogie deorum gentilium*, ed. V. Romano (Bari: Laterza, 1951), IV.31.

28. Aldo Bernardo, *Petrarch, Scipio and the Africa* (Baltimore: The Johns Hopkins University Press, 1962), pp. 147–48. My entire discussion of the *Africa* leans on this invaluable work.

29. See D'Arco Silvio Avalle, "La sémiologie de la narrativité chez Saussure," in his *Essais de la théorie du texte* (Paris: Galilee, 1973), pp. 20–56, for the discussion by Saussure of characters: "chacun des personnages est un symbole dont on peut varier . . . a) le nom, b) la position, c) le caractère, d) la fonction des actes." Saussure is referring to characters from the Nibelungenlied, Avalle to characters from Dante's *Commedia*. The adaptation to Ariosto is my own.

30. For a penetrating analysis of the symbolism of horses and their connections with aspects of human nature in *OF*, see A. Bartlett Giamatti, "Sfrenatura," in Scaglione, pp. 31–39.

31. For a good discussion of departures by Ariosto from Virgil, among other authors of classical epic, see Patricia A. Parker, *Inescapable Romance* (Princeton, N.J.: Princeton University Press, 1979), pp. 30–43.

32. I have used the fundamental edition of *Africa* by Nicola Festa (Florence: Sansoni, 1926). Citations are in the body of my text.

33. Morris Bishop, *Petrarch and His World* (Bloomington: Indiana University Press, 1963), p. 177.

34. Cited previously, note 28. For the palace of Syphax, or Truth, see especially pp. 126–60.

35. Bernardo, *Petrarch, Scipio, and the Africa*, p. 47.

36. Ibid., p. 49; see also p. 110.

37. Erich Auerbach, "Figura," in his *Scenes from the Drama of European Literature: Six Essays*, trans. Ralph Manheim (New York: Meridian Books, 1959), pp. 11–76.

38. For a discussion of the *adynaton* as a figure frequently appearing in Petrarch's poetry to connote or denote a realm of possibility beyond nature, see Marianne Shapiro, *Hieroglyph of Time: The Petrarchan Sestina* (Minneapolis: University of Minnesota Press, 1980), pp. 70–90.

39. For the translations of *Africa* I cite throughout from Thomas G. Bergin and Alice Wilson, *Petrarch's Africa* (New Haven, Conn.: Yale University Press, 1977).

40. Bernardo, *Petrarch, Scipio and the Africa*, p. 138.

41. In other versions of the myth Medusa is punished for having challenged the beauty of Athena's hair. See Fontenrose, *Python*, pp. 284–85.

42. The *Ovide moralisé* contains allusions to Medusa's former beauty

(IV.5666), following Fulgentius (in Whitbread, *Fulgentius the Mythographer,* p. 61), who also mentions her great wealth, increased by cultivation and husbandry. In his important article on Dante's Furies, "Dante's Medusa: The Letter and the Spirit," *Yearbook of Italian Studies,* 4 (1972), 1–18, John Freccero discusses the symbolism of Medusa as it was transmitted to Dante, with reference also to Boccaccio, *De genealogie,* X.9.

43. I cite Petrarch's *Canzoniere* from the edition of C. Ponte (Milan: Mursia, 1968).

44. Fulgentius (in Whitbread, *Fulgentius the Mythographer,* p. 62): "The first terror is indeed that which weakens the mind; the second, that which fills the mind with terror; the third, that which not only enforces its purpose upon the mind but also its gloom upon the face." Each of these is represented by a Gorgon sister, the third by Medusa.

45. Bernardo, *Petrarch, Scipio and the Africa,* p. 49.

46. For a synopsis of earlier views on the identity of this palace, see Nicola Festa, "Il palazzo della Verità e le lacune dell'*Africa,*" *Giornale dantesco,* 27 (1924), 197–201. E. H. Wilkins, who did not accept the full idea of a misplaced passage suggested by Festa, observes nevertheless that "it is probable that [the passage in question] occurred originally in a description . . . of a Palace of Truth built by Atlas" ("Descriptions of Pagan Divinities from Petrarch to Chaucer," *Speculum,* 32 [1957], 515).

47. Bernardo, *Petrarch, Scipio and the Africa,* p. 130.

48. Petrarch, *De secreto conflictu curarum mearum,* ed. Ponte, I.3–4.

49. *Africa,* ed. Festa, pp. lxviii.

50. This kind of interpretation originated in a Latin translation by Ennius of Euhemerus (c. 300 B.C.) who had maintained that the gods were ordinary mortals excelling in unusual prowess and pursuits. The doctrine reached its culmination in Lactantius and Isidore. See John D. Cooke, "Euhemerism: A Medieval Interpretation of Classical Paganism," *Speculum,* 2 (1927), 396–410.

51. Bernardo, *Petrarch, Scipio and the Africa,* p. 148.

# Chapter 3

1. Ovid, *Metamorphoses* IV.663–764.

2. Pio Rajna, *Le fonti dell'Orlando Furioso* (Florence: Sansoni, 1900), first drew the attention of modern scholars to this discovery by Pigna.

3. Cited by Eduardo Saccone, *Il soggetto del Furioso* (Naples: Liguori, 1973), p. 218.

4. For example, see Daniel Javitch, "Rescuing Ovid from the Allegorizers: The Liberation of Angelica, *Furioso* X," in *Ariosto in America: Atti del Congresso Ariostesco,* ed. Aldo Scaglione (Ravenna: Longo, 1976), pp. 85–100.

5. An interesting contemporary analysis of the intersecting trajectories in *OF* is provided between the lines of Italo Calvino, *Il castello dei destini incrociati* (Turin: Einaudi, 1976).

6. Virginio Ariosto, cit. C. P. Brand, *Ariosto: A Preface to Orlando Furioso* (Edinburgh: University of Edinburgh Press, 1974), p. 15.

7. For valuable information on art objects pertinent to the inventions in *OF,* as well as on the conflation of Bellerophonic and Perseid myths, see W. Rensselaer Lee, "Ariosto's Roger and Angelica in Sixteenth-Century Art: Some Facts and Hypotheses," in *Studies in Late Medieval and Renaissance Painting in Honor of Millard Meiss,* ed. Irving Lavin and John Plummer (New York: New York University Press, 1977), pp. 302–19.

8. For Ariosto's poem as a critique of literary authority, see Patricia A. Par-

ker, *Inescapable Romance* (Princeton, N.J.: Princeton University Press, 1979), pp. 30–43.

9. Mario Santoro, "L'Astolfo ariostesco: homo fortunatus," in his *Letture ariostesche* (Naples: Liguori, 1974), pp. 135–214, surveys the tradition of Astolfo in French and Italian poems before Ariosto's.

10. *Turpini historia Karoli magni et Rotholandi,* ed. Ferdinand Castets (Paris: 1880), chapters 11, 14.

11. For an extended discussion of Astolfo in the *Chanson d'Aspremont,* see Salvatore Battaglia, "Il 'compagnonaggio' di Orlando e Olivieri," *Filologia romanza,* 5 (1958), 34–68.

12. Antoine Thomas, ed., *Entree d'Espagne* (Paris: 1913). Here too the introduction provides a helpful orientation to the Astolfo tradition, stressing the late additions to his character, pp. lx–lxii.

13. Ibid., 11.1458–59.

14. Ibid., 11.1533–37.

15. *Li fatti di Spagna,* ed. Ruggero M. Ruggieri (Modena: Società Tipografica Modenese, 1951), p. 21: "S'al tuo signore l'aspeta su lo campo, meglio fosse che anchora non fosse nato. . . ." Astolfo is also called a *buffone* several times in chapter 22 of this work.

16. Luigi Pulci, *Morgante maggiore,* ed. Giuseppe Fantini (Turin: UTET, 1968), XXI.85.1–6.

17. Boiardo, *Orlando Innamorato* I.I.60.1–5.

18. Ibid., I.II.67.1–4.

19. Ibid., I.III.5.8: "Et a sè stesso non lo credea quasi."

20. Ibid., I.VII.39.5–6.

21. Ibid., I.VII.48.4.

22. Ibid., I.VII.63. *Orlando Innamorato* also emphasizes Astolfo's unusual handsomeness.

23. Ibid., II.VII.45.1–8.

24. In some versions of the myth the man Bellerophon had killed is his brother (variously named Piren, Deliades, or Alcimenes). For these, see Michael Simpson, ed. and trans., *Gods and Heroes of the Greeks: The Library of Apollodorus* (Amherst: University of Massachusetts Press, 1976), esp. p. 71. In other accounts Bellerophon killed Bellerus, tyrant of Corinth, thereby acquiring his name.

25. For the gift of Pegasus by Poseidon, see Pindar, *Olympian Odes* XIII.63–71; also the numerous sources cited by C. M. Bowra, *Pindar* (Oxford: Clarendon Press, 1964).

26. Pausanias, *Descriptions of Greece: Corinth* III.9. Bowra, *Pindar,* p. 116, points out that this source would strive to produce a favorable account of Bellerophon as a Corinthian, by contrast with Pindar, who uses Bellerophon as an example of pride's leading to its own fall (*Isthmian Odes* VII.44–48).

27. Pindar, *Olympian Odes* XIII.63–71, and Hyginus, *Fabula* 157.

28. Pindar, *Isthmian Odes* VII.44.

29. Apollodorus, *Library* II.iii.2. The wide diffusion of a happy ending for the Bellerophon myth testifies to the ambiguous character of this hero and suggests that Ariosto had ample opportunity to implement it in the case of Astolfo.

30. In this account Bellerophon ascends in triumph to his Lycian kingdom and marriage with Philonoë. There is no word of his attempted flight to Olympus.

31. The anecdote of the Xanthian women comes from Plutarch, *On the Virtues of Women* IX.

32. Francesco Petrarca, *De secreto conflictu curarum mearum III,* in *Opere,* ed. C. Ponte (Milan: Mursia, 1968), p. 548 (translation my own): "Think now of the pestilence that has corrupted your mind with contempt for everything, hatred of life,

desire for death, the love of wretched solitude, and the flight from all mankind; so it can be said as appropriately of you as of Bellerophon (according to Homer): qui miser in campis merens errabat alienis / ipse suum cor edens, hominum vestigia vitans (that he wandered in alien fields, eating his heart out and avoiding the traces of mankind)."

33. Nicola Zingarelli, ed., *Orlando Furioso* (Milan: Hoepli, 1959), p. 527.

34. Boccaccio, *De genealogie,* XIII.5: "Oltre ciò Bellerophonte ammazzo la Chimera, la quale è detta quasi Chimeron, cio è Fluttuatione d'amore. . . ."

35. For working inventories of Dantesque features and citations, see Cesare Segre, *Esperienze ariostesche* (Pisa: Nistri-Lischi, 1966), and Luigi Blasucci, *Studi su Dante e Ariosto* (Milan: Ricciardi, 1969).

36. In Apollodorus, *Library* II.iv.1, Danaë's father is Acrisius; note also Servius's commentary on the *Aeneid* III.286. Apollodorus also notes the variant of the myth that makes Proetus the father. Homer makes only scant mention of Perseus, Danaë, and the Gorgons without assigning a parent to Danaë.

37. Homer, *Iliad* XIV.319–20; Apollodorus, *Library* II.iv.1; Horace, *Odes* III.xvi.1; Ovid, *Metamorphoses* IV.610–11.

38. For Hermes' sickle, see Apollodorus, *Library,* II.iv.2. In Lucian, *Dialogues of the Sea Gods* XIV, the cap of invisibility, sandals, and wallet belong to the Graiae and the shield to Athena; see J. M. Woodward, *Perseus: A Study in Art and Legend* (Cambridge: Cambridge University Press, 1913), among other useful reference works; also M. Phillips, Jr., "Perseus and Andromeda," *American Journal of Archaeology,* 72 (1968), 1–23, pls. 1–20.

39. Apollodorus, *Library* II.iv.6, says that Perseus exchanged Argos for Tiryns with Proetus's son Megapenthes. In Hyginus, *Fables* LXIII and LXIV, Perseus rules over all of Argolis, having turned Proetus to stone with Medusa's head; the same transformation occurs in Ovid, *Metamorphoses* V.242–49, but without the development of the Megapenthes part of the myth.

40. Jean Seznec, *The Survival of the Pagan Gods in the Renaissance,* trans. Barbara F. Sessions (New York: Pantheon Books, 1953), p. 220.

41. Fulgentius's *Mythologies* went through at least twelve editions during the sixteenth century and was printed as early as 1498; see the introduction to the translated edition by Leslie George Whitbread, *Fulgentius the Mythographer* (Columbus: Ohio State University Press, 1971).

42. Leone Ebreo (Guida Abarbanel), *Dialoghi d'amore,* ed. Santino Caramella (Bari: Laterza, 1929), pp. 98–99, "De la comunità d'amore."

43. Boccaccio, *De genealogie,* XIV.10 and 12, where the Perseus myth is used to exemplify the threefold allegorical method of analysis. *De genealogie* had eight editions between 1472 and 1532, the year of the final version of *OF.* Well after Ariosto, Cartari still adduces testimony from this work; see E. H. Wilkins, "The Genealogy of the Editions of the *Genealogia Deorum,*" *Modern Philology,* 17 (1919), 28–36.

44. Cit. Fausto Ghisalberti, "L'*Ovidius Moralizatus* di Pierre Bersuire," *Sfudj Romanzi,* 23 (1933), 111, as edited in a volume inaccessible to me (published 1932).

45. For the sea monster, see Pliny, *Natural History* VI.35; and (further from the Ariostean context) Herodotus, *Histories* II.91. Ovid, *Metamorphoses* IV.706–29, includes descriptive terms whereby the hybrid nature of the monster may be inferred. Apollodorus, *Library,* II.II.iv.3, gives the full account of what Ovid refers to only as the "words" of Cassiopeia, or the product of her tongue ("maternae lingua," IV.670).

46. See Joseph Fontenrose, *Python: A Study of Delphic Myth and Its Origins* (Berkeley: University of California Press, 1959), a masterful work that discusses many ramifications of Medusa's myth and refers to variants in which Perseus, during

his rise to power, comes upon Medusa *in* Libya and leads an army against the Gorgon *nation* that dominated the western portion of that country, as well as other variants in which Perseus sailed with a fleet against the Atlantic island where Medusa reigned as queen of the Ethiopians (pp. 290–96).

47. Fontenrose, *Python,* pp. 276–79, analyzes the notion of Ethiopia entertained by ancient Greece, including its various locations in or near Syria or Phoenicia. The problem of "Ethiopia" is relevant to the context of *OF* insofar as that country figures there as a fabulous realm and thus expands in the conception of Africa that belongs to the pagan elements in the poem. Both the liminality and the opulence of "Africa" pass into Ovid's descriptions of it.

48. For Atlantis as an African kingdom, see Fontenrose, *Python,* p. 284.

49. Philip Slater, *The Glory of Hera: Greek Mythology and the Greek Family* (Boston: Beacon Press, 1968), p. 324.

50. Slater's analysis is restricted to Perseus alone (p. 325).

51. I can only briefly summarize the vast secondary literature explicating the conflation of Perseid and Bellerophonic myths. A good beginning might be T. W. Baldwin, "Perseus Purloins Pegasus," *Philological Quarterly,* 20 (1941), 363–65; valuable supplementary information is to be found in John M. Steadman, "Perseus upon Pegasus and *Ovid Moralized,*" *Review of English Studies,* N.S. 9 (1918), 407–10. Both include Lactantius and medieval allegorizers in their purview. See also Mary Lascelles, "The 'Rider on the Winged Horse,' " in *Elizabethan and Jacobean Studies Presented to Frank Percy Wilson* (Oxford: Oxford University Press, 1959), 173–76 and 185–88. As a standard reference work I have used W. H. Roscher, *Ausführliches Lexikon der griechischen und römischen Mythologie* (Leipzig: Teubner, 1884–1919), in conjunction with the texts cited elsewhere in this chapter. See also Fontenrose, *Python,* esp. pp. 274–306.

52. For iconography applied to St. George and the dragon as relevant to Perseus and Andromeda, see Lee, "Ariosto's Roger and Angelica," p. 305.

53. Rajna, *Le fonti,* pp. 114, 119; Lee, "Ariosto's Roger and Angelica," p. 306. In the latter, note the discussion of two medals showing Bellerophon on Pegasus with the Chimera below, turning its lion's head; this image is also found in Alciati's *Emblemata* (Paris, 1535), with the inscription "Consilio et virtute Chimaeram superari, hoc est, fortiores et deceptores." The wide influence of this image and others on the association of Bellerophon with Virtue and good counsel should be taken into account together with literary sources.

54. Virgil, *Eclogue* VIII.26–28 (translation emended).

55. Ovid, *Metamorphoses* IV.765–86.

56. Boiardo, *Orlando Innamorato,* III.V.37.7–8.

57. *OF* IV.61; VIII.67; XIV.99 ("Mauritano"); XXVII.51; XXXIII.100; XXXVIII.98.

58. Fulgentius, *Mythologies* I.26.

59. Boccaccio, *De genealogie,* X.xxvi (on Pegasus).

60. Fulgentius, *Mythologies* III.1.

61. Cit. Lascelles, "The 'Rider on the Winged Horse,' " 184.

62. Cf. *Satira* VI.154–58: "Ahi lasso! quando ebbi al pegaseo melo / l'età desposta, che le fresche guancie / non si vedeano ancor fiorir d'un pelo, / mio padre mi cacciò con spiedi e lancie / non che con sproni, a volger testi e chiose. . . ."

63. Ovid, *Metamorphoses* IV.616 ("stridentibus alis" [whirring wings]); 665–66 ("pennis ligat ille resumptis / parte ab utraque pedes teloque accingitur unco / et liquidum motis talaribus aera findit," [then Perseus bound on both his feet the wings he had laid by, gift on his hooked sword, and soon in swift flight was cleaving the thin air]).

64. Vatican Mythographer I, cit. K. O. Elliott and J. P. Elder, "A Critical

Edition of the Vatican Mythographers," *Transactions of the American Philological Association,* 77 (1941), 99; see also Baldwin, "Perseus Purloins Pegasus," p. 364. In this medieval account, however, Perseus does not ride Pegasus.

65. Boccaccio, *De genealogie,* X.xxviii: "Hunc insuper dicunt Bellerophontem adversa chimeram monstreum euntem tulisse. Sic et Perseum dum ad Gorgones ivit." (Those above say that Bellerophon rode [Pegasus] against the monster, Chimaera. The same with Perseus when he set out against the Gorgons.) Boccaccio emerges as an important contributor to the confusion of Perseus with Bellerophon as rider of Pegasus.

66. Cf. Ghisalberti, "L'*Ovidius Moralizatus,*" p. 86: "statim de sanguine eius natus est pegasus equus scilicet alatus sive pennatus et alis in pedibus praemunitus. Super quem cum perseus ascendisset portavit eum per aera circumquoque." (Immediately from her blood was born Pegasus, a horse either winged or feathered and provided with wings on its feet, on which when Perseus ascended it carried him all about the air.)

67. *Ovide moralisé,* 11.5475–76: "Et tant fu grans sa vaselages, / Qu'il s'en aloit par l'air volant." (And so great was his service that he went flying through the air.) Later Perseus flies Pegasus, and on his own wings: "Perseus, par l'air volant / Fuit le cheval plain de ferte" (Perseus flying through the air flees the proud steed), 11.5480–81.

68. Charles De Boer and J. T. M. van't Sant, eds., *Ovide moralisé (texte du quinzième siècle)* (Amsterdam: Koniklijke Akademie van Wetenschappen, 1954), p. 3.

69. For "ambition," Pindar, *Isthmian Odes* VII.44–48, suggests that it is not for man to aspire to the dwellings of the gods. This interpretation comes down to Natalis Comes (Natale Conte), *Mythologiae:* "Sed Bellerophon, quale est ingenium plerisque mortalium, tanta rerum gestarum felicitate nimium elatus in coelum quoque ascendere super equo Pegaso voluit, quam arrogantium Jupiter omnes temeritatis gravissimus vindex deprimendam esse ratus, oestrum illi equo immisit, quare Bellerophon praeceps in terram deturbator;" cit. Steadman, "Perseus upon Pegasus," p. 409. For Horace (*Ode* IV.xi), however, Bellerophon, like Phaeton, fell because of his inordinate desire of the unattainable ("ultra quam licet sperare"), a nuance that recurs in a different context in Ariosto's own *Satire.*

70. In his edition of Apollodorus (*Gods and Heroes,* pp. 86–88), Michael Simpson includes a highly suggestive discussion of the relation of encomiastic epic to the power of verbal art. Tracing a line of development from the *Odyssey* XXII.297, in which Medusa's head appears on the outer side of Athena's shield, to a striking parallel between Perseus and Medusa in Ovid, on one hand, and Aeneas and his *pietas* on the other, Simpson claims that "Ovid symbolizes Aeneas' *pietas* (and so Augustus' *pax*) with Perseus' head of Medusa" in a "savage satire" revealing a profound cynicism with regard to Virgil, his epic, and his motives for writing it, as well as the Augustan regime itself. A number of the important elements cited by Simpson—including the Medusa head itself—are not present in Ariosto's "reading" of Ovid, but it is appropriate to compare the Italian poem to "Ovid's Virgilian epic" (Simpson, *Gods and Heroes,* p. 88) and with Perseus-Ruggiero as Aeneas, the more so because of Ariosto's copious borrowings from and references to Virgil, both structural and nonstructural. Simpson's intriguing analysis of "what Ovid saw in Virgil's Aeneas that is analogous to the head of the Medusa" identifies this analogous element as his very *pietas,* "his sense of duty to his own which is transformed into a sense of mission to found Rome, whatever the cost, the compelling power of which, as it gathers force, corresponds to the power of Medusa's head. Virgil's epic, as readers know, is strewn with victims of Aeneas' *pietas.*" Now if Medusa represents Aeneas' *pietas* in the poem, the *Aeneid,* then the poem, the "stony" monument of art, represents in turn Augustus and his *pax:* thus Perseus and Medusa symbolize Aeneas

and his *pietas* in the Aeneid, but also Virgil's process of art by means of which he fixed forever in poetry "the criminality of Augustus, glossing it with *pietas,* and, of course, his own poetic charm" (p. 88). The force with which Ariosto implements the forms of ancient myth might fruitfully be analyzed in this light, as a modern instance of mythological "glossing over" of a difficult, internally contradictory *pace ferrarese* (this last evenhandedly discussed by Werner Gundersheimer, *Ferrara: The Style of a Renaissance Despotism* [Princeton, N.J.: Princeton University Press, 1975]).

71. The most readable, concise, and learned history of the Cinquecento debates regarding Ariosto's poem is still to be found in Bernard Weinberg, *A History of Literary Criticism in the Renaissance* (Chicago: University of Chicago Press, 1961), vol. 2.

72. Aristotle, *Poetics* 1450a.38–39.

73. Northrop Frye, *Anatomy of Criticism* (Princeton, N.J.: Princeton University Press, 1957), p. 136.

74. Ibid., p. 193.

75. Kenneth Burke, *Philosophy of Literary Form* (Baton Rouge: Louisiana State University Press, 1941), p. 63.

## Chapter 4

1. The attribution is that of Pio Rajna, *Le fonti dell'Orlando Furioso* (Florence: Sansoni, 1900), p. 347.

2. This fundamentally artificial distinction generated considerable debate during the sixteenth century. See Edward W. Tayler, *Nature and Art in the Renaissance* (New York: Columbia University Press, 1964), for a good general outline; but among primary sources such books as Castiglione's *Libro del cortegiano* are to be searched for evidence of the debate and its effect on opinion regarding manners and morals.

3. For a comparison of leprosy and madness, see Saul Nathan Brody, *The Disease of the Soul: Leprosy in Medieval Literature* (Ithaca, N.Y.: Cornell University Press, 1974).

4. The quotation is drawn from the shorter, English version of Michel Foucault, *Histoire de la folie, Madness and Civilization: A History of Insanity in the Age of Reason,* trans. Richard Howard (New York: Pantheon, 1965), p. 10.

5. In Pulci's *Morgante,* XXI.132, Orlando is said to know Arabic and "African" languages.

6. One of these is Giuseppe Della Palma, "Una cifra per la pazzia d'Orlando," *Strumenti critici,* 22 (1975), 367–76, who analyzes the use of the pair "Orlando e la giumenta," or mare, but concludes (371) that with the episode of madness "siamo in presenza del 'predominio della lettera,' punto di contatto capitale fra i linguaggi rispettivi della poesia e dell'inconscio" (we are in the presence of the "dominance of the letter," the crucial point of contact between the languages of poetry and the unconscious). Another recent example is Elissa B. Weaver, "Lettura dell'intreccio dell'Orlando Furioso," *Strumenti critici,* 34 (1977), 384–406; and to the extent that he makes Orlando's madness dependent upon his understanding of the inscriptions, Paolo Valesio, "The Language of Madness in the Renaissance," *Yearbook of Italian Studies,* 1 (1971), 199–234.

7. Gianfranco Contini, "Come lavorava l'Ariosto," in his *Esercizi di lettura,* rev. ed. (Turin: Einaudi, 1974), pp. 232–41.

8. See the discussion of the topos of public recitation by Robert M. Durling, *The Figure of the Poet in the Renaissance Epic* (Cambridge, Mass.: Harvard University Press, 1965), pp. 100–103 and 112–14.

9. These citations are but a sampling of a pervasive tendency of Ariosto to cite Petrarch directly (after the fashion of many a Cinquecento lyricist) when hope-

less love is at issue. For a fuller discussion see Emilio Bigi, "Petrarchismo ariostesco," in his *Dal Petrarca al Leopardi* (Milan: Ricciardi, 1954), pp. 63–66.

10. R. R. Bolgar, *The Classical Heritage* (Cambridge: Cambridge University Press, 1954), p. 265.

11. Plato, *Phaedrus* 275 d: (Socrates) "Then anyone who leaves behind him a written manual, and likewise anyone who takes it over from him, on the supposition that such writing will provide something reliable and permanent, must be exceedingly simple-minded . . . if he imagines that written words can do anything more than remind one who knows that which the writing is concerned with." *The Collected Dialogues of Plato,* ed. Edith Hamilton and Huntington Cairns (New York: Pantheon, 1963), p. 52.

12. Roman Jakobson, "On Linguistic Aspects of Translation," in *On Translation,* ed. Reuben Brower (Cambridge, Mass.: Harvard University Press, 1959), p. 233.

13. F. E. Sparshott, " 'As,' or The Limits of Metaphor," *New Literary History,* 6 (1974), 76.

14. For a discussion of the influence of the status of languages on Orlando's madness, see Valesio, "The Language of Madness," p. 230.

15. Michel Foucault, *The Order of Things,* trans. Richard Howard (New York: Pantheon, 1970), p. 47.

16. Ibid., p. 54.

17. I single out the resemblance to Dante's text in order to emphasize my belief that Ariosto's citations form a poetic world and are not mere tokens for recognition. The locus in *Orlando Furioso* may be an amalgam of two in *Purgatorio:* Statius's explanation of the mountain "earthquake" (*Purgatorio* XX.40–72): "Cosa non e che sanza / Ordine senta la religione / de la montagna, o che sia fuor d'usanza"; and Matelda's speech to Dante in the Earthly Paradise: "E saper dei che la campagna santa / Dove tu se' d'ogni semenza e piena . . ." (*Purgatorio* XXVIII.118–19).

18. See Carlo Ossola, "Métaphore et inventaire de la folie dans la littérature italienne du XVIe siècle," in *Folie et déraison à la Renaissance* (Brussels: Presses Universitaires, 1976), p. 185. Leonzio Pampaloni's "scholastic" edition of *Orlando Furioso* annotates madness as nonreason: "Tutto quanto nell'agire dell'uomo non è controllabile e giustificabile secondo ragione, diventa—nella terminologia ariostesca—pazzia" (Florence: La Nuova Italia, 1971), p. 209.

19. The literature on interlacing in the romance can scarcely be touched upon here. I cite only some of the most important works: Jean Frappier, *Étude sur la mort le Roi Artu* (Geneva: Droz, 1936), esp. pp. 38–46, 347–51, and 348, which refers to Ariosto as a master of interlace; "The Vulgate Cycle," in *Arthurian Legend in the Middle Ages,* ed. R. S. Loomis, (Oxford: Clarendon Press, 1959), pp. 195–318; Eugene Vinaver, *The Rise of Romance* (Oxford: Oxford University Press, 1971), pp. 68–98; Rosamond Tuve, *Allegorical Imagery* (Princeton, N.J.: Princeton University Press, 1966), pp. 362–70, 417–36. See also William W. Ryding, *Structure in Medieval Narrative* (The Hague: Mouton, 1971) and its review by Charles Altman, "Medieval Narrative Versus Modern Assumptions: Revising Inadequate Typology," *Diacritics,* 4 (1974), 12–19.

20. For a discussion of interlace in the visual arts as related to writing, see Otto Pacht, *The Rise of Pictorial Narrative in Twelfth-Century England* (Oxford: Clarendon Press, 1962); Mark Lambert, *Malory: Style and Vision in Le Morte d'Arthur* (New Haven, Conn.: Yale University Press, 1975); Susanna Greer Fein, "Thomas Malory and the Pictorial Interlace of *La Queste del Saint Graal,*" *University of Toronto Quarterly,* 46 (1977), 216–40.

21. Vinaver, *Rise of Romance,* pp. 68–122.

22. Fein, "Thomas Malory and the Pictorial Interlace," p. 225. For the picto-

rial representation, see J. G. Alexander, *Norman Illustration at Mont St.-Michel 966–1100* (Oxford: Clarendon Press, 1970), p. 75.

23. Paul Zumthor, *Langue, texte, énigme* (Paris: Seuil, 1975) devotes a chapter to "visual" poetry.

24. Anthony Welch, *Calligraphy in the Arts of the Muslim World* (Austin: University of Texas Press, 1979), p. 160.

25. These are the letters lam and aleph. See Meyer Schapiro, "On the Aesthetic Attitude in Romanesque Art," in his *Romanesque Art* (New York: Braziller, 1977), pp. 1–27.

26. Yasin Hamid Safadi, *Islamic Calligraphy* (London: Thames & Hudson, 1978), p. 11.

27. Ibid., pp. 11–12.

28. Welch, *Calligraphy,* p. 148.

29. Ibid., p. 17.

30. Ibid., p. 38.

31. Ibid., p. 101.

32. Franz Rosenthal, "Significant Uses of Arabic Writing," *Ars Orientalis,* 4 (1962), 15.

33. Annemarie Schimmel, "Schriftsymbolik im Islam," in *Aus der Welt der islamischen Kunst,* ed. Richard Ettinghausen (Berlin: Mann, 1959), pp. 244–54.

34. Welch, *Calligraphy,* p. 24.

35. Erika Cruikshank Dodds, "The Image of the Word," *Berytus,* 18 (1969), 35–58.

36. A. K. Žolkovskij, "Dell'amplificazione," in *I sistemi di segni e lo struttura-lismo sovietico,* ed. R. Faccani and U. Eco (Milan: Bompiani, 1969) p. 97 (my translation, from a translation of the Russian original into Italian).

37. Ibid., p. 94 (emphasis added).

# Chapter 5

1. I refer in particular (cf. Chapter 6) to the passages among the many ecphrases of the poem that specifically describe the Estense progeny and offer praise to their friends and beneficiaries: the Tomb of Merlin (III), and Hall of Merlin (XXXIII); the Fountain (XXVI) consisting of Merlin's marble sculptures; Atlante's tomb (XXXVI); the Fountain of sculptured Ladies (XLII) and the tapestry of Melissa (XLVI). Other important ecphrases describe Olimpia (XI), Alcina (VI), and Atlante's castle (X).

2. For a stimulating interpretation of this voyage, see David Quint, "Astolfo's Journey to the Moon," *Yale Italian Studies,* 4 (1980), 398–408.

3. Elsewhere in this book I make the point that Ariosto has transferred onto the plane of narrative Petrarch's conception of fluctuating, unstable mankind. Stylistic evidence of this transfer may be derived from Petrarch's own use of "Altri" in his *Canzoniere,* often to signify unspecified otherness and emphasize the sameness of the lover's experience. See Marianne Shapiro, "Revelation and the Vials of Sanity in *Orlando Furioso,*" *Romance Notes,* 22 (1982), 329–31.

4. The tradition of the mirror is well surveyed by Sister Ritamary Bradley, C.H.M., "Backgrounds of the Title Speculum in Medieval Literature," *Speculum,* 29 (1954), 100–115. See also Frederick Goldin, *The Mirror of Narcissus* (Ithaca, N.Y.: Cornell University Press, 1967), for an incisive analysis of the mirror image in medieval love lyric. The latter topic is of course to be related to the self-conception of the lovers in Ariosto's poem.

5. Donald S. Carne-Ross, "The One and the Many: A Reading of *Orlando Furioso,* Cantos I and VIII," *Arion,* 5 (1966), 195–234.

6. Marilyn Schneider, "Calvino's Erotic Metaphor and the Hermaphroditic Solution," *Stanford Italian Review,* 1 (1981), 95 and 105, posits Bradamante as an essentially hermaphroditic figure in *Orlando Furioso* as well as in Calvino's reinterpretation.

7. Virgil, *Aeneid* I.482: "diva solo fixos oculos aversa tenebat" (the goddess kept her eyes fixedly averted).

8. Virgil, *Georgics* III.8–29, announces his intention to bring the Muses home to Mantua, as a "victor" parallel to Caesar in war.

9. Carolyn Heilbrun, *Toward a Recognition of Androgyny* (New York: Knopf, 1973), pp. 242–43, deals briefly with twinning and the exchange of sexual identities in *Orlando Furioso.*

10. Morton Bloomfield, "The Problem of the Hero in the Later Medieval Period," in *Concepts of the Hero in the Middle Ages and the Renaissance,* ed. Norman T. Burns and Christopher T. Reagan (Albany: State University of New York Press, 1975), pp. 30–48.

11. Ibid., p. 33.

12. Ibid., p. 34.

13. Ibid., p. 32.

14. Ibid., p. 42.

15. Otto Rank, *The Double,* trans. and ed. Harry Tucker, Jr. (New York: New American Library, 1971), p. 69.

16. Ibid., p. 70.

17. For an effort at narrative analysis of *Orlando Furioso* in terms of bipartite and tripartite schemes, see Leonzio Pampalone, "Per un'analisi narrativa del Furioso," *Belfagor,* 26 (1974), 133–50. This article constitutes the only earlier attempt to decipher the narrative patterns of the poem.

18. The first poetic use of this expression known to me occurs in the well-known Provençal lyric beginning "Can vei la lauzeta mover" by Bernart de Ventadorn (fl. c. 1170). Its proverbial meaning is explained in Karl Appel, *Bernart von Ventadorn: Seine Lieder* (Halle: Niemeyer, 1915), p. 256: "A wise man does not fall (from his horse) on the bridge because he is able to control the reins." According to Appel the saying is one of the medieval *Proverbes au vilain,* 28: "Sages hon ne chiet ou pont."

19. Charles Peter Brand, *Ludovico Ariosto: A Preface to the Orlando Furioso* (Edinburgh: Edinburgh University Press, 1974), p. 147.

20. Ibid., p. 148.

21. The term and concept are taken from Ruggero M. Ruggieri, "I nomi parlanti nel *Morgante,* nell'*Innamorato* e nel *Furioso,*" in his *Saggi di linguistica italiana e italo-romanza* (Florence: Olschki, 1962), pp. 169–82.

22. These exemplary stories together constitute the precursor and source of Cervantes's "The Man Who Was Too Curious," incorporated within *Don Quixote,* I.4.6. The chief character, as in one of Ariosto's stories, is called Anselmo.

23. Donald Ward, *The Divine Twins: An Indo-European Myth in Germanic Tradition* (Berkeley: University of California Press, 1968), is a comprehensive survey of the theme, including Greek and Latin mythology (for example in the myth of Castor and Pollux).

24. Virgil, *Aeneid* IV.69.72–73: "qualis coniecta cerva sagitta . . . / illa fuga silvas saltusque peregrat / Dictaeos; haeret lateri letalis harundo." (even as a hind, smitten by an arrow . . . She in flight ranges the Dictaean woods and glades, but fast to her side clings the deadly shaft.)

25. The critic is Giorgio Barberi Squarotti, *Fine dell'idillio: Da Dante a Marino* (Genoa: Il Menangolo, 1978), pp. 110–19.

26. For a recent account of neofeudalism in the Ferrarese arts, see Werner Gundersheimer, *Ferrara: The Style of a Renaissance Despotism* (Princeton, N.J.:

Princeton University Press, 1973); also the clearly negative interpretation of the same trend by Antonio Piromalli, *La cultura a Ferrara al tempo di Ludovico Ariosto* (Rome: Bulzoni, 1975).

27. Kenneth Burke, *Terms for Order*, ed. Stanley E. Hyman (Bloomington: Indiana University Press, 1964), p. 84.

28. Rank, *The Double*, p. 82.

29. Ibid., p. 83.

30. Pausanias, *Descriptions of Greece* 9.31.6 (ed. W. H. S. Jones [Cambridge, Mass.: Harvard University Press, 1975], 4, 311), cited in Rank, *The Double*, p. 87.

31. Ovid, *Metamorphoses* III.504–5: "tum quoque se, postquam est inferna sede receptus, / in Stygia spectabat aqua." (And even when he had been received into the infernal abodes, he kept on gazing at his image in the Stygian pool.)

# Chapter 6

1. It is noteworthy that Alfonso d'Este had in his possession a translation of the *Imagines*, borrowed from his sister, Isabella. See Edgar Wind, *Bellini's Feast of the Gods* (Cambridge, Mass.: Harvard University Press, 1948), p. 56.

2. Plutarch is said to have estimated the date of Simonides' proverbialized expression. See the discussion in Jean Hagstrum, *The Sister Arts* (1958; rpt. Chicago: University of Chicago Press, 1974), p. 26.

3. For full review and discussion of the *Ut pictura* topos see W. Rensselaer Lee, *Ut pictura poesis* (New York: Norton, 1967), esp. the first five chapters.

4. Wendy Steiner, *The Colors of Rhetoric: Problems in the Relation between Modern Literature and Painting* (Chicago: University of Chicago Press, 1982), p. 5. This book concentrates on twentieth-century rapprochements of the arts, but the first chapter provides an excellent introduction to the chief problems.

5. Ibid., p. 6.

6. Ibid.

7. Leonardo da Vinci, *Notebooks*, trans. Edward McCurdy (New York: Modern Library, 1941), p. 852; from MS 2038 Biblioteca Nazionale 19 r. Leonardo's opinion, reiterated throughout the manuscripts, is based largely upon the assumption of art as mimesis: again, "When the poet ceases to represent in words what exists in nature, he then ceases to be the equal of the painter." McCurdy, p. 856, from *Quaderni* III.7r.

8. Svetlana Alpers, "Ecphrasis and Aesthetic Attitudes in Vasari's Lives," *Journal of the Warburg and Courtauld Institute*, 23 (1960), 190–215.

9. Aristotle, *Poetics* 1448a, for the distinction between the direct representation of events and narrative; see the bibliographies in various works of Gérard Genette dealing with the levels of narrative, as for instance, *Figures III* (Paris: Seuil, 1968), and "Aux frontieres du récit," *Communications*, 8 (1966), 152–63, in which he distinguishes ecphrastic or "non-signifying" description from significant description.

10. Aristotle, *Poetics* 1447a:2: "Just as colour and form are used as means by some, who (whether by art or constant practice) imitate and portray many things by their aid, and the voice is used by others; so also in the abovementioned group of arts, the means with them as a whole are rhythm, language and harmony." Cit. from *The Basic Works of Aristotle*, ed. Richard McKeon (New York: Random House, 1968), p. 1455.

11. Giorgio Vasari, *Vite de li piu eccellenti pittori e scultori*, ed. G. Milanesi (1878–85; rpt. Florence: Giunti, 1968).

12. Carlo Ridolfi, *Le meraviglie dell'arte, ovvero le vite degli illustri pittori veneti e dello stato* (Venice, 1648), ed. D. F. von Hadeln (Berlin: Grote, 1914–24), 1, 91.

13. Lodovico Dolce, *Dialogo della pittura, intitolato l'Aretino* (1557), in

*Scritti d'arte nel Cinquecento,* ed. Paola Barocchi (Milan: Ricciardi, 1962), 1, 781. Dolce also compares good painters to orators, using the example of Titian, and the more noted one of the Laocoön group, later disputed by Lessing. Among other theorists who assimilate other arts to painting are Pomponio Gaurico, *De sculptura,* in Barocchi, *Scritti d'arte,* p. 251, who terms painting a kind of writing, deriving them from the common grafein; and Mario Equicola, *Institutioni* (1541), in Barocchi, *Scritti d'arte,* p. 259 ("dove le lettere el il colloquio per la diversita de gli uomini non penetra, essa [pittura] dilettevolmente s'intromette"); and Giovan Paolo Lomazzo, discussed in the following note.

14. Giovanni Paolo Lomazzo, *Trattato dell'arte della pittura, della scoltura e dell'architettura* (1584), in Barocchi, *Scritti d'arte,* p. 352, which also cites Ariosto as a "painter." For similar views of Ariosto, see Paola Barocchi, "La fortuna dell'Ariosto nella trattatistica figurativa," in *Critica e storia letteraria: studi offerti a Mario Fubini* (Padua: Liviana, 1971), pp. 388–403.

15. Galileo Galilei, *Scritti letterari,* ed. Alberto Chiari (Florence: Le Monnier, 1943), pp. 87–88. See also Erwin Panofsky, *Galileo as a Critic of the Arts* (The Hague: Mouton, 1954), p. 16.

16. See also Lodovico Dolce, in Barocchi, *Scritti d'arte,* pp. 298–99, for a similar list of specific comparisons.

17. For the influence of oratory and writing about rhetoric on Alberti, see the English edition and translation by John R. Spencer, *On Painting* (1966; rpt. Westport, Conn.: Greenwood Press, 1976); also his article "Ut rhethorica pictura," *Journal of the Warburg and Courtauld Institute,* 20 (1957), 27–44.

18. Compare *De inventione* II.i.1–3.

19. Baldesar Castiglione, *Il libro del cortegiano,* ed. Bruno Maier (Turin: UTET, 1964), I.53, p. 181.

20. Alberti, *On Painting,* p. 96.

21. Alberti, *On Painting,* p. 37.

22. Ibid., p. 41.

23. Ibid., p. 78.

24. "Hi sunt actori, ut pictori, expositi ad variandum colores" (Thus are actors, like painters, subject to the need to vary their colors [translation mine]); *De oratore* III.lvii.216–17.

25. See Hans Baron, *The Crisis of the Early Italian Renaissance* (Princeton, N.J.: Princeton University Press, 1955), 1, 302–12.

26. Jean Seznec, *The Survival of the Pagan Gods: The Mythological Tradition and Its Place in Renaissance Humanism and Art* (Princeton, N.J.: Princeton University Press, 1953).

27. Ibid., pp. 205–6.

28. Ibid., p. 19.

29. Werner Gundersheimer, *Ferrara: The Style of a Renaissance Despotism* (Princeton, N.J.: Princeton University Press, 1973) provides a balanced account of the Estense achievements in foreign policy during the years of Ariosto's youth.

30. Ibid., p. 225.

31. Giulio Bertoni, *La biblioteca estense di Ferrara* (Turin: Loescher, 1903), discusses the popularity and importance of the earlier poem.

32. Edmund Gardner, *Dukes and Poets in Renaissance Ferrara* (New York: rpt. Haskell House, 1968), pp. 85–86. See also Elizabeth A. Chesney, *The Countervoyage of Rabelais and Ariosto* (Durham, N.C.: Duke University Press, 1981), pp. 7–8.

33. Johan Huizinga, *The Waning of the Middle Ages: A Study of the Forms of Life, Thought and Art in France and the Netherlands in the XIVth and XVth Centuries* (New York: Doubleday Anchor, 1956).

34. Ibid., p. 34.

35. Malcolm Vale, *War and Chivalry* (London: Duckworth, 1980), p. 67.

36. For surveys of the myth, see Harry Levin, *The Myth of the Golden Age in the Renaissance* (Bloomington: Indiana University Press, 1969), and for Italian literature, Gustavo Costa, *La leggenda dei secoli d'oro nelle lettere italiane* (Bari: Laterza, 1972).

37. See Paul Zumthor, *Merlin le prophète* (Geneva: Payot, 1943).

38. Seneca, *De beneficiis*, VII.1.15. I cite from the edition of William Hardy Alexander (Berkeley: University of California Press, 1950).

39. Ibid., III.18–21.

40. Ibid., I.7.

41. Owen B. Hardison, *The Enduring Monument: A Study of the Idea of Praise in Renaissance Literary Theory and Practice* (Chapel Hill: University of North Carolina Press, 1962), p. 37. This book deals almost exclusively with classical and English literature.

42. Ibid., p. 33, for discussion of the *Interpretationes virgilianae*.

43. Ibid., p. 35, for Petrarch's *Africa* as a poem of praise.

44. One of the best recent accounts of Ariosto's allegoresis is that of Patricia A. Parker, *Inescapable Romance* (Princeton, N.J.: Princeton University Press, 1979).

45. Chesney, *The Countervoyage*, p. 10.

46. Thomas M. Greene, "The Flexibility of the Self in Renaissance Literature," in *The Disciplines of Criticism*, ed. Peter Demetz et al. (New Haven, Conn.: Yale University Press, 1968), pp. 241–64.

47. Ovid., *Metamorphoses* V.227.

48. Ibid., XV.871–72; 875–76: "Iamque opus exegi, quod nec Jovis ira nec ignis / nec poterit ferrum nec edax abolere vetustas . . . parte tamen meliore mei super alta perennis / astra ferar, nomenque erit indelebile nostrum. . . ." (And now my work is done, which neither the wrath of Jove, nor fire, nor sword, nor the gnawing tooth of time shall ever be able to undo . . . . Still in my better part I shall be borne immortal far beyond the lofty stars and I shall have an undying name.)

49. Virginia A. Tufte, *The Poetry of Marriage* (Los Angeles: University of Southern California Press, 1970), p. 13.

50. For good discussions of Renaissance masques and courtly praise, see Stephen Greenblatt, *Sir Walter Raleigh: The Renaissance Man and His Roles* (New Haven, Conn.: Yale University Press, 1973); Wayne A. Rebhorn, *Courtly Performances: Masking and Festivity in Castiglione's Book of the Courtier* (Detroit: Wayne State University Press, 1978), esp. pp. 11–52, 117–51.

51. Rebhorn, *Courtly Performances*, p. 148, makes this point about the courtiers in Castiglione.

52. Boiardo, *Orlando innamorato*, III.1.5.

53. Piromalli, *La cultura a Ferrara*, p. 35.

54. Gundersheimer, *Ferrara*, pp. 279–80, describes this tendency to channel generic models into accounts of the Estensi.

55. Walter Binni, *Metodo e poesia in Ludovico Ariosto* (Florence: Olschki, 1947), p. 96.

56. One effort to equate Ariosto's methods with those of the painters he favored is that of Cesare Gnudi, "L'Ariosto e le arti figurative," *Atti dei Convegni Lincei* (Accademia Nazionale dei Lincei, 1975), 331–400. This study discusses nearly every painter with whom Ariosto could have been connected directly. Another article that finds a common spirit of purpose in "Ariosto and the Painters" is Robert Hanning, "Ariosto, Ovid and the Painters: Mythical Paragon in *Orlando Furioso*," in *Ariosto in America*, ed. Aldo Scaglione (Ravenna: Longo, 1976), esp. pp. 102–3, which stresses the free use of classical sources by artists such as Giovanni Bellini.

Edgar Wind, *Bellini's Feast of the Gods* (Cambridge, Mass.: Harvard University Press, 1948), p. 27, discusses the reinterpretation of subjects from Ovid's *Fasti* in the context of epithalamium.

57. *Progymnasmata* X, cit. under "Hermogenes," *Paulys Real-Encyclopädie der klassischen Altertumswissenschaft,* 8, 862–81.

58. As is known, Ariosto replaced "cinque canti" of the 1521 edition with a series of hyperbolic developments for Ruggiero and Bradamante. The poem's final section offers Ruggiero the crown of Bulgaria and arranges for the emperors of East and West to come to his wedding. See the studies of the "cinque canti" by Cesare Segre in his *Esperienze ariostesche* (Pisa: Nistri-Lischi, 1966), pp. 79–109, 121–77.

59. This idea is supported by my reading of Emilie Bergmann, *Art Inscribed: Essays on Ekphrasis in Spanish Golden Age Poetry* (Cambridge, Mass.: Harvard University Press, 1979), pp. 123–48. Hagstrum, *The Sister Arts,* provides a considerably narrower definition of ecphrasis but is useful especially with reference to writing that accompanies or forms part of pictorial illustration.

60. For Petrarch's interest in archeology and its relationship to philological accuracy and authenticity, see Thomas M. Greene, "Petrarch and the Humanist Hermeneutic," in *Italian Literature: Roots and Branches, Essays in Honor of Thomas Goddard Bergin,* ed. Giosè Rimanelli and Kenneth John Atchity (New Haven, Conn.: Yale University Press, 1976), pp. 201–24, esp. for "the resurrection of literary texts as they were discovered, copied, edited, disseminated, translated, and imitated by the humanist necromancer-scholar," compared to the resurrection of buried objects and buildings (p. 204).

61. Alan G. Paterson, "Ecphrasis in Garcilaso's *Egloga Tercera,*" *Modern Language Review,* 72 (1977), 90. Leo Spitzer, "The Ode on a Grecian Urn, or Content Versus Metagrammar," *Comparative Literature,* 7 (1955), 207, points out that this still motion is often depicted in circular form, as on Keats's urn, thereby implying perpetual repetition.

62. For discussion of ecphrasis in Poliziano's *Stanze,* see Warman Welliver, "The Subject and Purpose of Poliziano's *Stanze,*" *Italica,* 48 (1971), 34–51.

63. Ernst Gombrich, *The Image and the Eye: Further Studies in the Psychology of Pictorial Representation* (Oxford: Oxford University Press, 1982).

64. See Alpers, "Ecphrasis and Aesthetic Attitudes," p. 195, on the relationship between expression and imitation in ecphrasis.

65. Ibid.

66. On human speech as an all-inclusive language, see the classical work of Louis Hjelmslev, *Prolegomena to a Theory of Language,* trans. Francis J. Whitfield (Madison: University of Wisconsin Press, 1969).

67. Bradamante's reaction is to be compared with that of Aeneas to the scenes carved on Vulcan's shield (VIII.730–31). He is elated by its portrayal of future glories: "Miratur rerumque ignarus imagine gaudet, / attollens umero famamque et fata nepotum." (Though he knows not the deeds, he rejoices in their portraiture, uplifting on his shoulders the fame and fortunes of his children's children.)

68. Alberti, *On Painting,* p. 90: "A beautiful invention has such force, as will be seen, that even without painting it is pleasing in itself alone. Invention is praised when one reads the description of Calumny which Lucian recounts was painted by Apelles."

69. Alpers, "Ecphrasis and Aesthetic Attitudes," p. 200.

70. Alberti, *On Painting,* p. 76.

71. Ibid., p. 77.

72. Leonardo da Vinci, *Notebooks,* trans. Edward MacCurdy (New York: Random House, 1956), p. 121.

73. Ibid., p. 868.

74. Alberti, *On Painting,* p. 91: "Therefore I advise that each painter should make himself familiar with poets, rhetoricians and others equally well learned in letters. They will give new inventions or at least aid in beautifully composing the *istoria.* . . ."

75. Alpers, "Ecphrasia and Aesthetic Attitudes," p. 195, for numerous citations from Vasari in the light of the relationship between imitation and expression.

76. For discussion of the ideological utility of Platonistic doctrines in the Renaissance, see Pietro Floriani, *Bembo e Castiglione: studi sul classicismo del Cinquecento* (Rome: Bulzoni, 1976), esp. pp. 108–13: "The image of the courtier is isolated in a Paradise of Eternal Ideas While Rome is in the hands of Lutheran soldiers," p. 113 (translation my own).

77. Erwin Panofsky, *Idea: A Concept in Art Theory,* trans. Joseph S. Peake (Columbia: University of South Carolina Press, 1968), is the text on which this discussion leans.

78. See, for example, Marsilio Ficino, *In Parmenidem Opere* II.1142, cit. Panofsky, *Idea,* p. 210: "Et Plato in Timeo septimoque de Republica manifeste declarat substantias quidem veras existere, res vero nostra rerum verarum, id est idearum, imagines esse." (And Plato in the Timaeus and in the seventh book of the Republic, declares that true substances exist, which are the Ideas, while our earthly things are only images of them.) This is one of many examples from Panofsky of Quattrocento Platonistic concepts of the innate Idea.

79. Panofsky, *Idea,* p. 7.

80. Ibid., p. 50.

81. Ibid., p. 55.

82. Ibid., pp. 63, 66.

83. Ibid., p. 67.

84. Castiglione, *Il libro del Cortegiano,* I.1. For comparison of the mirror topos with that of the portrait in Castiglione, see my article, "Mirror and Portrait: The Structure of *Il libro del Cortegiano,*" *Journal of Medieval and Renaissance Studies,* 5 (1975), 37–62.

85. Castiglione, *Il libro del Cortegiano,* IV.73.

86. Panofsky, *Idea,* p. 48.

87. Giovanfrancesco Pico della Mirandola, *On the Imagination,* trans. Harry Caplan (1933; rpt. Westport, Conn.: Greenwood Press, 1971).

88. Ibid., p. 29.

89. Ibid., p. 39.

90. Ibid., p. 85.

91. Ibid., pp. 30, 33.

92. Ibid., p. 35.

93. Mario Praz, *Mnemosyne: The Parallel between Literature and the Visual Arts* (Princeton, N.J.: Princeton University Press, 1967), p. 16.

94. Pico, *On the Imagination,* p. 27.

95. Aristotle, *De anima* 428a, cit. Caplan in Pico, *On the Imagination,* p. 29.

96. Kenneth Burke, *A Rhetoric of Motives* (Berkeley: University of California Press, 1969), p. 78.

97. The most important of recent discussion of Plato's opinions of poetry is Eric A. Havelock, *Preface to Plato* (New York: Grosset and Dunlop, 1967).

98. Thomas Aquinas, *Summa Theologica,* 1.1.16.1, cit. Panofsky, *Idea,* p. 199.

99. Panofsky, *Idea,* p. 206, n. 17.

100. Alberti, *On Painting,* p. 93. The remark occurs in tandem with the Zeuxis story, which shows that the painter must seek out his model (however composite) in Nature.

101. Cited and discussed by Panofsky, *Idea,* pp. 6–7; also mentioned by Hans-Robert Jauss, *Aesthetic Experience and Literary Hermeneutics,* trans. Timothy Bahti (Minneapolis: University of Minnesota Press, 1982), p. 34.

102. Panofsky, *Idea,* p. 7.

103. Gotthold Ephraim Lessing, *Laocoön,* trans. Edward Allen McCormick (New York: Bobbs-Merrill, 1967), pp. 105–8.

104. Ibid., p. 110.

105. Ibid., p. 106.

106. Ibid., p. 86.

107. Ibid., p. 77.

108. The only similar statement occurring prior to Lessing's is by Dio Chrysostom (c. A.D. 40–?). See McCormick in Lessing, *Laocoön,* p. xiii.

109. Horace, *Ars poetica* 361–62.

110. Anthony Blunt, *Artistic Theory in Italy 1450–1600* (Oxford: Oxford University Press, 1974).

# Bibliography

Alberti, Leon Battista. *On Painting,* trans. John R. Spencer. 1966; rpt. Westport, Conn.: Greenwood Press, 1976.

Alexander, J. G. *Norman Illustration at Mont St-Michel 966–1100.* Oxford: Clarendon Press, 1970.

Allen, Don Cameron. *Mysteriously Meant.* Baltimore: The Johns Hopkins University Press, 1970.

Alpers, Svetlana. "Ecphrasis and Aesthetic Attitudes in Vasari's Lives," *Journal of the Warburg and Courtauld Institute,* 23 (1960), 190–215.

Altman, Charles. "Medieval Narrative Versus Modern Assumptions: Revising Inadequate Typology," *Diacritics,* 4 (1974), 12–19.

Appel, Karl. *Bernart von Ventadorn: Seine Lieder.* Halle: Niemeyer, 1915.

Ariosto, Ludovico. *Orlando Furioso,* ed. Cesare Segre. Milan: Mondadori, 1964.

———. *Orlando Furioso,* ed. Leonzio Pampaloni. Florence: La Nuova Italia, 1971.

———. *Orlando Furioso,* ed. Nicola Zingarelli. Milan: Hoepli, 1959.

———. *Satire,* ed. Cesare Segre. Turin: Einaudi, 1976.

Aristotle. *The Basic Works,* ed. Richard McKeon. New York: Random House, 1968.

Arouet, François-Marie. *Oeuvres complètes,* 2d ed. Paris: Baudouin, 1825–28.

Auerbach, Erich. *Mimesis,* trans. Willard F. Trask. Princeton, N.J.: Princeton University Press, 1953.

———. *Scenes from the Drama of European Literature: Six Essays,* trans. Ralph Manheim. New York: Meridian Books, 1959.

Avalle, D'Arco Silvio. *Essais de la théorie du texte.* Paris: Galilee, 1973.

Baldwin, T. W. "Perseus Purloins Pegasus," *Philological Quarterly,* 20 (1941), 361–70.

Barocchi, Paola. "La fortuna dell'Ariosto nella trattatistica figurativa," in *Critica e storia letteraria: studi offerti a Mario Fubini*, pp. 388–403. Padua: Liviana, 1971.

Baron, Hans. *The Crisis of the Early Italian Renaissance*. Princeton, N.J.: Princeton University Press, 1955.

Battaglia, Salvatore. "Il 'compagnonaggio' di Orlando e Olivieri," *Filologia romanza*, 5 (1958), 34–68.

Bergin, Thomas G., and Alice Wilson, trans. *Petrarch's Africa*. New Haven, Conn.: Yale University Press, 1977.

Bergmann, Emilie. *Art Inscribed: Essays on Ekphrasis in Spanish Golden Age Poetry*. Cambridge, Mass.: Harvard University Press, 1979.

Bernardo, Aldo. *Petrarch, Scipio and Africa*. Baltimore: The Johns Hopkins University Press, 1962.

Bertoni, Giulio. *La biblioteca estense di Ferrara*. Turin: Loescher, 1903.

Bigi, Emilio. *Dal Petrarca al Leopardi*. Milan: Ricciardi, 1954.

Binni, Walter. *Metodo e poesia in Ludovico Ariosto*. Florence: Olschki, 1947.

Bishop, Morris. *Petrarch and His World*. Bloomington: Indiana University Press, 1963.

Blasi, Giorgio de. "L'Ariosto e le passioni (studio sul motivo poetico fondamentale dell'*Orlando Furioso*)," *GSLI*, 129 (1952), 318–62; 130 (1953), 178–203.

Blasucci, Luigi. *Studi su Dante e Ariosto*. Milan: Ricciardi, 1969.

Bloomfield, Morton. "The Problem of the Hero in the Later Medieval Period," in *Concepts of the Hero in the Middle Ages and the Renaissance*, ed. Norman T. Burns and Christopher T. Reagan, pp. 30–48. Albany: State University of New York Press, 1975.

Blunt, Anthony. *Artistic Theory in Italy 1450–1600*. Oxford: Oxford University Press, 1974.

Boccaccio, Giovanni. *De genealogie deorum gentilium*, ed. V. Romano. Bari: Laterza, 1951.

Boiardo, Matteo Maria. *Orlando Innamorato*, ed. Giuseppe Anceschi. Milan: Garzanti, 1968.

Bolgar, R. R. *The Classical Heritage*. Cambridge: Cambridge University Press, 1954.

Bowra, C. M. *Pindar*. Oxford: Clarendon Press, 1964.

Bradley, Sister Ritamary, C.H.M. "Backgrounds of the Title Speculum in Medieval Literature," *Speculum*, 29 (1954), 100–115.

Branca, Daniela Delcorno. *L'Orlando Furioso e il romanzo cavalleresco medievale*. Florence: Olschki, 1973.

Brand, C. P. *Ariosto: A Preface to Orlando Furioso*. Edinburgh: Edinburgh University Press, 1973.

Brody, Saul Nathan. *The Disease of the Soul: Leprosy in Medieval Literature*. Ithaca, N.Y.: Cornell University Press, 1974.

Burke, Kenneth. *A Rhetoric of Motives*. Berkeley: University of California Press, 1969.

———. *Philosophy of Literary Form*. Baton Rouge: Louisiana State University Press, 1941.

———. *Terms for Order*, ed. Stanley E. Hyman. Bloomington: Indiana University Press, 1964.

Calvino, Italo. *Il castello dei destini incrociati*. Turin: Einaudi, 1973.

Capellani, Nino. *La sintassi narrativa dell'Ariosto*. Florence: La Nuova Italia, 1952.

Caretti, Lanfranco. *Ariosto e Tasso*. Turin: Einaudi, 1961.

Carne-Ross, Donald S. "The One and the Many: A Reading of *Orlando Furioso*, Cantos I and VIII," *Arion*, 5 (1966), 195–234.

Castiglione, Baldesar. *Il libro del cortegiano*, ed. Bruno Maier. Turin: UTET, 1964.

Cesati, Luigi. "Contatti e interferenze tra il ciclo brettone e carolingio prima del Boiardo," *Archivum Romanicum*, 11 (1927), 108–17.

Chesney, Elizabeth A. *The Countervoyage of Rabelais and Ariosto*. Durham, N.C.: Duke University Press, 1981.

Contini, Gianfranco. *Esercizi di lettura*. Turin: Einaudi, 1974.

Cooke, John D. "Euhemerism: A Medieval Interpretation of Classical Paganism," *Speculum*, 2 (1927), 396–410.

Costa, Gustavo. *La leggenda dei secoli d'oro nelle lettere italiano*. Bari: Laterza, 1972.

DeBlasi, Giorgio. "L'Ariosto e le passioni (studio sul motivo poetico fondamentale dell'*Orlando Furioso*)," *GSLI*, 129 (1952), 318–62; 130 (1953), 178–203.

De Boer, C., ed. *Ovide moralisé*. Amsterdam: Maatschappij, 1919–38.

DeBoer, C., and J. T. M. van't Sant. *Ovide moralisé (texte du quinzième siècle)*. Amsterdam: Koniklijke Akademie van Wetenschappen, 1954.

Della Palma, Giuseppe. "Una cifra per la pazzia d'Orlando," *Strumenti critici*, 32 (1975), 367–76.

Dodds, Erika Cruikshank. "The Image of the Word," *Berytus*, 18 (1969), 35–58.

Durling, Robert M. *The Figure of the Poet in the Renaissance Epic*. Cambridge, Mass.: Harvard University Press, 1965.

Ebreo, Leone (Guida Abarbanel). *Dialoghi d'amore*, ed. Santino Caramella. Bari: Laterza, 1929.

Elliott, K. O., and J. P. Elder. "A Critical Edition of the Vatican Mythographers," *Transactions and Proceedings of the American Philological Association*, 78 (1947), 189–207.

Fedi, Roberto. "Petrarchismo prebembesco in alcuni testi lirici dell'Ariosto," in *Lodovico Ariosto: lingua, stile e tradizione*, ed. Cesare Segre, pp. 283–302. Milan: Feltrinelli, 1974.

Fein, Susana Greer. "Thomas Malory and the Pictorical Interlace of *La Queste del Saint Graal*," *University of Toronto Quarterly*, 46 (1977), 216–40.

Festa, Nicola. "Il palazzo della Verità e le lacune dell'Africa," *Giornale dantesco*, 27 (1924), 197–201.

Floriani, Pietro. *Bembo e Castiglione: Studi sul classicismo del Cinquecento*. Rome: Bulzoni, 1976.

Fontenrose, Joseph. *Python: A Study of Delphic Myth and Its Origins*. Berkeley: University of California Press, 1959.

Foucault, Michel. *Madness and Civilization: A History of Insanity in the Age of Reason*, trans. Richard Howard. New York: Pantheon, 1965.

Frappier, Jean. *Étude sur la mort le Roi Artu*. Geneva: Droz, 1936.

———. "The Vulgate Cycle," in *Arthurian Legend in the Middle Ages*, ed. R. S. Loomis, pp. 295–318. Oxford: Clarendon Press, 1959.

Freccero, John. "Dante's Medusa: The Letter and the Spirit," *Yearbook of Italian Studies*, 4 (1972), 1–18.

Frye, Northrop. *Anatomy of Criticism*. Princeton, N.J.: Princeton University Press, 1957.

Gaeta, F. "L'avventura di Ercole," *Rinascimento*, 5 (1954), 227–60.

Galileo Galilei. *Scritti letterari*, ed. Alberto Chiari. Florence: Le Monnier, 1943.

Gardner, Edmund. *Dukes and Poets in Renaissance Ferrara*. New York: Haskell House, 1968.

Genette, Gerard. "Auz frontières du récit," *Communications*, 8 (1966), 152–63.

———. *Figures III*. Paris: Seuil, 1968.

Ghisalberti, Fausto. "L'*Ovidius Moralizatus* di Pierre Bersuire," *Studj romanzi*, 23 (1933), 5–132.

Giamatti, A. Bartlett. "Sfrenatura," in *Ariosto in America: Atti del Congresso ariostesco*, ed. Aldo Scaglione, pp. 31–39. Ravenna: Longo, 1976.

———. *The Earthly Paradise in the Renaissance Epic*. Princeton, N.J.: Princeton University Press, 1966.

Gnudi, Cesare. "L'Ariosto e le arti figurative," in *Atti dei Convegni Lincei*, pp. 331–400. Rome: Accademia Nazionale dei Lincei, 1975.

Goldin, Frederick. *The Mirror of Narcissus*. Ithaca, N.Y.: Cornell University Press, 1967.

Gombrich, Ernst. *The Image and the Eye: Further Studies in the Psychology of Pictorial Representation*. Oxford: Oxford University Press, 1982.

Greenblatt, Stephen. *Sir Walter Raleigh: The Renaissance Man and His Roles*. New Haven, Conn.: Yale University Press, 1973.

Greene, Thomas M. "Petrarch and the Humanist Hermeneutic," in *Italian Literature: Roots and Branches, Essays in Honor of Thomas Goddard Bergin*, ed. Giosè Rimanelli and Kenneth John Atchity, pp. 201–24. New Haven, Conn.: Yale University Press, 1976.

———. *The Descent from Heaven: A Study in Epic Continuity*. New Haven, Conn.: Yale University Press, 1963.

———. "The Flexibility of the Self in Renaissance Literature," in *The Disciplines of Criticism*, ed. Peter Demetz et al., pp. 241–64. New Haven, Conn.: Yale University Press, 1968.

Gundersheimer, Werner. *Ferrara: The Style of a Renaissance Despotism*. Princeton, N.J.: Princeton University Press, 1975.

Hagstrum, Jean. *The Sister Arts*. 1958; rpt. Chicago: University of Chicago Press, 1974.

Hanning, Robert. "Ariosto, Ovid and the Painters: Mythical Paragon in *Orlando Furioso*," in *Ariosto in America: Atti del Congresso ariostesco*, ed. Aldo Scaglione, pp. 100–116. Ravenna: Longo, 1976.

Hardison, Owen B. *The Enduring Monument: A Study of the Idea of Praise in Renaissance Literary Theory and Practice*. Chapel Hill: University of North Carolina, 1962.

Havelock, Eric A. *Preface to Plato*. New York: Grosset and Dunlap, 1967.

Hegel, Georg Wilhelm Friedrich. *Aesthetics*, trans. T. M. Knox. Oxford: Clarendon Press, 1975.

Heilbrun, Carolyn. *Toward a Recognition of Androgyny*. New York: Knopf, 1973.

Hjelmslev, Louis. *Prolegomena to a Theory of Language*, trans. Francis J. Whitfield. Madison: The University of Wisconsin Press, 1969.

Huizinga, Johan. *The Waning of the Middle Ages: A Study of the Forms of Life, Thought and Art in France and the Netherlands in the XIVth and XVth Centuries*. New York: Doubleday Anchor, 1956.

Jakobson, Roman. "On Linguistic Aspects of Translation," in *On Translation*, ed. Reuben Brower, pp. 232–39. Cambridge, Mass.: Harvard University Press, 1959.

Jauss, Hans-Robert. *Aesthetic Experience and Literary Hermeneutics*, trans. Timothy Bahti. Minneapolis: University of Minnesota Press, 1982.

Javitch, Daniel. "Rescuing Ovid from the Allegorizers: The Liberation of Angelica," in *Ariosto in America: Atti del Congresso ariostesco*, ed. Aldo Scaglione, pp. 85–100. Ravenna: Longo, 1976.

Kennedy, William J. "Modes of Allegory in Ariosto, Tasso and Spenser." Diss. Yale, 1969.

———. *Rhetorical Norms in Renaissance Literature*. New Haven, Conn.: Yale University Press, 1978.

Kremers, Dieter. *Der rasende Roland des Ludovico Ariosto: Aufbau und Weltbild*. Stuttgart: Kohlhammer, 1973.

Lambert, Mark. *Malory: Style and Vision in Le Morte D'Arthur*. New Haven, Conn.: Yale University Press, 1975.

Lascelles, Mary. "The 'Rider on the Winged Horse,'" in *Elizabethan and Jacobean Studies Presented to Frank Percy Wilson*, pp. 173–98. Oxford: Oxford University Press, 1959.

Lee, W. Rensselaer. "Ariosto's Roger and Angelica in Sixteenth-Century Art: Some Facts and Hypotheses," in *Studies in Late Medieval and Renaissance Painting in Honor of Millard Meiss*, ed. Irving Lavin and John Plummer, pp. 302–19. New York: New York University Press, 1977.

————. *Ut pictura poesis: The Humanistic Theory of Painting*. New York: Norton, 1967.

Leonardo da Vinci. *Notebooks*, trans. Edward McCurdy. New York: Modern Library, 1941.

Lessing, Gotthold Ephraim. *Laocoön*, trans. Edward Allen McCormick. Indianapolis: Bobbs-Merrill, 1967.

Levin, Harry. *The Myth of the Golden Age in the Renaissance*. Bloomington: Indiana University Press, 1969.

Levin, Samuel R. "Allegorical Language," in *Allegory, Myth and Symbol*, ed. Morton Bloomfield, pp. 23–38. Cambridge, Mass.: Harvard University Press, 1981.

*Li fatti di Spagna*, ed. Ruggero M. Ruggieri. Modena: Società Tipografica Modenese, 1951.

Marinelli, Peter. "Redemptive Laughter: Comedy in the Italian Romances," *Genre*, 9 (1976), 505–26.

Mommsen, Theodore. "Petrarch and the Story of the Choice of Hercules," *Journal of the Warburg and Courtauld Institute*, 26 (1953), 178–92.

Nelson, William. *Fact and Fiction: The Problem of the Modern Storyteller*. Cambridge, Mass.: Harvard University Press, 1973.

Niccolo da Padova. *L'entree d'Espagne*, ed. Antoine Thomas. 2 vols. Paris: Firmin-Didot, 1913.

Ossola, Carlo. "Dantismi metrici nel Furioso," in *Lodovico Ariosto: lingua, stile e tradizione*, ed. Cesare Segre, pp. 65–95. Milan: Feltrinelli, 1974.

————. "Métaphore et inventaire de la folie dans la littérature italienne du XVe siècle," in *Folie et déraison a la Renaissance*, pp. 171–96. Brussels: Presses Universitaires, 1976.

Ovid. *Metamorphoses*. 2 vols., ed. Frank Justus Miller. Cambridge, Mass.: Harvard University Press, 1976.

Pacht, Otto. *The Rise of Pictorial Narrative in Twelfth-Century England*. Oxford: Clarendon Press, 1962.

Pampalone, Leonzio. "Per un'analisi narrativa del *Furioso*," *Belfagor*, 26 (1971), 133–50.

Panofsky, Erwin. *Galileo as a Critic of the Arts*. The Hague: Mouton, 1954.

————. *Hercules am Scheidewege*. Leipzig: Teubner, 1930.

————. *Idea: A Concept in Art Theory*, trans. Joseph S. Peake. Columbia: University of South Carolina Press, 1968.

————. *Studies in Iconology*. 1939; rpt. New York: Torchbooks, 1962.

Parker, Patricia A. *Inescapable Romance*. Princeton, N.J.: Princeton University Press, 1979.

Paterson, Alan G. "Ecphrasis in Garcilaso's *Egloga Tercera*," *Modern Language Review*, 72 (1977), 73–92.

*Paulys Real-Encyclopädie der klassischen Altertumswissenschaft*. rev. ed. Georg Wissowa and Wilhelm Kroll. Vol. 8. Stuttgart: Metzler, 1913.

Pausanias. *Descriptions of Greece*, trans. W. H. S. Jones. Cambridge, Mass.: Harvard University Press, 1975.

Petrarca, Francesco. *Africa*, ed. Nicola Festa. Florence: Sansoni, 1926.

————. *Opere*, ed. C. Ponte. Milan: Mursia, 1968.

Phillips, K. M., Jr. "Perseus and Andromeda," *American Journal of Archaeology*, 72 (1968), 1–23.

Pico della Mirandola, Giovanfrancesco. *On the Imagination*, trans. Harry Caplan. 1933; rpt. Westport, Conn.: Greenwood Press, 1971.

Piromalli, Antonio. *La cultura a Ferrara al tempo di Ludovico Ariosto.* Rome: Bulzoni, 1975.

Plato. *The Dialogues,* trans. Benjamin Jowett. New York: Random House, 1920.

Praz, Mario. *Mnemosyne: The Parallel between Literature and the Visual Arts.* Princeton, N.J.: Princeton University Press, 1967.

Pulci, Luigi. *Morgante maggiore,* ed. Giuseppe Fatini. Turin: UTET, 1968.

Quint, Daivd. "Astolfo's Voyage to the Moon," *Yale Italian Studies,* 1 (1977), 398–408.

————. "The Figure of Atlante: Ariosto and Boiardo's Poem," *MLN,* 94 (1979), 77–91.

Rajna, Pio. *Le fonti dell'Orlando Furioso.* Florence: Sansoni, 1900.

Rank, Otto. *The Double,* trans. and ed. Harry Tucker, Jr. New York: New American Library, 1971.

Rebhorn, Wayne A. *Courtly Performances: Masking and Festivity in Castiglione's Book of the Courtier.* Detroit: Wayne State University Press, 1978.

Ridolfi, Carlo. *Le meraviglie dell'arte, ovvero le vite degli illustri pittori veneti e dello stato,* ed. D. F. von Hadeln. Berlin: Grote, 1914–24.

Roscher, Wilhelm H. *Ausführliches Lexikon der griechischen und römischen Mythologie.* Leipzig: Teubner, 1884–1919.

Rose, William Stewart, trans. *Orlando Furioso,* ed. Stewart A. Baker and A. Bartlett Giamatti. Indianapolis: Bobbs-Merrill, 1968.

Rosenthal, Franz. "Significant Uses of Arabic Writing," *Ars Orientalis,* 4 (1961), 15–23.

Ruggieri, Ruggero. *Saggi di linguistica italiana e italo-romanza.* Florence: Olschki, 1962.

Ryding, William W. *Structure in Medieval Narrative.* The Hague: Mouton, 1971.

Saccone, Eduardo. *Il soggetto del Furioso e altri saggi.* Naples: Liguori, 1974.

Safadi, Yasin Hamid. *Islamic Calligraphy.* London: Thames & Hudson, 1978.

Santoro, Mario. *Letture ariostesche.* Naples: Liguori, 1974.

Schapiro, Meyer. *Romanesque Art.* New York: Braziller, 1977.

Schimmel, Annemarie. "Schriftsymbolik im Islam," in *Aus der Welt der islamischen Kunst,* ed. Richard Ettinghausen, pp. 244–54. Berlin: Mann, 1959.

Schneider, Marilyn. "Calvino's Erotič Metaphor and the Hermaphroditic Solution," *Stanford Italian Review,* 1 (1981), 93–118.

*Scritti d'arte nel Cinquecento,* ed. Paola Barocchi. Milan: Ricciardi, 1962.

Segre, Cesare. *Esperienze ariostesche.* Pisa: Nistri-Lischi, 1966.

————. "Nel mondo della luna ovvero Leon Battista Alberti e Ludovico Ariosto," in *Studi in onore di A. Schiaffini,* pp. 1025–33. Citta di Castello: Nistri-Lischi, 1965.

Seneca. *De beneficiis,* ed. William Hardy Alexander. Berkeley: University of California Press, 1950.

————. *Works,* VIII: *Tragedies,* 1, ed. Frank Justus Miller. Cambridge, Mass.: Harvard University Press, 1979.

Servius. *Servianorum in Vergilii Carmina Commentariorum,* ed. E. K. Rand et al. Lancaster, Pa.: Harvard University Press, 1964.

Seznec, Jean. *The Survival of the Pagan Gods in the Renaissance,* trans. Barbara F. Sessions. New York: Pantheon Books, 1953.

Shapiro, Marianne. *Hieroglyph of Time: The Petrarchan Sestina.* Minneapolis: University of Minnesota Press, 1980.

————. "Mirror and Portrait: The Structure of *Il libro del Cortegiano,*" *Journal of Medieval and Renaissance Studies,* 5 (1975), 37–62.

————. "Revelation and the Vials of Sanity in *Orlando Furioso,*" *Romance Notes,* 22 (1982), 329–31.

Shapiro, Michael, and Marianne Shapiro. *Hierarchy and the Structure of Tropes.* Bloomington: Indiana University Press, 1976.

Shklovskij, Viktor. "On the Connection between Devices of *Syuzhet* Construction and General Stylistic Devices," in *Russian Formalism: A Collection of Articles and Texts in Translation,* ed. Stephen Bann and John E. Bowlt, pp. 48–72. New York: Harper and Row, 1973.

Simpson, Michael, ed. and trans. *Gods and Heroes of the Greeks: The Library of Apollodorus.* Amherst: University of Massachusetts Press, 1976.

Slater, Philip. *The Glory of Hera.* Boston: Beacon Press, 1968.

Sparshott, F. E. " 'As,' or The Limits of Metaphor," *New Literary History,* 6 (1974), 75–94.

Spencer, John R. "Ut rhetorica pictura," *Journal of the Warburg and Courtauld Institute,* 20 (1957), 27–44.

Spitzer, Leo. "The Ode on a Grecian Urn, or Content Versus Metagrammar," *Comparative Literature,* 7 (1955), 203–25.

Squarotti, Giorgio Barberi. *Fine dell'idillio: Da Dante a Marino.* Genoa: Menangolo, 1978.

Steadman, John M. "Perseus upon Pegasus and *Ovid Moralized,*" *Review of English Studies,* N.S. 9 (1958), 407–10.

Steiner, Wendy. *The Colors of Rhetoric: Problems in the Relation between Modern Literature and Painting.* Chicago: University of Chicago Press, 1982.

Tayler, Edward W. *Nature and Art in the Renaissance.* New York: Columbia University Press, 1964.

Tietze-Conrat, Erica. "Notes on Hercules at the Crossroads," *Journal of the Warburg and Courtauld Institute,* 24 (1951), 305–9.

Tufte, Virginia A. *The Poetry of Marriage.* Los Angeles: University of Southern California Press, 1970.

*Turpini historia Karoli magni et Rotholandi,* ed. Ferdinand Castets. Paris: Maisonneuve, 1880.

Tuve, Rosamond. *Allegorical Imagery.* Princeton, N.J.: Princeton University Press, 1966.

Vale, Malcolm. *War and Chivalry.* London: Duckworth, 1980.

Valesio, Paolo. "The Language of Madness in the Renaissance," *Yearbook of Italian Studies,* 1 (1971), 199–234.

Vasari, Giorgio. *Vite de li piu eccellenti pittori e scultori,* ed. G. Milanesi, 3 vols. 1878–85; rpt. Florence: Giunti, 1968.

Vinaver, Eugene. *The Rise of Romance.* Oxford: Oxford University Press, 1971.

Virgil. *Aeneid,* trans. H. Rushton Fairclough. Cambridge, Mass.: Harvard University Press, 1928.

Ward, Donald. *The Divine Twins: An Indo-European Myth in Germanic Tradition.* Berkeley: University of California Press, 1968.

Weaver, Elissa B. "Lettura dell'intreccio dell'*Orlando Furioso,*" *Strumenti critici,* 34 (1977), 384–406.

Weinberg, Bernard. *A History of Italian Literary Criticism in rhe Renaissance.* 2 vols. Chicago: University of Chicago Press, 1961.

Welch, Anthony. *Calligraphy in the Arts of the Muslim World.* Austin: University of Texas Press, 1979.

Welliver, Warman. "The Subject and Purpose of Poliziano's *Stanze,*" *Italica,* 48 (1971), 34–51.

Whitbread, Leslie George, ed. and trans. *Fulgentius the Mythographer.* Columbus: Ohio State University Press, 1971.

White, Hayden. *Metahistory.* Baltimore: The Johns Hopkins University Press, 1973.

Wilkins, Ernest Hatch. "Descriptions of Pagan Divinities from Petrarch to Chaucer," *Speculum,* 32 (1957), 511–22.

——. "The Genealogy of the Editions of the *Genealogia Deorum,*" *Modern Philology,* 17 (1919), 28–36.

Wind, Edgar. *Bellini's Feast of the Gods.* Cambridge, Mass.: Harvard University Press, 1948.

———. *Pagan Mysteries in the Renaissance.* New York: Norton, 1969.

Woodward, J. M. *Perseus: A Study in Art and Legend.* Cambridge: Cambridge University Press, 1913.

Zumthor, Paul. *Langue, texte, énigme.* Paris: Seuil, 1975.

———. *Merlin le prophète.* Geneva: Payot, 1943.

Zolkovskij, A. K. "Dell'amplificazione," in *I sistemi di segni e lo strutturalismo sovietico,* ed. Remo Faccani and Umberto Eco, pp. 91–98. Milan: Bompiani, 1969.

# Index

Marianne Shapiro (A.M., Harvard; Ph.D., Columbia) has taught at Yale and Berkeley. In addition to over fifty articles she is the author of Woman Earthly and Divine in the Comedy of Dante (1975) and Hieroglyph of Time: The Petrarchan Sestina (1980); and the co-author (with her husband, Michael Shapiro) of Hierarchy and the Structure of Tropes (1976) and the forthcoming Figuration in Verbal Art.

The manuscript was edited by Susan Thornton. The book was designed by Don Ross. The typeface for the text is Sabon. The display type is Garamond. The book is printed on 55-lb. Booktext and is bound in Joanna Mills' Arrestox over binder's boards.

Manufactured in the United States of America.